MASKS

OUTRAGEOUS AND AUSTERE

Culture, Psyche, and Persona
in Modern Women Poets

CHERYL WALKER

INDIANA UNIVERSITY PRESS
Bloomington and Indianapolis

The paper used in this publication meets the minimum requirements of American
National Standard for Information Sciences—Permanence of Paper for Printed
Library Materials, ANSI Z39.48-1984.

⊚™

Manufactured in the United States of America

Library of Congress Cataloging-in-Publication Data

Walker, Cheryl, date.
 Masks outrageous and austere : culture, psyche, and persona in
modern women poets / Cheryl Walker.
  p. cm.
 Includes index.
 ISBN 0-253-36322-5 (alk. paper). — ISBN 0-253-20666-9 (pbk. :
alk. paper)
  1. American poetry—Women authors—History and criticism. 2. Self
in literature. 3. Women and literature—United States—
History—20th century. 4. American poetry—20th century—History
and criticism. 5. Persona (Literature) I. Title.
PS310.S34W35   1991
811'.52099287—dc20   91-6294

1 2 3 4 5 95 94 93 92 91

To my Mother
Virginia Marilyn Iversen Lawson
September 22, 1906–May 29, 1990

In Memoriam

Let No Charitable Hope

Now let no charitable hope
Confuse my mind with images
Of eagle and of antelope:
I am in nature none of these.

I was, being human, born alone;
I am, being woman, hard beset;
I live by squeezing from a stone
The little nourishment I get.

In masks outrageous and austere
The years go by in single file;
But none has merited my fear,
And none has quite escaped my smile.

Elinor Wylie

CONTENTS

Acknowledgments

One of the disadvantages of taking almost ten years to complete this book is that I am now no longer in a position to thank all of the people who have contributed to it one way or another. They are many, and I offer those who are not mentioned, but who know they were involved, my apologies and sincere thanks.

The following group of people read drafts of what follows or contributed information of substantial importance to this project. I owe them a special debt of gratitude: T. J. Jackson Lears, Rachel Blau DuPlessis, Susan Stanford Friedman, Alicia Ostriker, Nancy Milford, Elizabeth Frank, Ruth Limmer, William Drake, Lucy Freibert, Barbara Guest, Dan and Helen Horowitz, Gloria Bowles, Gloria Hull, Michael Harper, and Elizabeth Barnett.

My friends who saw me through a very difficult time in my life also deserve credit for making this book possible: John Peavoy, Frances McConnel, Clive and Sophia Miller, Carol De Poix, Marjory Williams, Frances Ferguson, Sara Adler, David Claus, Kitt McCord, Dion Scott-Kakures, Steven and Kersten Koblik, Rick Berg, Sue Houchins, Hadley and Jeannette Reynolds, Martha Gramlich, Michael Cunningham, Sylvia Gray, and Pat Voges.

For financial support and time to write, I am grateful to the Graves Foundation for a fellowship in 1986–87 and to Scripps College, which has over the years provided numerous grants and stipends for research, travel, books, and sabbaticals.

I wish to say special thanks to my secretary, Nancy Burson. Without her support (and unflagging goodwill) I could not have accomplished the final stages of this project so painlessly.

My family has probably been most important in keeping this work going. My son Ian and my daughter Louisa know how much they are loved and how much their love has meant to me during these past years. My husband, Michael F. Harper, saw me through all but the earliest stages of this project, edited the entire manuscript (some parts more than once), and provided the ultimate faith in me I often did not have myself. As William Carlos Williams wrote to his wife, so I write now: "We are older, I to love and you to be loved; we have, no matter how, by our wills survived to keep the jeweled prize always at our fingertips. We will it so and so it is, past all accident."

renewed 1945, 1948 by Mamie T. Wheless; 1954, 1961 by Guaranty Trust Co. of New York.

The poems of Elinor Wylie in *The Collected Poems of Elinor Wylie*, copyright 1932 by Alfred A. Knopf, Inc. and renewed 1960 by Edwina Rubenstein. Reprinted by permission of Alfred A. Knopf, Inc.

The poems of H. D. reprinted by permission of New Directions Publishing Corporation: *The Collected Poems of H. D.: 1912–1944*, copyright 1982 by the Estate of Hilda Doolittle. *Helen in Egypt*, copyright 1961 by Norman Holmes Pearson. *Hermetic Definition*, copyright 1972 by Norman Holmes Pearson.

The poems of Edna St. Vincent Millay from *Collected Poems* (Harper and Row, 1956) and in *Letters of Edna St. Vincent Millay* (Harper and Row, 1952). The poems are copyrighted 1917, 1921, 1922, 1923, 1931, 1939, 1945, 1948, 1950, 1951, 1954, 1958, 1967, 1982 by Edna St. Vincent Millay and Norma Millay Ellis. Reprinted by permission of Elizabeth Barnett, Literary Executor.

The poems of Louise Bogan from *The Blue Estuaries*, copyright 1923, 1929, 1930, 1931, 1933, 1934, 1935, 1936, 1937, 1938, 1941, 1949, 1951, 1952, 1954, 1957, 1958, 1962, 1963, 1964, 1965, 1966, 1967, 1968 by Louise Bogan. Reprinted by permission of Farrar, Straus and Giroux, Inc.

The poems of Lisel Mueller from *The Need to Hold Still* reprinted by permission of Louisiana State University Press. Copyright 1980 by Lisel Mueller. "Why We Tell Stories" originally appeared in *Poetry*.

The poems of Carolyn Kizer from *Mermaids in the Basement*, copyright 1984 by Carolyn Kizer. "Pro Femina" also copyrighted 1965; "Afterthoughts of Donna Elvira" also copyrighted 1974. Reprinted by permission of Copper Canyon Press.

"Aphrodite," by Louise Gluck, copyright 1976, 1977, 1978, 1979, 1980 by Louise Gluck. From *Descending Figure*, first published by the Ecco Press in 1980. Reprinted by permission.

"Glitter Box," by Jana Harris, from *Manhattan as a Second Language and Other Poems*, by Jana Harris. Copyright 1982 by Jana Harris. Reprinted by permission of Harper Collins Publishers.

"Rearranging My Body," by Cleopatra Mathis, from *An Aerial View of Louisiana*, by Cleopatra Mathis, copyright 1979. Reprinted by permission of Sheep Meadow Press and Cleopatra Mathis.

"Photograph of the Girl," by Sharon Olds, from *The Dead and the Living*, copyright 1983 by Sharon Olds. Reprinted by permission of Alfred A. Knopf, Inc.

"Figure from an Elder Lady," by Dave Smith, from *Cumberland Station*, copyright 1976 by Dave Smith. Reprinted by permission of University of Illinois Press.

"A Young Woman, A Tree," by Alicia Ostriker, from *Green Age*, copyright 1989 by Alicia Suskin Ostriker, reprinted by permission of the University of Pittsburgh Press.

"Genetic Expedition," by Rita Dove, from *Grace Notes*, copyright 1989 by Rita Dove. Reprinted by permission of W. W. Norton and Co., Inc.

Unpublished material by Hilda Doolittle (H. D.) reprinted by permission of Yale University, the Collection of American Literature, Beinecke Rare Book and Manuscript Library.

Portions of chapter 5 appeared first in an essay entitled "H. D. and Time" in *Taking Our Time: Feminist Perspectives on Temporality*, edited by Frieda Johles Forman with Caoran Sowton (Oxford: Pergamon Press, 1989).

The photograph of Sara Teasdale is from the Yale Collection of American Literature, reprinted courtesy of the Beinecke Rare Book and Manuscript Library, Yale University

The photograph of Amy Lowell is from the Houghton Library and is reprinted by permission of the Library and Harvard University

The photograph of Elinor Wylie is from the Yale Collection of American Literature, reprinted courtesy of the Beinecke Rare Book and Manuscript Library, Yale University

The photograph of H. D. is from the Yale Collection of American Literature, reprinted courtesy of the Beinecke Rare Book and Manuscript Library, Yale University

The photograph of Edna St. Vincent Millay is reprinted courtesy of the Vassar College Library

The photograph of Louise Bogan is reprinted courtesy of Rollie McKenna, Photographer, Stonington, Connecticut

MASKS

OUTRAGEOUS AND AUSTERE

INTRODUCTION

"Oh, the times, oh the customs! Oh, indeed, the times! The customs! Their own, specifically, but part and parcel of the cosmic, comic, crucifying times of history."[1] So begins H. D.'s novel about the experiences of her social set during the First World War, experiences which created a significant context for fifty years of literary production. Nevertheless, until recently few critics would have thought it worthwhile to investigate this kind of context as an interpretive strategy for reading those crystalline lyrics H. D., Elinor Wylie, and Louise Bogan all wrote in the 1910s and 1920s.

Fortunately, the contemporary critical scene is more aware of the cultural and historical dimensions of literature. In our time a poem need no longer appeal to us like a snowflake whose only interest lies in the uniqueness of its pattern. Poems may also contribute to our explorations of the archeologies of culture.

In order to learn to read poetry this way, however, we need to know a great deal more about the past than what has previously passed for literary history. We need to consider how a poet lived, what books she read, what race and class she belonged to, how living in the city affected her, what made her go to and what made her leave college, how she experienced a world torn apart by war, whom she loved. In the modern era we might ask if she was influenced by the temporal theories of Henri Bergson, when she saw the beginnings of department store consumerism, what views she held about communism. In the end we must know how a life which intersected in so many now invisible ways with the ideas, the economic realities, the social norms, the political practices of its generation *also* contained the production of certain poems which reveal more than that individual mind, poems that evoke the psyche of an era or show us how a particular group wished to see itself represented.

Literature, like all the arts, draws our attention to cultural history because, at its best, it does not simply bear the imprint of "the times, the customs" but reenvisions them in memorable ways. As Giles Gunn has written recently, in *The Culture of Criticism and the Criticism of Culture* (1987), "Instead of mirroring the social, culture particularizes, complicates, and deepens it."[2]

Yet, to see a given text in the context of culture requires a complicated process of listening to its various voices, a process given memorable description by Alan Trachtenberg:

> "Culture" distances the reader from the "text" pure and simple—and calls attention to what is absent, the missing mediation of the text's history, or as we

might put it, the texture of transactions by and through which we know it as a cultural artifact. Thus does culture replace the familiar literary object with an unfamiliar reading, . . . the aim of such a distanced reading being not to understand the presumed text in its presumed autonomy, but the network of relations into which the cultural text subsumes and reconstitutes the literary text.[3]

In the arguments that follow, I have attempted to supply some of the texts' missing mediations. I have also intervened in my own representations of these to show some of the determinants of my particular readings, determinants created by my historical and biographical positioning. Therefore, the distance from the text achieved by placing it in the larger frames of history may once again seem to be foreshortened in the process.

As a feminist critic, my primary concern is with the interrelationships between culture and gender and the way these interrelationships express themselves in poems (and readings) by American women. In my first book, *The Nightingale's Burden: Women Poets and American Culture before 1900*, I investigated the way the work of a series of women before the twentieth century coalesced into what I called "the nightingale tradition," a generally white, middle-class, stringent, and melancholy set of poetic voices which both defined for the general society what it meant to be a "woman poet" and was deeply affected by assumptions about women current at the time.[4]

Confrontation with this tradition allows us to see how women writers in the past both conformed to conventional expectations and challenged those assumptions in startling and even humorous ways. Though many poems fit perfectly with our prejudices about the "poetesses" of the nineteenth century, others—like Frances Osgood's "Woman," Lucretia Davidson's "Auction Extraordinary," and Emily Dickinson's "My life had stood—a loaded gun"—revitalize that category and make us rethink it. However, I was less concerned to focus on the genius of individual women in that book than I was to suggest how a cultural phenomenon—the sudden appearance of a large number of women poets—might be understood in terms of cultural and social histories, the histories of American women.

Therefore, the "archetypal poems" I was able to isolate from thousands of pages of women's poetry were meant to be suggestive as illustrations of the way women shared responses to their historical situation and invented conventions for representing them. This book, though it also concerns itself with bourgeois ideology and an exemplary set of American women poets, operates in a somewhat different fashion.

For the modern women poets in this book, bourgeois ideology affects both culture and gender in complicated ways, issuing not in some set of archetypal poems (though there are typical poems) but in versions of the female which I have called *persona poems*. Such poems are in complex ways mediated by the social and psychic. By necessity, these poets fall prey to the ideological formations with which they also struggle. It is important for me in this book to suggest both receptivity and resistance, exploring both psychological and wider cultural realms to which these poems address themselves. As Cora Kaplan says:

Women's fiction and poetry is a site where women actively structured the meaning of sexual difference in their society, especially and powerfully as it applied to difference between women. Nevertheless, these writings properly considered undermine the programmatic way in which bourgeois ideology is used as shorthand by male marxist critics for a unified, genderless, hegemonic system of ideas.[5]

My way of structuring the examination of culture and poetry I undertake in this volume is necessarily complicated. I have chosen six poets who wrote a significant body of work before 1945 and who seem to me to represent the development and full flowering of the nightingale tradition I outlined in my previous book. Further, I have identified a particular persona for each which I feel was mediated by conventions of cultural representation and which appears predominantly in her poetry. The development of this persona also seems to me linked in important ways to psychosocial development, so I have included relevant biographical material to suggest how, when, and why the persona is connected to the particular author's life. Finally, I have situated the discussion of the intersection of culture, psyche, and persona within larger theoretical frames. Though there is a great deal of overlap in terms of these general theoretical issues, which I have tried also to suggest, I feel that each of the poets I have chosen is *the best example* of that particular theoretical concern.

Therefore, there are basically three strands to each of the chapters: (1) a psychobiographical strand; (2) a cultural strand; and (3) a poetic strand. My intention is to make these vivid in the overarching discussion of persona.

Primarily, however, this book is meant to be a work of cultural criticism. For all the poets in this study, American culture was a vital though not always constantly utilized set of discourses. Some of the features of this set of discourses are continuous with European forms, particularly in the social prominence given to heterosexual romance and marriage and the model of femininity as predominantly nurturing, unintellectual, and sentimental.

Yet American culture does have a peculiar configuration that makes it interesting to ponder in connection with the special burden American women poets have had to bear. In America there is perpetually the myth of specialness—here things are better, more just, more egalitarian. America is on an errand to redeem the rest of the world by its example. Sacvan Bercovitch recalls:

> Indeed, what first attracted me to the study of Puritanism was my astonishment, as a Canadian immigrant, at learning about the prophetic errand of America. Not of North America, for the prophecies stopped short at the Canadian and Mexican borders, but of a country that, despite its arbitrary territorial boundaries—despite its bewildering mix of race and genealogy—could believe in something called America's mission, and could invest that patent fiction with all the emotional, spiritual, and intellectual appeal of a religious quest.[6]

Embued with this spirit of specialness, American culture conveys a message of privilege to many groups. For at least two centuries we have been told that American women are the freest in the world. Alexis de Tocqueville was struck by the liberties allowed to young girls in the nineteenth century, struck by the freedom with which they were encouraged to think and speak. Henry James's Isabel Archer is an embodiment of Tocqueville's American ingenue, her thoughts "a tangle of vague outlines which had never been corrected by the judgment of people speaking with authority." Isabel dramatizes America's belief in its own liberality. James, of course, sees the potential for both liberation and enslavement in the fact that "in matters of opinion she had had her own way."[7]

We can see these dual themes of promise and peril not only in the works of men like James but also in women's assessments of the American scene. In 1917 Lola Ridge, poet and political activist, gave a lecture on "Woman and the Creative Will." Fired by the Russian Revolution and the arguments for women's suffrage, she felt it was time to acknowledge the weakness of women's past literary achievements and to lay the blame on the psychological, social, and political restrictions under which women have always labored. Her conception of history led her to believe that progressivism was not enough. The human race would destroy itself unless an effort was made "not merely toward reorganization and reform, but toward the construction of a completely new social and economic fabric."[8]

Yet, when she turns to the position of women in America, she seems unduly optimistic. Though she sees Strindberg's misogyny as having caused "ripples of pleasurable excitement in some intellectual circles—particularly in England and Germany," she suspects its appeal was limited in the United States "I do not think it had much effect in this country: there is very little sex-antagonism in American men."

Of course, hand in hand with this notion that America provides a more favorable climate for the free play of the female imagination has been an equally indigenous reaction against the strength of women's participation on the cultural scene. From Hawthorne's "damned mob of scribbling women" to the hostile arguments about effeminate culture in Melville, Twain, Emerson, and Santayana, American writing is full of irritation at the way women have imposed an ethic privileging domestic virtues and a spiritual heart over rugged independence, frontier courage, and an intellectual head.

Harold Stearns, writing about "The Intellectual Life" in *Civilization in the United States* (1922), comments: "To an extent almost incomprehensible to the people of older cultures, the things of the mind and the spirit have been given over, in America, into the almost exclusive custody of women." Stearns claims that the First World War, coeducation, and professional activity by women have resulted in a world where men and women meet on terms of intellectual camaraderie. However, "where men and women in America today share their intellectual life on terms of equality and perfect understanding, closer examination reveals that the phenomenon is not a sharing but a capitulation. The men have been feminized." By this he seems to mean that intellectual life is no longer intellectual at all but rather sociological: "what women usually understand by the intellectual life is the application of modern scientific methods to a sort of enlarged and subtler course in domestic science."[9]

Where critics like these see a loss of male control of literary culture, however, women have repeatedly acknowledged feelings of constraint. In the early nineteenth century, Sara Josepha Hale—a conservative woman and author of "Mary Had a Little Lamb"—remarked: "The path of poetry, like every other path in life, is to the tread of woman, exceedingly circumscribed. She may not revel in the luxuriance of fancies, images and thoughts, or indulge in the license of choosing themes at will, like the lords of creation."[10] Even Lola Ridge, despite her belief that gender-antagonism is relatively undeveloped in American men, admits that "for centuries the women of all races have been under the pressure of social fear."[11]

Yet the repeated cautions of astute critics of culture have never entirely eradicated the myth that women in America are free to say what we will, to write as we choose. In this land of opportunity, so the story goes, the only real limitations upon our success are said to be those of inherent talent. Since the market has been comparatively receptive to its women poets since the 1840s—with many popular poets like Lydia Sigourney, Frances Harper, Ella Wheeler Wilcox, Amy Lowell, and Edna Millay selling thousands of volumes apiece—it is difficult to see what the problem is. And this, it seems to me, is the real disadvantage of the cultural legacy. Enjoined to believe that success is possible, even patriotic in the sense that to be an American means at some level to try to achieve success, women poets have sometimes missed the underlying message: the most popular among us have rarely been respectable at the highest levels of culture, unlike Henry Wadsworth Longfellow, William Cullen Bryant, Walt Whitman, Robert Frost, and T. S. Eliot, who have had both popularity and prestige. Even today, the standard college anthologies—though improving—are hardly evenhanded in their treatment of male and female poets.

In light of these reflections, one might characterize the particular dilemma of the woman poet in America as deriving from the mixed messages she has always received. The culture has said that women are freer here than elsewhere. It has also implicitly denied the value of female representations that call attention to gender. Like African-Americans after the Civil War, like immigrants and indigenous peoples of color, many women have had to ask themselves if "freedom" without dignity is enough.

For those who ignore the politics of literary reception, it is possible to judge a poet's talent without reference to such considerations. Talent is its own certification, so the story goes. However, one need only read John Crowe Ransom's article "The Poet as Woman" (1937) to confront in unvarnished form the opinions of the male literary establishment that made and still make the talent theory inadequate. Though this article has been discussed by others, it is worth reviewing because of its prominence in the world inhabited by the poets under examination here.

In this article Ransom is condescending in the extreme toward women poets, whom he treats very much as a nineteenth-century anthropologist might treat an elusive tribe of aborigines. He overlooks or refuses to acknowledge the role of culture in shaping his own views. Although Ransom strikes a coy pose, calling his own remarks "doubtless tedious, perhaps invidious," it is clear that he has the weight of institutions behind him, the weight of tradition and education, all of which allow him to present himself as the embodiment of the intellectual. "To be intellectual is to be disciplined in technique and stocked with learning."[12] The woman poet, we are told, can't quite manage this even when she has had a good education, reads Latin, and carries her Vergil along with her clothes in her suitcase. "Less pliant, safer as a biological organism, she remains fixed in her famous attitudes, and is indifferent to intellectuality."

During the course of his argument, Ransom voices every commonplace of nineteenth-century patriarchal criticism as he surveys Edna St. Vincent Millay's work and concludes that she represents "the poet as woman." She is childlike and spontaneous in her affections. "She has the innocence of the amateur who tries too early to be ingenious." She is "seduced" into acts of fancy instead of pursuing the tougher, lonelier road of imagination. The male critic misses something in her poetry, and Ransom says: "I used a conventional symbol, which I hope was not objectionable, when I phrased this lack of hers: deficiency in masculinity. It is true that some male poets are about as deficient; not necessarily that they are undeveloped intellectually, but that they conceive poetry as a sentimental or feminine exercise." Intellect is masculine. Sentimentality and femininity are interchangeable.

Ransom feels that Millay's best subjects are the ones usually associated with women poets—death, personal moods, and natural objects—those her tender sensibility fixes upon, for "a woman lives for love, if we will but project that term to cover all her tender fixations upon natural objects of sense." It is clear enough that Ransom's intermittently self-deprecatory remarks are only the blandishments of a Southern gentleman who knows the distance between the cabins and the Big House. His tone is full of the complacency of power.

> [Millay] is not a good conventional or formal poet, and I think I have already suggested why: because she allows the forms to bother her and to push her into absurdities. I imagine there are few women poets of whom this is not so, and it would be because few are strict enough and expert enough to manage forms, in their default of the intellectual disciplines.

This last sentence is worth pausing over for the picture it furnishes us of the patriarchal mind in operation. When he says, "I imagine," he suggests, "I don't know enough women poets to be sure about it but I imagine this to be the case." He would never make a comparable remark about male poets, for it would make him susceptible to the charge of ignorance. Women poets, however, one need not know well. One can imagine, and (this is particularly important) one can generalize about women poets as a group not because one has read them but simply by deductive reasoning.

But isn't he only "a gentleman in a dustcoat waiting," slightly fussy, definitely old-fashioned, whom we need not take seriously? Alas, no; his firmly entrenched convictions are still around, as we can see by the fact that Norman Mailer made the same kinds of sweeping generalizations about women writers' lack of intellectual substance as recently as 1986, when he directed the P. E. N. Conference.

Though women publish at least half the volumes of poetry selected by the prestigious boards of university presses, women poets are still seriously underrepresented in most anthologies. Only rarely does a male editor find as much room for women poets as he does for men, though the justifications for this imbalance break down when one takes seriously the formalist arguments usually produced. Neither the form nor the content of women's poems justifies the marginalizing treatment they have received.

If patriarchal criticism disparages the personal when that personal is gendered female, it also sometimes misses the point of women's writing. For instance, Ransom revises a carpe diem couplet of Millay's ("Youth, have no pity; leave no farthing here / For age to invest in compromise and fear"), by denigrating the value of the word *compromise*. He says: "*Fear* is better alone than compounded with *compromise*," and he offers instead: "For age to invest it, and in what but fear."

His revision, however, is inferior in more than one way. First of all, it is awkward, and noticeably padded. (Isn't it Ransom here who is being pushed into absurdities because of the form?) More relevant to our concerns, the poem's premise, as an address by a young woman to her heart, makes compromise a significant and separate term. As Millay's "Sonnets from an Ungrafted Tree" demonstrate, compromise may suggest the willingness to enter into the circle of another's desire at the expense of one's own, rather than fear itself. Both have been important in limiting the options of women.

It comes as no surprise that the woman poet Ransom exempts from his critique is Marianne Moore, whom Florence Howe calls one of the "tokens—those women especially selected by males (or accepted by them) as women/artists."[13] Moore never called attention to herself as a woman, though her poems are being mined today for material relevant to the poet's life and gender.

I have no quarrel with the argument that Moore was a brilliant poet capable of some impressive fancy footwork. Her temperament seems to have been consistent with her art, eccentric but not demonstrative. In terms of judging her abilities as a poet, it doesn't really matter that she failed to insist upon her femaleness. Furthermore, many male poets have led quiet lives, applauded gentility, preferred intellectual reflection over gestures of social outrage, and amused themselves with playful experiments. Though Moore's was not a voice of outrage, it was capable of powerful analytic interventions as well as bricolage.

Still, it does concern me that, liking Moore, critics feel they must denigrate Millay as though poetry might not flourish in several media. No theory can establish absolute standards for acceptable form or content; nor can we determine with precision how a society which is both "open" and "closed" to women has affected their creative work. But there is a growing body of evidence that it has. Feminist literary criticism has found an enthusiastic audience eager for speculation on how it has, and this has resulted in an important interest in recovering lost female texts. If Marianne Moore continues to find readers today, so do H. D., Edna Millay, and Louise Bogan.

Before I leave the subject of American culture and the critical reception of women poets, I wish to address a tendency in some recent feminist criticism to focus on only those aspects of a poet's work which seem to suggest conflict with patriarchy. Like comparable arguments in Marxist and ethnic theory, this approach tries to create a class of nonhegemonic or counterhegemonic individuals whose stories provide models for revision or revolution. However, as Jackson Lears says in his helpful article "The Concept of Cultural Hegemony: Problems and Possibilities," no such pure models exist. Whether we are looking at folk culture, the working class, or women poets in America, careful study reveals that, though hegemony is never absolute, alternative cultures are never entirely immune from invasion by either traditional or dominant cultural elements. "Subordinate groups may participate in maintaining a symbolic universe, even if it serves to legitimate their domination."[14]

The point to be emphasized is that there is always complicity as well as duplicity. Since feminist criticism has moved away from portraying women as victims, it has begun to chafe at indications of complicity on the part of women, immediately seeing irony or covert antagonism in any evidence that women enjoyed or exploited the roles assigned to them. No woman writer is worth her salt who did not defy patriarchy whenever and wherever possible. This, it seems to me, has led to a warping of historical representation. For instance, Emily Dickinson is now frequently represented in feminist criticism as centrally and prevailingly preoccupied with herself as a woman and with the deforming structures of patriarchal discourse. Though there is some highly interesting material illuminating Dickinson's gender-consciousness, it must be acknowledged that a great deal of her written work—letters and poems—is not addressed to this essentially twentieth-century set of concerns.[15]

In my own work, I have continued to try to argue that there is as much to be learned from seeing the way women poets have operated within conventional expectations as there is in defining them as radicals. Our hunger for heroines has made some of us want to ignore those figures who bear the imprint of patriarchy most clearly. The nightingale tradition is therefore at risk of being silenced in favor of clearly independent and experimental figures like Gertrude Stein, Mina Loy, Marianne Moore, and H. D.

As will be clear from chapter 5, I think H. D. belongs among the nightingale poets because she used the material of her own experiences as a woman to write her most impressive poems. I continue to be interested in the nightingale tradition because it most clearly reveals the conflicts women have encountered in trying to reconcile their lives with their art. Each of these women—Amy Lowell, Sara Teasdale, Elinor Wylie, H. D., Edna Millay, and Louise Bogan—has been read passionately by an audience made up in large part of women. Such women have found in these poets a voice for their own struggles.

Yet the stories of these poets' creative lives rebuke us when we try to appropriate them too absolutely for our purposes. All of these poets were born before the turn of the century (one of my criteria for including them in this book), and none can be used to provide a blueprint for our particular moment in American history.

Nevertheless, I remain interested in trying to locate lost mediations which connect these poetic texts to biography and history. In this sense I clearly belong to what has been called the Anglo-American side of feminist criticism. The "death-of-the-author" critics who have insisted that we only pay attention to "the texts themselves" seem prepared to see us lose some rich approaches within the field of cultural criticism.[16]

My interest in this book is to construct stories about women poets that emphasize their horizontal relations within a particular time period: 1910–1945. To do this I have used a number of different kinds of texts: poetry, biography, letters, feminist theory, cultural commentary. I am not arguing that this is the only way to read women poets or that the author always intended—that is, consciously installed—the meanings I find in her texts. In many cases, the need "to avoid the bitterness of understanding," as Elinor Wylie spoke of it, prevented these women from making the connections I wish to make.

My desire to tell the stories in the way I do is political. I think we still have a lot to learn about the factors which determine or inhibit creativity. If we do not consider the conditions under which women have written, if we do not consider the authors themselves, we run the risk of ignoring important elements of our own history. If we find only heroines in our past, we expose ourselves to the dangers of concluding either that patriarchy has not been and is not now a virulent force in the lives of creative women or that we cannot afford to confront our own complicity, our own failures of nerve and power. Must being read depend upon being a "heroine"? Without knowledge of our failures, past and present, what possibilities for real change do we have?

Implicit in my treatment of these women are attitudes toward history, self, and creativity. Presenting history as multiform, disjunctive with the present and yet always open to reconstructions from a later period, I have tried to convey a sense of my own connection to the past. I hope that by telling six basically different stories about women who all lived during the same formative period, I have illustrated my belief that culture is not monolithic and that historical experience can be reconstructed in a number of different ways. I want to make clear my own distance from the world of these women as well as my sense of the ways the past seems to me continuous with the present.

If historical specificity tends to distance these poets from our own time, psychological penetration tends to bring them closer. Each woman's intersection with culture, psychological makeup, and creative bent gave her a different orientation to a similar set of problems. Yet many of the themes of these women's lives resonate profoundly with issues that still concern me and the women I know.

Part of my desire to retrieve the relations between poet and poem comes from my frustration over the fact that each new surge forward in women's writing in America has occurred without benefit of a sense of history. The nightingales of the nineteenth century drew little inspiration from their eighteenth-century sisters, about whom they seem to have known very little. Similarly, for most of the women dealt with here, the actual poets of the nineteenth-century nightingale tradition were forgotten, with the exception of Dickinson. Twentieth-century women poets, beginning with Amy Lowell, started out by asserting their lack of continuity with the past.

Yet, by seeking to distance themselves from the past, modern women poets failed to come to terms with the legacy that each in spite of herself inherited. What could be more reminiscent of the nineteenth-century nightingale context than this sudden outbreak from Teasdale? "A woman ought not to write. Somehow it is indelicate and unbecoming. She ought to imitate the female birds, who are silent—or, if she sings, no one ought to hear her music until she is dead."[17] Significantly, Vachel Lindsay would write to her: "I only wish I could take you harvesting. It would give you a rest from this nightingale business."[18]

Each of the poets under study in this volume thought herself more modern and less limited than the poetesses. Yet each chose a mask that reveals her relation to earlier women poets even as it also represents her orientation to modernity. For the mask is embedded in ritual and culture. It always invokes the past. Furthermore, it requires a certain costume, certain appropriate ornaments as accompaniment, becoming at last an organizer of experience rather than merely a form within it.

Amy Lowell's androgynous mask has analogies to Emily Dickinson's. Sara Teasdale's dainty eroticism bears considerable relation to Frances Osgood's. Elinor Wylie shares the image of the woman warrior with Louise Guiney and Julia Ward Howe. Guiney and H. D. immersed themselves in past cultures which seemed to offer more reliable values than the present, choosing women of the past to speak for them. Edna St. Vincent Millay and Emily Dickinson alternated between fits of self-indulgence in their hunger for experience and bouts of abstemiousness and renunciation. Like Ella Wheeler Wilcox, Millay shocked and delighted her generation with explicit poems of passion. As a stoic, Louise Bogan was strongly influenced by Guiney and Lizette Woodworth Reese: her poem "Women" is a rewriting of Reese's and she continued to value Guiney's "Talisman" all her life.

However, the superficiality of these connections requires us to acknowledge disjunction as well as continuity with the past. The typical poems reappear but with a difference. Like the poetesses, Sara Teasdale, Elinor Wylie, Edna Millay, H. D., and Louise Bogan all write sanctuary poems, in which they imagine safe, enclosed spaces as protection against incursions from a hostile reality outside the walls. Unlike their nineteenth-century sisters, however, they also discredit these sanctuary-longings not out of a sense of guilt at trying to avoid their duty but out of a recognition that sanctuaries are suffocating and self-destructive. In the twentieth century the home is no longer a stable image of self-protection and withdrawal.

In what follows I have tried to develop a procedure of historical inquiry that acknowledges both change and continuity. Because of my own immersion in an historical moment in feminist criticism, my critical practice is also an example of both change and continuity.

I have paid more attention to theory in this book than I did in the last. Each of the following chapters addresses a theoretical issue: women and female poetic traditions, women and selfhood, women and aggression, women and time, women and the body, women and the mind. However, unlike some of the theoreticians I use, such as French feminists, I do not wish to make large, ahistorical generalizations about these issues. Instead, I have tried to fashion an argument that suggests why and how these issues become significant for these women poets in their particular times and places. In some cases, particularly in my combination of French feminist theory with Marxist and Anglo-American critical approaches, I am aware that the structure I have created to bring them together is fragile. My prevailing belief is that persona criticism—with its emphasis upon intersections—justifies the creation of these delicate arrangements and keeps them all in play without insisting on the submersion of one within the pattern of the other.

If the theoretical orientation of these chapters opens the discussion of these issues to larger, more transhistorical perspectives, the focus on mask or persona narrows the historical range. Women poets in the twentieth century have been consciously concerned with masks or mask analogs to a degree unknown before. Elinor Wylie is the best example, a woman for whom self-protection and contrivance were everything. But Amy Lowell made "Patterns" a tremendously popular poem about masks and H. D. adopted the masks of the past to resolve the torments of the present. Louise Bogan wrote several mask poems, speaking in "Heard by a Young Girl" of "the secret and the delicate mask" which the lover will presumably try to remove. Patrick Moore sees her "Masked Woman's Song" as an expression of anger against men who have "forced women to live, out of fear, at a distance, masked from the varieties of experience and the wellsprings of life."[19]

Though the focus on mask is always in part psychological, it should be clear that this focus is not meant to imply either that the task of the critic is to unmask the poet by discovering what she "really" meant (too often the implication of psychological criticism) or that language can never reveal truths about women's experiences, as some deconstructive critics would have it. It is rarely the case, among the women I write about, that the mask is seen as an inevitable or delightful aspect of human experience. More often, these women want like Melville to strike through the pasteboard mask to get at something which they find difficult to articulate. As Alicia Ostriker says: "When masks and disguises govern the poems, . . . it is not to entertain us but because the mask has grown into the flesh. It is the fact that the question of identity is a real one, for which the thinking woman may have no satisfactory answer, that turns her resolutely inward."[20]

In this sense, persona and mask are not always the same. Persona becomes the operative and complex discourse about the mask though this is likely to occur only after the poet has achieved a certain degree of self-consciousness, with which she is aware of choosing among models to represent the particular image of herself she desires to project. When persona becomes distinguishable from mask, the poet has usually developed a sense of irony about her literary self that deserves recognition.

Yet, despite the importance of a female poet's recognition of her own multiplicity, I have trouble subscribing to Sandra Gilbert's notion that the female modernists are more comfortable with masks and with a decentered subject than their male counterparts who oppose false mask to true self.[21] If anything, my research has led me to the opposite conclusion: that authenticity is a burning concern for some women precisely because of their awareness of the limitations of the particular masks they are constrained to wear. Her analysis may work for Virginia Woolf, for

Moore and Stein, but most of the women I have studied are in search of a stable and strong sense of selfhood. Contrary to Gilbert, I find William Butler Yeats less ready to oppose false mask to true self, less concerned that his vital energies will be lost under the costumes of representation.

In "The (US)es of (I)dentity: A Response to [Elizabeth] Abel on (E)merging Identities," Judith Kegan Gardiner makes an argument that agrees in outline with what I have to say about Elinor Wylie further on. Gardiner recommends a critical approach to women's novels that "leads us to view women's writing as a process connecting the author, her characters, and her readers. These novels make us complicit; teaching us to know as she does, engaging us in the process whereby *the self creates itself in the experience of creating art.*"[22] The particular closeness between women authors and their works may be related to the need to create a legitimate stance within patriarchal culture.

This is not to say, however, that we should read women's poetry as simply autobiographical, transparently referential, or essentially private in its concerns. The nightingale tradition takes its name from the nightingale of myth, Philomela, whose rape and subsequent mutilation by Tereus, her brother-in-law, renders her unable to speak. Her story, woven into a tapestry, reveals not only her own victimization but the nature of power under patriarchy. Tapestry art is, in its traditional form, the rendering of a world of interconnections: social, political, biological, and artistic. Its content is always drenched with history, as is the mask's.

Though the focus of this project is in part historical, converging on the years between 1910 and 1945, some caveats are in order. The subject of this study remains the nightingale tradition. Thus, it will not focus on either the populists (like Lola Ridge, Genevieve Taggard, and Muriel Rukeyser) or the radical modernists (like Gertrude Stein, Mina Loy, and Marianne Moore). Some choices have to be made in any project of this sort. I have chosen to focus on a group of women all born before 1900, all of whom transform personal experience into poetry about women, and who train themselves to be poets by working in disciplined, traditional, and highly condensed forms. Half of them—Amy Lowell, H. D., and Edna Millay— give up adherence to these forms later on, but half—Sara Teasdale, Elinor Wylie, and Louise Bogan—do not. For all of them, the narrow lyric is a significant early choice because, like the mask, it seems to offer power and protection.

I have neither included nor excluded women because of their politics. Mina Loy, for instance, was a feminist and wrote defiantly of women's experience in "Parturition," as Virginia Kouidis shows.[23] Marianne Moore had her moments of feminist insight in poems like "Marriage" and "Sojourn in the Whale." Were I only concerned with poets who have expressed what might be called "politically correct" views, I might have included Gertrude Stein, who is more and more the subject of feminist critical interest because of poems like "Patriarchal Poetry" and "Storyette: H. M." Her lesbian love poems, though still opaque to many of us, address themselves to an issue of interest in this book, women and the body. However, none of these women inherits the legacy of the nightingale tradition as outlined in *The Nightingale's Burden*: the combination of lyric reflection in the use of the first person to explore issues relating to women and power, a deep sense of frustration, and at least an early poetic that emphasizes discipline, condensation, and traditional forms.

As not all poets capable of feminist insight belong to the nightingale tradition, neither is the tradition itself necessarily feminist, if by feminist we mean the translation of isolated insights into a coherent sociopolitical philosophy. Amy Lowell, Elinor Wylie, Sara Teasdale, H. D., and Louise Bogan were all antagonistic to feminism as a political movement to benefit women in general. Yet each was conscious of gender as a significant issue in the life of a creative woman.

A final word is in order here about black women poets. An important book still needs to be written, relating black women poets like Alice Dunbar-Nelson, Angelina Weld Grimke, and Georgia Douglas Johnson to prominent white women poets like Edna Millay and Sara Teasdale, to whom Johnson, at least, was specifically compared. This is not that book.

In "Afro-American Women Poets: A Bio-Critical Survey," Gloria Hull reminds us that black women do not fit neatly into white traditions but create a synthesis of their own:

> Since black women poets are African people kidnapped to America, they did not simply fall heir to an Anglo-Saxon tradition but gave birth to an Anglo-African one which forced together African and English modes of thought and expression. . . . It remains indisputably true that for all of the foregoing reasons Afro-American women poets, by and large, have had to "go it alone" as only children or support and nurture each other in an underground sisterhood. Thus they have forged and developed their own unique tradition.[24]

However, the fascinating part of reading Hull's book, *Color, Sex, and Poetry: Three Women Writers of the Harlem Renaissance* (1987), was its revelation of how often these poets were writing poems which do sound like they belong within the nightingale tradition. Furthermore, these were essentially middle-class women, though, as Hull points out, "large amounts of ambivalence, white blood, and caste privilege did not obliterate the basic race-color reality of these three women's existence." Like the nightingale poets, they were all born before the turn of the century, and like Teasdale, Wylie, and most of their nineteenth-century predecessors, they were "reared as proper, middle-class, almost Victorian" women who valued modesty and privacy. Hull says that it is hard to know to what extent they saw themselves as belonging to a feminine literary tradition. But their subjects, their use of conventional forms, Grimke's seclusion and her image of the harp all provoke fascinating speculations about their reading of white women poets. Furthermore, Hull's comment that "all these women were released into the freedom of the self only through the lyric 'I' persona"[25] invites further consideration of the ways identity-formation and poetic production were achieved similarly and differently by the two groups.

We now know that African-American women wrote a great deal of poetry during the years between the First and Second World Wars. In Erlene Stetson's *Black Sister: Poetry by Black American Women, 1746–1980*, one can find at least

thirteen poets who were doing interesting work during this time.[26] Alice Dunbar-
Nelson's poem "I Sit and Sew"—which expresses anger at her domestic imprisonment and hunger for the more compelling drama of the war front—suggests the
kind of gendered reaction to the European conflict that Gilbert and Gubar explore
in "Soldier's Heart" in the second volume of *No Man's Land*.[27]

A striking example of a poem invoking the nightingale tradition is Georgia
Douglas Johnson's "The Heart of a Woman," published in 1918.

> The heart of a woman goes forth with the dawn,
> As a lone bird, soft winging, so restlessly on,
> Afar o'er life's turrets and vales does it roam
> In the wake of those echoes the heart calls home.
>
> The heart of a woman falls back with the night,
> And enters some alien cage in its plight,
> And tries to forget it has dreamed of the stars
> While it breaks, breaks, breaks, on the sheltering bars.[28]

This poem has all the elements of the nineteenth-century nightingale mode: emphasis on special female experience, rejection of aspiration, suggestion of the dual
nature of sanctuary ("sheltering bars"), a prison image, a sense of deep frustration.
Though I can no longer see such poems purely as "archetypal," the free bird poem,
written first by Felicia Hemans and then reworked by many American white women,
certainly provides a broader context for this lyric than race alone.

However, the problem with trying to examine seriously the issues of how black
women poets both fit into and depart from the tradition I am examining is that
there are so many gaps in what we know. Hull's book is the first full-length study
and it only begins to scratch the surface, making no attempt itself to relate Alice
Dunbar-Nelson, Angelina Grimke, and Georgia Johnson to contemporary white
female voices, though Hull has said that black women read the popular white
women poets. We will need to wait until more material is available before beginning
the necessary task of reconceiving the relations between the two cultures.

What is clear, however, is that for women these definitely *were* two cultures.
As far as we know, the nightingales paid no attention to the poetry being published
by their black sisters. By the same token, Hull has very little to say about cross-
references from black to white, except where Georgia Douglas Johnson intriguingly
mentions that Edna St. Vincent Millay visited a black salon in Washington in
order to see Jean Toomer.

Nothing is more indicative of the differences between our world and the world
of these nightingale women than the level of mutual recognition which is characteristic of the literary scene today. Diversity rather than uniformity characterizes
our literary milieu with women of all colors taking active part.

And what has happened to the nightingale tradition? For some reason, until
the Second World War most people associated women poets with its most prominent members: Emily Dickinson, Amy Lowell, Elinor Wylie, and Edna St. Vincent
Millay. (Marianne Moore was considered an oddity, not a representative figure.)

Since the 1950s the tradition even in its twentieth-century manifestation has lost its centrality. Instead, we have a multiplicity of female voices (which didn't, of course, prevent three male anthologers in 1976 from excluding all but a few.)[29] African-American and Native American women, in particular, seem to have come into their own in both poetry and prose.

In the last chapter of this book, I will talk further about the postwar period, though without attempting anything like a survey of contemporary women poets on the scale, say, of Alicia Ostriker's impressive *Stealing the Language: The Emergence of Women's Poetry in America.*[30] The masks have certainly changed. But occasionally behind the new, more liberated models, one catches an eye, sombre, restless, with a trace of ancestral longing, and thinks suddenly of the settling of old wings on hard perches. We have yet to see the dawn of a day in which women do not know the fears and frustrations of gender.

2. WOMEN AND FEMININE LITERARY TRADITIONS
Amy Lowell and the Androgynous Persona

Among the nightingale poets, there are few individuals likely to appear as forbidding as the formidable Amy Lowell, walking her garden path at Sevenels, her mansion in Brookline, Massachusetts. To many of us, her name is familiar but her life and her poetry are shadowy presences left over from a brief excursion into an anthology, perhaps, where "Patterns" hovers in an antique haze. The most frequently reprinted photograph of Amy Lowell, in which she appears austere and scowling, does nothing to bring her closer to our own time, emphasizing instead her affiliations with Queen Victoria and a world we have lost. A world well lost, some would say.

> I walk down the garden paths,
> And all the daffodils
> Are blowing, and the bright blue-squills.
> I walk down the patterned garden-paths
> In my stiff brocaded gown.
> With my powdered hair and jewelled fan,
> I too am a rare
> Pattern. As I wander down
> The garden paths.[1]

To a young Robert Lowell, his kinswoman was no less intimidating, since she was typically described as "irreproachably decent." Still, in the context of his essay "Life Studies," she represents to Robert the attraction of a disruptive force within the family's oppressive configuration. We are invited to feel the young poet's fascination with a figure so mysteriously in need of defense. "Amy Lowell was never a welcome subject in our household. Of course, no one spoke disrespectfully of Miss Lowell. She had been so plucky, so *formidable, so beautifully and unblushingly immense*, as Henry James might have said."[2] As feminists, we too may see Amy Lowell as one of our forebears, but there are certain relatives with whom one doesn't bother to communicate, and unfortunately Amy Lowell has become one of those.

But "Patterns" is not a poem about an austere, supercilious figurine. The eighteenth-century persona who imagines herself as "just a plate of current fashion /

Tripping by in high-heeled ribboned shoes" will soon begin to disrobe. "For my passion / Wars against the stiff brocade." She will confound us with a picture of her nakedness bruised by the buttons of her lover's waistcoat. We will feel her lover's hand like the water stroking "the softness of a woman bathing in a marble basin." And if we know something more about Amy Lowell, we may be shocked that this woman infamous for her obesity should invite us to so intimate an encounter, as one of the members of her audience at a poetry reading reported feeling shocked when Lowell read one of her many poems about disrobing. She didn't like the sensation of imagining Amy Lowell *deshabillée*.

Despite Lowell's repeated attempts to remove her cultural garments, however, it remains true that, like Emily Dickinson's Nature, "those who know her, know her less the nearer her they get." This study of Amy Lowell's persona and its intersection with American culture at the turn of the century will not attempt to lay bare the real Amy Lowell since such a task would inevitably prove futile. Instead, I will examine the forms of self-representation Lowell chose, suggesting where appropriate the convergence of these representations and cultural models available to such women. For it is not only in the first-person poems that Lowell explored ways of representing a female sensibility frustrated with the narrow conventions of ladyship. She also used masks, both male and female, which are sometimes striking in their difference from Lowell's perceived public presence even as they reveal aspects of a poetic self symmetrical with a larger conception of her psyche. If women poets have made their psyche from their need, as Alicia Ostriker has suggested,[3] Amy Lowell's complicated poetic psyche is made up from both ends of the traditional nightingale spectrum, in masks outrageous as well as austere. How many of us would recognize Lowell in the wife of "Appuldurcombe Park," who chants: "I am a woman, sick for passion"? Yet this was one of Amy Lowell's masks. She exploited the traditional woman poet's voices of frustration and melancholy even as she insisted that she belonged to a completely different school.

The public persona Lowell chose for herself was the androgyne, a figure with both "masculine" and "feminine" attributes but emphasizing the masculine.[4] Though Lowell vacillated between presenting herself as a "lady" and as an overweening man, as early as Lowell's second book, *Sword Blades and Poppy Seed* (1914), the poet imagined a conflagration consuming the two halves of her androgynous psyche—the intellectual and passionate "male" side (a poet) and the languid, sensitive artisan side, constructed as female. In this poem Annette, the romantic female lead, seems at first the less interesting of the two as she sits with her basket, nervously exclaiming: "My work is taxing and I must have sight! I MUST!" She creates rich patterns with thread and cloth like Philomela, and like the earlier poets in the nightingale tradition, she is nervous and full of frustration. Yet when the conflagration devours her house at the end, the vision is transferred to Peter the poet, who becomes her eye. In this final fusion we see Lowell's desire to melt her categories, male and female; though the male gaze absorbs Annette's vision, his last word is a cry for his lost female other.

The division between the two personae, first asserted where "the shadow of the man is divided from the shadow of the woman by a silver thread," turns out to be as fragile as this image suggests. One might call the silver thread romantic but succeeding it is a surrealistic passage of great power and mystery. Written in polyphonic prose, a form in which line as a unit is abandoned but recurrent patterns of sound and syntactical units remain, it startles us with its excursion into the grotesque. The basket this bright-haired virgin carries is not a basket of moonlight as her lover has imagined. (He says: " 'The Basket Filled with Moonlight,' what a title for a book!") Instead, it is a work-basket whose very grotesquerie shatters the tradition of romance into which the lover has tried manfully to inscribe his beloved. In his revery about the basket, "He has forgotten the woman in the room," though she is intensely there.

Instead of nuts or moonlight, Annette's basket holds human eyes, eyes which he cannot see because of his own altering gaze.

> They are eyes, hundreds of eyes, round like marbles! Unwinking, for there are no lids. Blue, black, gray, and hazel, and the irises are cased in the whites, and they glitter and spark under the moon. The basket is heaped with human eyes. She cracks off the whites and throws them away. They ricochet upon the roof, and get into the gutters, and bounce over the edge and disappear. But she is here, quietly sitting on the window-sill, eating human eyes. (58–60)

The woman who masks her inner violence under the modesty of a ladylike appearance, as Emily Dickinson's persona also does in "I Tie my Hat, I Crease my Shawl," is one version of Amy Lowell. The man, "tormented with pricks," who burns to consummate his passion and who transforms his experience into literature, is also Amy Lowell. The poem's ending remains obscure, however. Annette disappears in the "fire" of his devouring and deflowering passion, but "he" becomes one of "her" eyes: "he ricochets, gets to the edge, bounces over and disappears," only to return as a gazer at "deflowered windows," the burnt-out ruin of her structure of sensibility.

What is the relationship between Lowell's choice of a male persona to represent the poet and her sense of herself as a woman alienated from the masculine models available to her in the great tradition of English poetry, forced to become a self-consuming artifact, all eyes without text? The answer to this question is complex and provides the substance of this chapter, which will attempt to examine in some depth the relationship between Lowell's androgynous stance and her problematic heritage as a woman writer.

Yet this is not only Amy Lowell's story. Most of the women in this study share her discomfort. Elinor Wylie frequently imagined herself as a male and chose the persona of the woman warrior to suggest her desire for literary cross-dressing. H. D. had little respect for women poets other than Sappho and a few others. She preferred to see herself as belonging to an intermediate sex, neither wholly male nor wholly female, and thus safely removed from the threat of being considered a poetess. Edna Millay always spoke of the poet as male despite her respect for other women writers. She had herself photographed in masculine clothes and preferred the name "Vincent" to "Edna." Louise Bogan was deeply ambivalent about other women poets, condescending about poetess art, and unwilling until very late to define her poetic inheritance along female lines.

But it is to Amy Lowell that I have allocated this chapter on women and feminine traditions because she represents the clearest example of the strains many women poets have experienced in their desire to be taken seriously as poets and, at the same time, to use poetry as a medium to express their female frustrations with their cultural positioning. Her androgynous persona was more outrageous because more masculinized than H. D.'s, Elinor Wylie's, or Edna Millay's. At the same time, Peter's cry for his lost female other at the end of "The Basket" echoes through her work, tragically foreshadowing Lowell's late desire to redeem the feminine half of her sensibility too long overshadowed by what one of her friends called "that forthright, buccaneering maleness of hers."[5] Through an examination of Lowell's androgynous persona, we can see both gender and culture as they intersected in the first two decades of our century in the self-presentation of one of our most lively women poets.

AMY LOWELL AND FEMININE PRECURSORS

Amy Lowell was the first American woman poet to see herself inheriting a female tradition and to say in print that she was somewhat dismayed by the prospect. Her ambivalence about her poetic foremothers calls into question recent feminist critical conclusions, including my own, that women poets have not been particularly susceptible to what Harold Bloom has called "the anxiety of influence."[6] Since women have needed one another to legitimate their claims to poetic achievement, so the argument goes, they have more often delighted in one another's work and been less prone to feel diminished by their predecessors' success. The oedipal model Bloom uses has been criticized by feminist scholars as inappropriate to women who are more likely to be motivated by an ethic of cooperation and reciprocity. For example, Paula Bennett, in *My Life a Loaded Gun: Female Creativity and Feminist Poetics* (1986), says:

> The highly poeticized and extremely limited Freudian romance that Bloom depicts in books like *The Anxiety of Influence*—while clearly paralleling the woman poet's struggle for separation and individuation—is at best only indirectly relevant to that struggle. The woman writer's principal antagonists are not the strong male or female poets who may have preceded her within the tradition, but the inhibiting voices that live within herself.[7]

Though I would agree with parts of this statement, I think it needs modifying. Bennett acknowledges the struggle for separation but does not take seriously enough the poet's encounters with her poetic precursors, preferring to concentrate on the battleground within.

Another version of this argument is made by Alicia Ostriker in *Stealing the Language* (1986). Ostriker sees women poets acknowledging continuities with one another on the model of Demeter and Kore, returning and reviving rather than killing and superseding. To the extent that a past woman operates as a muse for the present poet, "the female muse functions as a giver of confidence and a representative of 'an alternative line to the dominant male canon.' "[8] Other arguments against Bloom have been made by Sandra Gilbert and Susan Gubar, Joanne Feit Diehl, and myself.[9]

More recently, however, some feminist scholars have felt a need to revise their earlier assumptions about relationships between poetic sisters. In " 'Forward into the Past': The Complex Female Affiliation Complex," Gilbert and Gubar acknowledge that modern women writers find themselves in a different position than their nineteenth-century sisters. Whereas the need for affiliation predominated in an earlier period, twentieth-century women writers, confronting their foremothers, find it necessary to compete with as well as revere them. "We are now convinced that female artists, looking back and revering grandmothers, are also haunted and daunted by the autonomy of these figures. In fact, we suspect that the love women writers send forward into the past is, in patriarchal culture, inexorably contaminated by mingled rivalry and anxiety," they admit.[10] This argument is especially relevant to the complicated figure of Amy Lowell, in whose work we can see a whole series of poetic behaviors amenable to this explanation.

When Lowell wrote her important poem "The Sisters," late in her life, she went back to Sappho, Elizabeth Barrett Browning, and Emily Dickinson. In "The Sisters" she certainly acknowledges the positive contribution each of these women made and she also revives them literally in her imagination, enjoying a romp with each, using the social energies that made her such a famous hostess. However, she also writes that they leave her "sad and self-distrustful." It must be said that Lowell, like H. D. and Louise Bogan, among others, was interested in superseding as well as giving acknowledgment to a feminine literary tradition. Furthermore, she associates such a feminine tradition with marginality, ascribing to men the primary authority for poetry. Lowell begins:

> Taking us by and large, we're a queer lot
> We women who write poetry. And when you think
> How few of us there've been, it's queerer still.
> I wonder what it is that makes us do it.
> Singles us out to scribble down, man-wise,
> The fragments of ourselves.
>
>   (459–61)

Since Lowell's poem is such an important breakthrough, the first grand attempt by a woman poet in America to situate herself within a feminine literary tradition, "The Sisters" is worth pausing over. From the eighteenth century forward, women have acknowledged the importance of other women poets, but usually their focus has been on a single individual like Sappho, Elizabeth Barrett Browning, or Felicia Hemans.

Here Lowell brings together three strong poets instead of one. She also acknowledges the autobiographical focus of women's poetry when she says that these poets scribble down the fragments of themselves. Of the Lesbian poet she writes:

> Ah me! I wish I could have talked to Sapho,
> Surprised her reticences by flinging mine
> Into the wind. This tossing off of garments
> Which cloud the soul is none too easy doing
> With us to-day.

In addition to what may have been Lowell's sense of continuity with Sappho as a lesbian, she also sees both the freedom and the limitations inherent in a poetic mask. For Browning, Lowell has particular sympathy because "her heart was squeezed in stiff conventions," just as Lowell's was at times.

However, Browning's connection with a powerful male poet (which might have helped her scribble down "man-wise" her fragments) leads Amy Lowell into dangerous territory. She imagines Elizabeth deferring to her husband, "for Robert is a genius." This makes Amy uncomfortable and she adds that she doesn't much like "the turn this dream is taking." Yet this dream moment is significant. The daunting presence of male achievement continued to haunt Lowell's imagination throughout her career, rendering her deferential as well as defiant.

Leaving Elizabeth Barrett Browning, Lowell imagines an afternoon with Emily Dickinson, which seems to delight her more. (In fact, she began a biography of Dickinson though she never got very far with it.) Despite the fact that her assessment of Dickinson is skewed by the early twentieth-century vision of the Amherst poet as a frustrated spinster, Lowell intuitively grasps the complexity of the earlier poet's demanding psyche.

> I think she'd be exacting,
> Without intention, possibly, and ask
> A thousand tight-rope tricks of understanding.
> But, bless you, I would somersault all day
> If by so doing I might stay with her.

Each of these poets excites Lowell's admiration and respect. However, at the end of "The Sisters," Lowell insists that she will not be restricted by the heritage they represent. Her "answer," she says, will not be any one of theirs. Why did Amy Lowell summon these women poets only to reject the traditions they represent? In the last lines one can actually hear Lowell imperiously hurrying her guests to leave, as she might have done at the end of an evening at Sevenels. "Put on your cloaks, my dears, the motor's waiting." Then, shooing them out the door with assurances that they "have not seemed strange to me, but near, / Frightfully near, and rather terrifying," she breathes a sigh of relief as she wishes them "Good night!"

Clearly, her need to separate herself from these women was complicated. In addition to her ambition to compete with a masculine tradition to which, she perceived, they did not belong, she also found that they made her self-distrustful, wondering as she did after writing the Keats biography if her commitment to invading the masculine sphere was the right one.

However, her desire to distance herself from these women also derives in part from her discomfort with the female roles they represent. Sappho's is the least objectionable. Yet Lowell admits that she knows only "a single slender thing about her"—that she was a lover. The role of the lover, especially the lesbian lover, is one Amy held dear. And, in fact, she may be singling Sappho out for special intimacy: "we two were sisters / Of a strange, isolated family." Yet Lowell wanted to be more than a love poet. She wanted to compete in the intellectual realm, a territory traditionally belonging exclusively to men.

Elizabeth Barrett Browning she sees in the guise of the female invalid, a common figure in the nineteenth century. She pities Browning for being bound by Victorian conventions, yet she admires her "over-topping brain." Then, with typical Lowell perversity, she actually criticizes Browning for being overly intellectual, saying she needed to escape "to freedom and another motherhood / Than that of poems." The love sonnets are the first Browning poems Lowell finds "fertilized" for, she concludes, "A poet is flesh and blood as well as brain." In her demand for balance between heart and head, we can hear the androgynous Amy speaking. Yet she finds Browning in any case "vastly unlike" herself, for the earlier poet was "very, very woman." Did Lowell insist on seeing her this way in order to be able to dismiss an intellectual rival? Did she see herself as also potentially guilty of one-sidedness?

Dickinson, the great experimenter, is the closest to Lowell in many ways, and therefore—as Bloom might predict—she comes in for the harshest reproach. Though Sappho "spent and gained," and Browning, after a miserly youth, "cut the strings / Which tied her money-bags and let them run," Emily

> hoarded—hoarded—only giving
> Herself to cold, white paper. Starved and tortured,
> She cheated her despair with games of patience
> And fooled herself by winning. Frail little elf,
> The lonely brain-child of a gaunt maturity,
> She hung her womanhood upon a bough
> And played ball with the stars—too long—too long—

None of these women fully represents the poet that Lowell wished to be: intellectual but passionate, sensitive to self and others but able to capture, as she praised D. H. Lawrence for doing, "the real throb, and misery and gusto" of life. For Lowell this meant choosing an androgynous persona. The spinster self was a greater liability, despite her capacity to "play ball with the stars," than the tough, manly self whom Lowell had never yet seen represented in a woman poet.

THE ANDROGYNOUS PSYCHE

What were the psychological factors that contributed to Lowell's choice of an androgynous persona, making her sensitive to her feminine literary heritage while she at the same time hoped to supersede it through imitation of and competition with men? Lowell's psyche was certainly shaped by the special circumstances of her upbringing.

The first issue that comes to mind when one thinks of the Lowells is apt to be class, as in the familiar epigram: "Cabots speak only to Lowells and Lowells speak only to God." Lowell privilege is proverbial, though Amy's immediate kin were not directly involved with the famous Lowell mills, founded by her great-grand-father. Inherited wealth made it possible for her family to live well. Furthermore, her father was a shrewd businessman who consolidated the family's fortunes and brought them to a peak of prosperity.

Privilege in one quarter did not mean privilege in all, however. Amy Lowell's childhood, like other women poets', was overshadowed by dark presences. Her father, "remote, taciturn, and bound to a strict routine,"[11] sounds eerily like Emily Dickinson's or Lucy Larcom's. All three men were severe Victorian patriarchs, though each could soften upon occasion. Lowell's father was a committed gardener who loved to tend his flowers, as Amy herself would do after his death. In both business acumen and love of flowers, she followed in his footsteps.

Her mother was a semi-invalid during most of Amy's childhood. This pairing—familiar enough in early women poets' lives—seems to have made Amy associate strength with men and sensibility with women. In "The Swans" she speaks "Of men passing—passing—every hour, / With arms of power, and legs of power, / And power in their strong, hard minds" (439). Such equations are, of course, as much a part of our cultural heritage as they are the result of particular experiences and hardly need biographical specification.

In fact, Amy's biography is surprisingly conventional in some respects. Though a tomboy at heart, she was not immune to longings for the beauty and charm other little girls had. Alternating between the rough-and-tumble of sports and attempts to conform to expectations for girls, Lowell never found an identity paradigm that fully suited her.

On the one hand, "Amy was deeply grieved that she was not a boy."[12] Yet she received little encouragement in her rebellions. S. Foster Damon says, "Mrs. Lowell thought Amy should be more feminine and tried to interest her in dolls and sewing, things which Amy abhorred" (Damon, 60). On the other hand, Amy internalized the voice of the critical parent and was prone to self-castigation. In her composition book fourteen-year-old Amy reflects the dilemma of being the androgynous tomboy in her culture. Her answers to a series of assigned questions show her caught between conflicting desires for self-assertion and self-protection. When asked to name her favorite heroine, she put down Jo from *Little Women*— the forthright tomboy she most seemed to resemble. However, the heroine she disliked most was Joan of Arc, whom she deemed "too masculine." The quality she liked best in a man was "manliness"; in a woman, "modesty." Faced with only conventional sex-role categories, she was forced to sum herself up as "a great rough masculine, strong thing" (Damon, 89).

Thus, the androgynous characteristics Amy Lowell was to highlight in future self-representations surfaced early and brought with them ambiguous consequences.

A glandular disturbance, undiagnosed and untreated, soon made her noticeably overweight. Her teen years were extremely painful, full of crushes on boys which were never reciprocated. In her fifteenth year she began a diary in which she recorded her longings and harsh self-criticism about her body. "Really, you know, I am appaulingly [sic] fat," she wrote (Gould, 45). Later she would demand that the mirrors in her hotel rooms be covered by drapes so that she need not be reminded of her body. She paid no attention to the dancing lessons she was given until quite unexpectedly she learned she had an aptitude for dancing and found that instead of being a wallflower she might be a popular partner.

Throughout her life Lowell was not unhappy to support the conventions of femininity when they suited her purposes. Louis Untermeyer tells the story of an argument Lowell once carried on with Heywood Broun in which she actually attacked feminists for attempting to revise the position of women in society. The argument concerned the Lucy Stone League, then much in the news for its insistence that women be allowed to keep their natal surnames after marriage. Untermeyer remembers:

> Broun's wife, Ruth Hale, was a . . . feminist, a charter member of the Lucy Stone League, and Broun attempted to defend the movement. "Amy Lowell leaned back," said Broun, "in a big, easy chair, puffing one of her Manila cigars. "I have (puff, puff) no patience," said Miss Lowell, "with the new-fashioned woman (puff, puff) and her so-called rights. I believe (and here she drew deep of the cigar) in the old-fashioned conservative woman and all her limitations.[13]

Without further information one might conclude that Lowell was mocking her audience since it was Haywood Broun and not his wife who was making the argument. Punctuated by the cigar, her comments suggest self-irony at the least. In *A Critical Fable* she does acknowledge the difficulties of name-changing for a writer like Sara Teasdale who, after her marriage, is expected to become a Mrs. Filsinger.

However, Lowell was in many ways deeply conservative. The left-wing causes of Greenwich Village—socialism, psychoanalysis, and women's suffrage—left her cold. In this way class had its influence on her. She certainly saw herself as a member of the ruling classes, she denounced the left-wing orientation of poets like Carl Sandburg and Louis Untermeyer, and she preferred to struggle against conventions by identifying more consistently with men than she did with women. Like H. D. and Elinor Wylie, she was concerned less with the lives of quiet desperation lived by women as an underclass than with exceptionally gifted spirits (like herself) who happened to be born female and thus were disadvantaged.

Obviously, identification through the male side of her heritage seemed to give her more opportunities for power and influence. Her father was eminently successful in the world of State Street. One brother was a famous astronomer and the other became president of Harvard. Furthermore, James Russell Lowell, her elder cousin, was her first image of a poet.

The women in Lowell's family were comparatively retiring, and when Amy began to move into the limelight of the new movement in poetry, her family were appalled. Her father had always felt that, like her sister's painting, Amy's poetry should be a pastime engaged in at home, not a public self-presentation. Yet from an early period Amy Lowell wanted to have it both ways. She wanted the power of the male, as she saw it, without losing touch with that same overburdened feminine sensibility that, at the turn of the century, resulted in neurasthenia in so many talented women, like Alice James and Marion Hooper Adams.

In 1889 she recorded in her diary, "Lotty told me last Sunday that I affected hoydenness, & was really the opposite, I did not let on, but I knew it was true" (Gould, 44). Thus, she began to see her self-presentation as both artificial and necessarily self-protective, a set of masks she would continue to chafe under and exploit throughout her life.

It is tempting to feel, as Glenn Ruihley does in *The Thorn of the Rose: Amy Lowell Reconsidered*,[14] that the "real" self was the more vulnerable one which Amy always associated with her female side. This was the part of her that responded so strongly to seeing the torture device from Nuremburg known as the "Iron Virgin," a traumatic experience she was to remember all her life. As a young woman watching beside her mother's deathbed and enduring her mother's agonizing screams, she feared she would go mad. And throughout her life, Lowell was prone to terrible depressions. At least one mental breakdown (in 1898) took her seven years to get over.

In all of these instances, she called the "feminine" side of her personality the one that responded in such a violent and helpless way to pain and anguish. But her conception of femininity was as artificial and constraining, as limited in its potential for self-expression, as its opposite. Her denigrating attitude toward the "mauve joys" and "purple sins" of 1890s poetry conveys a side of Lowell's personality as characteristic as the neurasthenic one. In a letter to Donald Evans, she wrote: "Of course we need more beauty in the world; of course that is what we must make the world safe for. But do not let us lisp this creed in a kind of dying languor; *let us shout it lustily—and dare to be happy—and dare to be robust—and dare to be a thousand things which mean poetry just the same*" (emphasis hers; Gould, 241).

Each side of this binary opposition which she attempted to unite in the androgyne was a mask to the extent that it presented itself as the "real" one, inhospitable to its shadow self. In this same letter to Evans, so full of Lowell bravado, one feels the presence of artificiality in the poet's very denial of her own need to pose. She says: "I detest pose, and have never found the need of being other than straightforwardly what I am." Yet we still don't know who Amy Lowell was. Even the mask of the androgyne left her uncomfortable in the end.

One consequence of her determination to privilege the so-called male side of her complex psyche was the necessity of uniting herself with a feminine other through whom she could live out her desires to be both maternal and pampered, as her own mother had been. This individual needed a make-up the reverse of Amy's: practical and self-sustaining independence controlled within a feminine model of demeanor. Ada Dwyer Russell was the deeply appropriate complement to Amy's androgynous spirit, an actress familiar with role playing (like Amy) but devoted to the duties of nurturance.

Amy met Ada in 1912. She soon realized that the actress could become the necessary complement to her fragmented psyche, the female other she had dreamed of since she was a child "whom I should love better than any other girl in the world, and who would feel so toward me" (Gould, 42), as she had phrased her longing in her diary. In 1914, after some hesitation, Ada agreed to leave the stage and move in with Amy, where she lived for the rest of the poet's life. The relationship appears to have been both passionate and mutually satisfying. Ada balanced Amy's roughness with her gentleness and tact, often smoothing the ruffled feathers of guests who might otherwise have left distraught. Most of Amy's letters from friends sent fond regards to Mrs. Russell, who had been divorced long before but had a daughter. H. D. and Bryher seem to have recognized in Ada and Amy a parallel to their own bond. Though Lowell nicknamed her companion "Peter," it was obvious that Ada played the wife to Amy's husband, as Alice B. Toklas played the wife to Gertrude Stein. In effect, Ada made it possible for Amy to carry on with her work. She read her drafts and managed the household, leaving the poet free to direct her energies toward her literary work.

Part of that work was the psychological perpetuation of a dominating persona that paid off in a certain kind of literary success. When the poet first approached a publisher with a book of poems, Ferris Greenslet of Houghton Mifflin was overwhelmed by the woman in the mannish suit who demanded so much with so little success behind her. In England Lowell managed to make a deal with Macmillan in which 90 percent of their profit would go to her and only 10 percent to them. Late in her life she brought in 1,160 pages on Keats. When her publisher suggested deletions, she simply steamrolled him into acceptance, telling him he knew nothing about biography. This was the public Amy whom everybody recognized, the woman Hugh Kenner describes as "a big blue wave."[15]

And the big blue wave was successful in a way that seemed to confirm Lowell's belief that success required a masculine persona. The story Margaret Widdemer tells suggests that Lowell saw the poetess as a dangerous option. According to Widdemer, Ezra Pound had boasted to Lowell that Harriet Monroe, editor of *Poetry Magazine* and one of Pound's early allies, was his slave. Amy Lowell did not want to be a slave. She found Pound extremely rude in their second encounter in London and she recalled to Widdemer:

"I said nothing: that is aloud. What I said to myself was, 'This young man takes me for one more literary spinster who is thrilled to be bullied into subjection by male brutality. All right, young man. I won't tell you what *I* think of *you*. But when I'm through with you, *your* Imagist movement will be *my* Imagist movement.' And," Amy ended, "it was."[16]

The "literary spinster"—a term she applied to Emily Dickinson—was vulnerable to male aggression because of her sensibility. She might be "thrilled" at precisely the moment when she should be defiant. Dickinson's method of defiance was too unworldly for Lowell, who wished to be powerful and recognized in her own time.

But Amy won the battle for imagism while losing the war; Pound simply forfeited this disputed territory and moved into other realms. Later in this chapter, we will consider Lowell's response to what she realized was literary defeat. This late perception caused her to see her literary position as one determined by that very fact she had wanted to ignore: gender.

ANDROGYNY IN CULTURAL CONTEXT

Though all of the poets in this study struggled against a feminine gender-identification to some degree, none but Amy chose the androgyne, as I earlier defined this term, for her poetic persona. "That forthright, buccaneering maleness" Elizabeth Sergeant describes was determined in part by the psychological imperatives of this poet's particular background and genetic makeup. However, equally important was her location in the culture of her time and place. At the turn of the century, the figure of the androgyne was available as a model to be appropriated.

In *No Place of Grace: Antimodernism and the Transformation of American Culture, 1880–1920,* Jackson Lears argues that popular literature of this period glorified the "masculine" woman because of her vitality. Androgynous women were acceptable within the antimodern "martial ideal":

> For some, the martial ideal promised fresh possibilities. Even if military adventure remained a male prerogative, as in the polemics of Agnes Repplier and Elizabeth Bisland, idealized war-making could embody desires for intensified experience. But military adventure did not remain a male prerogative, at least not in the realm of historical romance. The heroines of chivalric fiction could sometimes ride, fight, and organize an army as well as any man. Joan of Arc was one such figure; another was [Francis] Crawford's Eleanor of Guienne, who rides unflinchingly to face the Turk. Bored by her giggling ladies-in-waiting, she cries, "Oh, I often wish I were born a man!" That sentiment haunted educated women at the turn of the century, and suggested one reason for the popularity of self-willed chivalric heroines: they represented liberation from restrictive femininity.[17]

An earlier poet, Louise Imogen Guiney had used elements of the martial persona in her turn-of-the-century poems. Though Amy Lowell was rather critical of her work, she—like Guiney—grew up longing to be male. She not only read chivalric literature, she also went on to write numerous poems about military heroes like Napoleon and Lord Nelson, identifying her own interests in many places with those of military men. In "The Foreigner," printed in her second book, we can hear Amy Lowell's defiant intentions to make her presence felt by the literati. In this poem she tells us, "my heart / Is the heart of a man." Reminding us of her literary battle with Ezra Pound, she declares:

> before I have done,
> I will prick my name in
> With the front of my steel,

And your lily-white skin
Shall be printed with me.
For I've come here to win!
(40–41)

Unwilling to be the text or the muse, roles often assigned to women by creative men, Lowell announces her intentions with an *en garde* directed at the dandified male poets of the 1890s. Using the voice of the rough-hewn bohemian soldier, she pokes fun at the aristocratic, effeminate dress of her enemies. In this we can see her willingness to appropriate the language and costume of a virile persona, not to redeem the feminine but to escape it. In fact, she turns her enemy into a text by claiming that his "lily-white skin"—a description conventionally feminine—"shall be printed with me." In this way she appropriates the metaphors of male prerogative to turn the tables on the male literary establishment.

"The Foreigner" accomplishes cross-dressing as a form of "re-dressing," a strategy not uncommon among talented women at the turn of the century. Lowell uses the imagery of clothes in the poem to emphasize her appropriation of conventional categories: masculinity conveys power, femininity weakness. Thus, in this peculiar world of multiple role reversals, the female poet represents herself as male and superior, denigrating her male enemies as effeminate and inferior.

Like the Foreigner, both Amy Lowell and Gertrude Stein defied the conventions of their cultures by wearing odd man-tailored clothes. But they were hardly alone in this gesture. Dr. Mary Walker had been recommending that women's dress become more masculinized since the middle of the nineteenth century. In two books, *Hit* and *Unmasked; or the Science of Immorality*, Walker argued that the constriction of women's bodies in corsets, crinolines, small shoes, and other devices of fashion were damaging to women's health. During the Civil War, Walker pursued her medical career in men's trousers. She was certainly eccentric but her eccentricities were given wide recognition. Susan Gubar tells us, "In *Hit*, Dr. Walker's emphasis on the martial arts of women like Joan of Arc, Margaret of Anjou, Boadicea, and Isabella of Spain matches the taste for danger, exertion and patriotism that won her the only Medal of Honor given to a woman."[18] As Gubar points out, the adoption of male costume suggests a desire for the mystique of adventure and power associated with male heroes. Elinor Wylie's aunt, an English teacher at Bryn Mawr, also dressed in men's clothing, and all of these women were—by some standards of their culture—successful.

However, the assumption of the guise of the Other may also carry darker significance. Gubar says: "Male mimicry that presents itself as an act of assertion can, paradoxically, partake of 'feminine' self-denial, even self-hatred, for the male facade or persona may be an attempt born of shame to deny, hide, or disgrace the female self."[19] Such emotions were common to Amy Lowell as we can see from the derogatory role assigned to the feminine in "The Foreigner." In other poems as well, she both ridiculed and identified with her shy, overly sensitive, and distinctly unassertive female characters.[20]

Clearly, the androgyne grew out of changes in the feminine ideal which emerged in the last part of the nineteenth century under the banner of the New Woman, a controversial figure frequently attacked in the 1890s. In "The New Woman as Androgyne," Carroll Smith-Rosenberg writes: "A second generation of New Women confronted these new attacks upon their right to enter the 'male' world and assume 'male' power. They did so, however, in a new and complex manner. Seizing the men's most central symbolic constructs they invested them with female intent and thus inverting, repudiated them."[21] Smith-Rosenberg also sees the darker side of this maneuver, however. Like Susan Gubar, she notes that cross-dressing runs the risk of involving the woman writer in an act of fundamental alienation, relieving only intermittently a woman's pervasive sense of powerlessness.

Obviously, the culture into which Amy Lowell thrust herself with the phenomenal success of her second book in 1914 was a complex matrix of warring ideologies: bohemian rebellion and bourgeois restraint; modernist artistic salvos and post-Victorian reminders of a respectable past. William Dean Howells and Lizette Woodworth Reese were still publishing. Writers who came to prominence in the 1890s were still being read, even as the new writers—Robert Frost, Ezra Pound, Amy Lowell—were first being published.

Amy Lowell's position, however, was clear. Like George Santayana, who excoriated the "genteel tradition" in 1931, she saw the 1890s of her youth as having produced only dead artifacts, effeminate and gutless. In "Two Generations in American Poetry" she made the contrast which confirmed her alignment with masculinity. The new experimental poetry with which she sought to identify, "whether written by men or women, was in essence masculine, virile, very much alive. Where the nineties had warbled, it was prone to shout."[22]

Her rejection of the older generation was both a rejection of feminine influence on the arts and a rejection of part of Amy Lowell's past, part of herself. The sensitive romantic young woman she had been in the 1890s was perhaps too visible in Lowell's first book, *A Dome of Many-Coloured Glass*. It was this young woman, after all, whose loss of a male lover had contributed to a nervous breakdown and years of depression.[23]

Furthermore, the older kind of poetry had allied itself, Lowell felt, with precisely the kind of sensibility which spelled danger for an ambitious, unconventional woman. During the 1890s Lowell had felt herself to be a disconnected soul. As alienated artists drew together in the cities and began to have a powerful influence on the arts, she saw a chance to redeem an earlier dispiriting sense of failure.

> This little handful of disconnected souls, all unobtrusively born into that America which sighed with Richard Watson Gilder, wept with Ella Wheeler Wilcox, permitted itself to dance delicately with Celia Thaxter, and occasionally to blow a graceful blast on the beribboned trumpet of Louise Imogen Guiney, was destined to startle its progenitors.[24]

One of the women poets Lowell read from her early years was Alice Meynell, the British poet whose work—like Guiney's—was influenced by both Catholicism and late Victorianism. Like the little band Lowell both welcomes and dismisses in "The Sisters," Alice Meynell reappears in Lowell's late work, in a poem called "On Looking at a Copy of Alice Meynell's Poems, Given Me, Years Ago, By a Friend." Again she puts distance between her early feminine languishing self, who so loved to quote the verses of Meynell, and her later, more robust, avatar.

> How strange that tumult, looking back.
> The ink is pale, the letters fade.
> The verses seem to be well-made,
> But I have lived the almanac.
>
> (537)

Again she shoos an earlier woman poet out the door. "Between us I must shut the door. / The living have so much to do."

But was it true that Amy Lowell could exorcise so easily the ghosts of her early affiliations with the nightingale tradition? As late as *Pictures of the Floating World* (1919), there is an evident echo of Louise Imogen Guiney in the phrasing of the second stanza of "La Vie de Bohème," suggesting that Lowell still heard nightingale melodies in her inner ear.

Guiney's poem, "Borderlands," evokes a mystical encounter with an invisible Presence.

> Yet in the valley,
> At the turn of the orchard alley,
> When a wild aroma touched me in the moist and moveless air,[25]

she encounters her long-desired Friend. In Amy Lowell's poem, "La Vie de Bohème," she speaks of herself as "a defender / Of undesired faiths," sounding a note of self-pity and failure which one hears increasingly in the late poems. The purposes to which Lowell puts the earlier poet's phrasing are distinctly different from Guiney's and yet the echo is unmistakable.

> But in its narrow alleys,
> The low-hung, dust-thick valleys
> Where the mob shuffles its empty tread,
> My soul is blunted against dullard wits,
> Smeared with sick juices,
> Nicked impotent for other than low uses.
>
> (226)

Horace Gregory claims that Lowell's "true affinities were of a nineteenth-century origin, gathered from her readings in her father's library at Sevenels and among the book shelves of Boston's Athenaeum."[26] There is much to support this view, even in Lowell's own estimation of herself in a late poem like "New Heavens for Old," published in the posthumous *Ballads for Sale*. In this poem she contrasts the new women of the 1920s who:

bare the whiteness of their lusts to the dead
    gaze of the old housefronts,
They roar down the street like flame,
They explode upon the dead houses like sharp, new fire

with her own, old-fashioned, persona:

> But I—
> I arrange three roses in a Chinese vase:
> . . . .
> I fuss over their arrangement.
> Then I sit in a South window
> And sip pale wine with a touch of hemlock in it,
> And think of Winter nights,
> And field-mice crossing and re-crossing
> The spot which will be my grave.
>
> (574)

Just as Amy Lowell's culture was a complex mixture of late-nineteenth and early twentieth-century elements, of Victorianism, progressivism, and modernism, Lowell herself interacted with her culture both as a progressive and as a reactionary.

On the one hand, she criticized Victorian prudishness, defending D. H. Lawrence's *Women in Love* against charges of obscenity. She herself wrote many poems shocking in their suggestiveness, like "Fool O' the Moon," where she speaks of desire "pounding dully from my eyes" and details the appeal of the female body, "a single breast uncovered. / The carnation tip of it / Urgent for a lover's lip" (465). The image of the naked female body bathing seems particularly potent for Lowell, and in "The Bronze Horses" she comes very close to conflating images of lesbian love with images of masturbation when she brings before us a vision of the upper-class sybaritic lady at the Roman baths.[27]

A brief example from *Sword Blades and Poppy Seed* will help to illustrate the kind of risks Lowell was willing to take with erotic imagery. "Aubade" is forthrightly sensuous.

> As I would free the white almond from the green husk
> So I would strip your trappings off,
> Beloved.
> And fingering the smooth and polished kernel
> I should see that in my hands glittered a gem beyond counting.
>
> (73)

Ironically, Ella Wheeler Wilcox, who in her own day had been accused of obscenity, attacked this book in the *Boston American* for indecent exposure.

On the other hand, Lowell felt her culture had gone mad, in the wake of Freud's theories, on the subject of sex and especially its perversions. She lived an unconventional life in a Boston marriage of notorious intensity with Ada Dwyer Russell, yet she criticized feminism and warned Elinor Wylie after her third marriage that if she insisted upon changing partners again, Amy would cut her dead and all of society would do the same.

Similarly, her masculine poetic persona, chosen in part with an ear to the voice of her generation, alternated with older models of feminine sensibility so much a part of the nightingale tradition. Even the obdurate Amy Lowell was capable of reveling in postures of self-surrender. In her "Free Fantasia on Japanese Themes" she writes:

> And my heart is still and alert,
> Passive with sunshine
> Avid of adventure.
>
> I would experience new emotions—
> Submit to strange enchantments—
> Bend to influences,
> Bizarre, exotic,
> Fresh with burgeoning.
>
> (219)

Is she the actor—alert, avid, burgeoning—or the passive receiver of influences—still, submitting, and bending? This poem shows us the softer side of the androgyne, its ability to remind us of someone as seemingly distant as Frances Osgood, who also wavers between masculine and feminine identifications in "The Cocoa-Nut Tree" half a century earlier.

Some of Lowell's love poems even suggest the masochism linked to self-surrender that inspires so many nineteenth-century poetesses in the nightingale tradition.

> To make a pavement for your feet I stripped
> My soul for you to walk upon, and slipped
> Beneath your steps to soften all your ways.
>
> (19)
>
> I pray to be the tool which to your hand
>   Long use had shaped and moulded till it be
>   Apt for your need, and unconsideringly,
> You take it for its service. I demand
> To be forgotten. . . .
>
> (36)
>
> I touch the blade of you and cling upon it,
> And only when the blood runs out across my fingers
> Am I at all satisfied.
>
> (558)

As in Emily Dickinson's "Me from Myself to Banish," self-disgust darkens "Sultry": "I stare back at myself / And see myself with loathing" (470). The nineteenth-century image of the sanctuary is there as well (in "Behind a Wall") as is the ghostly lover ("Haunted") and the death wish ("Trees"). There are numerous poems on the forbidden lover, the secret sorrow, suicide, and madness. As much as any nineteenth-century woman poet, Amy Lowell was attracted to the theme of the unattained, and "In a Time of Dearth" combines a horror of limitation, a masochistic fantasy, a retreat to a sanctuary, and suggestions of madness—the dark side of the nineteenth-century female repertoire.

My intention in pointing to these inconsistencies in Lowell's poetic persona is not to suggest either that Lowell should be read entirely as a Victorian or that her poetic program was incoherent. As we focus more directly on the androgynous literary persona she created, we must simply keep in mind that it represents the intersection of culture with psyche, influenced both by the models of deviance her culture provided in the "mannish" woman and by older models of feminine sensibility given voice in the nightingale tradition.

THE ANDROGYNOUS LITERARY PERSONA

Though the energy Amy Lowell was able to deploy in the role of androgynous woman poet served her in good stead for a number of years, the darker side of assuming a masculinized role defeated her in the end. Looking at the contours of Lowell's career, one sees both success and failure imaged in her persona.

As the energetic proponent of a new movement in poetry, called imagism, she certainly made a name for herself. Backing the publication of several editions of *Some Imagist Poets* with her considerable personal fortune, she was able to find an outlet for her own poetry and also to appear as the only imagist this side of the Atlantic available for lectures and poetry readings, since the others were all in England. After the publication of several editions of *Some Imagist Poets*, *Pictures of the Floating World* (1919) was so popular that the publishers could not keep the volume in stock. The literary world was clamoring for Amy Lowell. In a letter to the *New York Tribune* from this period, the poet described what she felt to be the magnitude of her achievement. The letter downplays the importance of the poet's wealth, which in many small ways did open doors for her, but it is accurate about the way her energy paid off.

> I started in the world with one of the greatest handicaps that someone could possibly have. I belonged to the class which is not supposed to be able to produce good creative work. I was writing in an idiom which was entirely new and to most people extremely disagreeable. I knew not a single editor and had entrance to no magazine nor paper. Will you say that I have engineered myself badly in five short years? (Gould, 257)

Lowell was right to say that she had certainly not done badly even in what was really, by 1919, nine years of writing poetry. During the next six she was to publish four more volumes of verse and a monumental biography of John Keats, an enormous output even for an energetic writer. Through these years, she was in nearly constant pain because of her obesity, high blood pressure, retina deterioration, sporadic gastritis, and heart trouble. In 1916 she had given herself an umbilical hernia by lifting up her carriage, which was mired in the mud. She had four operations for the hernia and in her last years she found it painful even to get downstairs for dinner. However, her letters reflect only irritation at the enormous inconvenience of all this. She would have been the last person to take refuge in ill health.

At the beginning of the 1920s, Lowell found herself the leader of a movement whose force had waned. She herself had moved away from the strict requirements of imagism, writing long poems in polyphonic prose. As she looked around now, she saw a new generation emerging whose best writers, she felt, were Elinor Wylie and Edna Millay. Lowell was jealous of Millay and tended to downgrade her reputation. Still, in "Two Generations of American Poetry," she called her "that delightfully clever exponent of the perennial theme of love." Elinor Wylie she admired as a tougher spirit. She spoke of her as "one of the most intellectual and well-equipped of American poets." Her own role was hard to evaluate in light of this new group. Amy Lowell had made her bid to join a literary establishment dominated by men: Ezra Pound, T. S. Eliot, Robert Frost, Carl Sandburg, John Gould Fletcher, Vachel Lindsay, and D. H. Lawrence. She hoped to count like H. D. as "one of the boys." But she did not expect to see women moving to the forefront by speaking in their own voices. She was surprised. "For, while the older movement was innately masculine, the new one is all feminine. It is, indeed, a feminine movement, and remains such even in the work of its men."[28]

In 1922, only three years before her death, Amy Lowell published A Critical Fable, a long poem evaluating the state of contemporary poetry using the humorous device of a conversation between representatives of the past and the present. It was published anonymously, Lowell herself sparking controversy about the identity of the author by her speculations about who it might be. However, she left broad hints in the text for those who read it carefully, not least of which was the central position she gave to her own work.

From one point of view, A Critical Fable reaffirmed her commitment to her self-insertion within a male tradition. It was, after all, based upon the model of James Russell Lowell's A Fable for Critics. When Amy Lowell had considered the possibility of becoming a poet in her teens, the Covering Cherub of James Russell Lowell had obliterated that fantasy. Though her version of the satire is not the monologue delivered by Apollo that her elder cousin had chosen, the dialogue, between an elderly gentleman poet (Lowell himself) and a young man who defends the new generation, repeats Amy's impulse toward cross-dressing. Though the young man (Amy) pokes fun at his elder, he also acknowledges his own position as a Bloomian late-comer.

> . . . Poor old gentleman, should I be tempted
> To tell him the fault was that he had preempted,
> He and the others, the country's small stock
> Of imagination? The real stumbling-block

Was the way they stood up like Blake's angels, a chorus
Of geniuses over our heads, . . .

                                                                    (395)

Amy Lowell clearly did feel herself in the shadow of an older generation of male
poets like Lowell and Robert Browning. In "The Immortals" she repeats this lament,
saying to her "Masters": "Our Gethsemane / Is planted with your immortality. /
We walk with feet of lead" (541).

However, *A Critical Fable* is not simply a filiopietistic imitation. Whereas the
elder Lowell used almost entirely masculine endings in his poem, Amy generously
sprinkles hers with feminine rhymes, asserting her own style. Furthermore, her
decision to use a dialogue instead of a monologue along the lines of Apollo's suggests
both her uneasiness about masculine models of traditional authority and her late
desire to challenge the past in defense of a more feminine present.

Finally, the younger persona chides the old gentleman for having underrated
Dickinson (unknown in his time) and Margaret Fuller. One interchange on this
subject is particularly revealing and deserves quotation at length. The old gentleman
speaks first.

> "For the men, I'll admit there is room for dispute;
> But the choice of Miss Dickinson I must refute."
> Then seeing me shrug, he observed, "I am human,
> And hardly can bear to allow that a woman
> Is ever quite equal to man in the arts;
> The two sexes cannot be ranked counterparts."
> "My dear Sir," I exclaimed, "if you'd not been afraid
> Of Margaret Fuller's success, you'd have stayed
> Your hand in her case and more justly have rated her."
> Here he murmured morosely, "My God! how I hated her!
> But have you no women whom you must hate too?
> I shall think all the better of you if you do,
> And of them, I may add." I assured him, "A few.
> But I scarcely think man feels the same contradictory
> Desire to love them and shear them of victory?"
> "You think wrong, my young friend," he declared with a frown,
> "Man will always love woman and always pull down
> What she does."

                                                                    (409)

This passage is interesting on several counts. In addition to the defense Amy
Lowell mounts for Emily Dickinson and Margaret Fuller, against what she perceives
as entrenched male prejudice, we also see here that the mask slips. After all, the
young man can hardly be wondering what men think and the old gentleman's
gratification is explicable only if it is a woman admitting that she feels competitive
envy of women as well.

The insights into the politics of patriarchal criticism which Lowell displays in this poem are certainly worth noting. Furthermore, A *Critical Fable* is a much livelier, funnier, and wittier poem than James Russell Lowell's, though its judgments are flawed, both with respect to Amy Lowell's assessment of contemporary women poets (whom she introduces once again only to dismiss) and in regard to strong male competitors like Pound. Even with Pound, however, Lowell is willing to grant that

> Few men have to their credit more excellent verses
> Than he used to write, and even his worse is
> Much better than most people's good.
>
> (431)

Neither James Russell Lowell nor Pound himself was inclined to be as generous to his enemies.

Of course, Lowell also used her poem to make an extended defense of her own poetry. She argues that the complex surfaces and knick-knackery of her poems conceal an impassioned heart that awaits the touch "of a man who takes surfaces only as such." She predicts that the future will exonerate her: "She'll be rated by time as more rather than less." Yet she can poke fun at herself too, as when she imagines herself competing with Vachel Lindsay to gain converts to new literary theories.

> While Amy Lowell, close by the library door,
> Announces her theories and tries hard to score
> More disciples than Lindsay; though, with his and her medium,
> It's a matter of choice which produces least tedium.
>
> (429)

Though A *Critical Fable* contains many felicities worth further attention, its significance for this argument is that it reveals Lowell's growing desire to reorient the androgynous persona in the direction of feminine alliances.

In spite of her growing doubts, however, Amy Lowell made one last grand attempt to compete in the male sphere by writing a biography of Keats. She began the project partly because she had always admired the romantic poet and she had built up one of the best private collections of Keats manuscripts in the world. However, at a deeper psychological level the biography was undertaken as a last-ditch effort to show that she could compete with educated literary men.

In the world of her youth, poetry (considered somewhat effeminate as a career) had been contrasted with history (a more virile pursuit). Writing a biography was the quintessential androgynous undertaking, connecting her once again to James Russell Lowell. In 1922 she wrote: "It is a curious thing that James Russell Lowell planned to write a life of Keats and never did so. I like to imagine that the task had been deputed to me in his stead" (Damon, 677).

Still, Lowell did not want to write a so-called virile biography of Keats which would situate him in the political and cultural history of his time. She wanted to do a psychological study of the relation between the poet's nature and his art. Defining her project in this way, she sought to transform what she understood as a male undertaking into a work where she could bring her female sensitivities to bear.

The strain of this transformation took its toll on her. Many critics have referred to the passage in one of her letters, where Amy Lowell says, "Keats is nearly killing me." She ruined her health working on the enormous manuscript at a time when her worsening hernia condition demanded that she take it easy. Her obsession with the project undoubtedly derived in part from her struggle to find a more comfortable form of self-representation than had hitherto been available. Unfortunately, as far as she was concerned, the effort proved vain. Though the Keats biography was positively reviewed in America, the English reviews were devastating.

Pulling herself together for her last major effort, Amy Lowell went back to poetry. *What's O'Clock* is her most lyrical, personal, female-oriented work, and the one which would win her the Pulitzer Prize after her death. It contains many love poems to Ada as well as the celebrated "Lilacs" and "The Sisters." It also locates Lowell's serious doubts at the end of her life about the value of her earlier androgynous ambitions.

In a little-known poem called "La Ronde du Diable," Lowell reflects on her role in the competitive literary politics of her time and suggests that the real victims of this kind of charade are women. She groups herself with her poetic sisters.

> "Here we go round the laurel-tree."
> Do we want the laurels for ourselves most,
> Or most that no one else shall have any?
> We cannot stop to discuss the question.
> We cannot stop to plait them into crowns
> Or notice whether they become us.
> We scarcely see the laurel-tree,
> The crowd about us is all we see,
> And there's no room in it for you and me.
> Therefore, Sisters, it's my belief
> We've none of us very much chance at a leaf.
>   (473)

This poem raises the question of whether a male tradition of poetic glory, epitomized by the laurels, is really appropriate to women. Engaging in such competition distracts attention from the question of whether this tradition is congenial to a woman's temperament or whether it divides women from one another. The really interesting thing about Amy Lowell's work is that it does confess to urges to compete both with men and with women, but, in the end, it provides a shrewd analysis of its own earlier tendencies. Many of the poems in *What's O'Clock* admit feelings of failure, like those in "The Watershed."

Even the title of this collection suggests the perspective of "New Heavens for Old," the sense Lowell had at the end of her life that time had passed her by. Here was a new generation of women writers like Millay and Wylie, in no way seeking to obscure their gender, but claiming popularity and respect nonetheless. However, if the spectacle of these younger women made Lowell sad and self-distrustful, it also gave her courage to write poems more directly concerned with her position as a woman poet confronting a male tradition.

One of the most significant of these is also one of her most obscure works, called "Which, Being Interpreted, Is As May Be, Or Otherwise" (453–59). The poem is a long narrative written in blank verse. It concerns old Neron, one of Lowell's many male self-portraits. He has retreated to a garret sanctuary in the attic of a church. Like Lowell in this period, he feels that he has flung clear of his times, and he regards his past and younger selves with derision.

> And Neron felt a queasy sort of pride
> In mocking his old wounds with jibes that pricked
> To a delicious flood of memory.
> The hurt outgrown was tonic to his ears.

One easily recognizes Lowell's own painful journeys downstairs after her hernia operations in Neron's daily descent to get the basket of food left by the verger.

> He hated it, the aching journey down
> And up again, he hated even his bones
> Whose insolence in so demanding food
> Sent him to get it at whatever cost
> To old, unable feet and quaking knees.

Like so many of Lowell's personae in the last books, Neron loses his grip on reality. ("For might he not be going mad? Yes, mad!") He discovers two statues in his garret, one of a king and one of a queen. In the descriptions of the two we find all the ambivalence about roles poetic and personal that Lowell herself seems to have felt. The king is described first:

> The beard held Neron's eyes.
> Waist-long and vast, its heaviness of hair
> Stamped the king's sullen masculinity
> With something of grave terror. Neron felt
> An instant loathing, tingled with shrewd fear;
> And yet, although he shuddered, a sly spark
> Of admiration twinged him like a pain.
> This was a terrible and virile king.

The queen might be a representative of the nineteenth century's ideal woman. She is the image of submission.

> Her eyes were kind,
> But wise withal, and hooded with fatigue.

> She drooped in standing, yet remained upright
> Wistfully conscious of an effort so.

Neron constructs a story about their relationship, a story which reflects Lowell's often repeated poetic concern with rape and violation, a concern which also prompted her to buy a gun she kept loaded in the library table.

> He wrought them both
> Into a tale of tragic circumstance,
> Of bargained marriage hurried on through lust,
> Of desolate surrender where no hope
> Of moving iron wills could have a place,
> Of girlhood torn upon the state of queen.

The masculine image of power would always be attractive, but Lowell feared the insensitivity, even the brutality, she suspected men were prone to. Like many women poets, Elinor Wylie, Edna Millay, and H. D. among them, she not infrequently expresses a horror of male violence and lust. Her women are often cast in the roles of victims, and she vacillates between profound sympathy for that role and anger against the women who submit. Here, in the guise of Neron, she contrasts "bitter-bearded king, mighty in power, / And gentle queen all weariful repose." Her goal here seems to be to intervene between these two and redeem the queen (and the state of femininity) through love.

Neron makes love to the queen in his fantasy: "Fully persuaded that he served her cause / By this he had in mind." But the king has his own dreams which conflict with Neron's. The king refuses to be won over, and in this conflict of wills imagination is set against imagination. Against Neron's are "black dreams peculiar to a bearded king." And

> They injured Neron in his own esteem,
> Chafing him to achieve a greater thing
> Than he had yet conceived. His ardour grew
> To match himself against the king, and crack
> The shell of high omnipotence in two.

For a brief moment Neron's dreams are realized. The queen responds. The two are lost in love,

> Being removed past any reach of speech
> Into that silent space of holiness
> Where flesh creates the everlasting world.

But the king breaks in upon them and the final battle between dreams and wills takes place. At first Neron's dream "towered up / Tremendous in its brilliance." But in the end the king, "To save his dream, threw his black beard upon it, / The heaviness of hair shut out the brilliance." Neron is found by the verger "dead as last year's fly."

A great deal that Amy Lowell felt deeply about is dealt with in this poem. It is curious that, for all Lowell's carefulness with manuscripts, written usually between midnight and 5:00 A.M. and typed by her secretaries during the day, somehow this poem got lost. Like Edna Millay after the loss of *Conversation at Midnight*, the poet felt strongly enough about it to try to recompose it but she was never as satisfied with the second version. In Lowell's case, the misplacement and loss of the poem suggest that it may have been unusually distressing to the poet.

One critic, Clement Wood, sees in this poem a lesbian fantasy coupled with a portrayal of Lowell's struggle with the world.[29] Both of these themes are in the poem. However, the choice of the male persona is not simply a gesture of disguise. It also represents Lowell's serious indictment of women's cultural roles. She could not agree to submission so she chose the male role for her own. Yet like Neron she hungered for the female she had denied in herself, hungered to redeem the woman of her imagination "from weariful repose." Like Peter's cry for Annette at the end of "The Basket," this fantasy indicates that she wished to unite male and female elements but could imagine only disaster ensuing if she liberated her feminine half "from weariful repose."

Still, one must not ignore the fact that the patriarchal figure of the king is what makes the poet want "to achieve a greater thing / Than [she] had yet conceived." She wanted to take on the whole male poetic Establishment "and crack / The shell of high omnipotence in two." The queen in this interpretation becomes poetry or the muse. Her late desire to make poetry the voice of feminine sensibility and yet to give it power is crushed by the patriarchal king, who throws his beard (the symbol of masculinity and masculine "wisdom") across the poet's dream.

Amy Lowell died on May 12, 1925. To many she appeared at the climax of her career, and the loss of this powerful personality was so sudden it seemed her ghost would surely haunt the literary scene for years. Yet, significantly, it didn't. Obscurity swallowed her up in a decade. Winfield Townley Scott made an interesting appraisal of what had happened to Amy Lowell in an article in *New England Quarterly* titled "Amy Lowell after Ten Years." He saw that the poetic climate had changed. Male and female poets seemed to have split the readership for poetry. Edna Millay dominated one part, T. S. Eliot the other. Curiously, though rightly I think, Scott places Lowell more genuinely in the female tradition than in the male. He claims that her poetry was one of "feelings and moods; never is it a poetry of thought and ideas." The distinction may be unfair, but Lowell is better at evoking an atmosphere, at suggesting emotions under tension, than she is at imitating Carl Sandburg's "Chicago" in "The Congressional Library." Scott, like D. H. Lawrence, admires particularly the poems where "she wrote not to hide but to reveal herself."[30] Whatever we think of the problems of actually revealing the self in poetry, Lowell sometimes does sound too much like an epigone, unable to find an authoritative voice.

She tried to imitate too many other writers: Robert Browning, Robert Frost, Edna Millay, Carl Sandburg, James Russell Lowell, D. H. Lawrence, among others.

Furthermore, in spite of the imagist credo to avoid copying old rhythms or old moods, to use absolutely no word which does not contribute to a single effect, and to work toward compression above all, her poetry is open to attack on the basis of its archaism, discursiveness, and merely decorative effects. Lowell herself knew this. In "Poetic Justice," published the year of her death, she calls her poems "petals shrewdly whirled about an empty center" (581).

On the other hand, Lowell did accomplish a good deal previously untried by women. She opened up the world of women's poetry to vivid encounters with the body, some quite startling in their explicitness. Edna Millay took over this territory in more muscular terms and yet somehow missed the sensuousness of Lowell's loving portrayals of women.

Furthermore, where Lowell's wit and humor come through, as in parts of *A Critical Fable*, for instance, her exuberance is refreshing. There is nothing in the nightingale tradition quite like Lowell's gusto. In her willingness to imagine a female tradition and in her frankness, both about its strengths and its limitations, she anticipates much later work by feminists. Who but Amy Lowell, in "Footing Up a Total," would attack one of her peers for a "charming weariness of tone" and then end her poem, "The future is the future, therefore— / Damn you!" (441).

Lowell's poems do not successfully investigate politics or rethink epistemology or work out the mythic potential of a world under stress. However, at her best, Lowell's poems have psychological resonance, lyric beauty and a courageous, recognizable voice. One of my favorites is "Merely Statement," from *What's O'Clock*.

You sent me a sprig of mignonette,
Cool-coloured, quiet, and it was wet
With green sea-spray, and the salt and the sweet
Mingled to a fragrance weary and discreet
As a harp played softly in a great room at sunset.

You said: "My sober mignonette
Will brighten your room and you will not forget."

But I have pressed your flower and laid it away
In a letter, tied with a ribbon knot.
I have not forgot.
But there is a passion-flower in my vase
Standing above a close-cleared space
In the midst of a jumble of papers and books.
The passion-flower holds my eyes,
And the light-under-light of its blue and purple dyes
Is a hot surprise.

How then can I keep my looks
From the passion-flower leaning sharply over the books?
When one has seen
The difficult magnificence of a queen
On one's table,
Is one able

> To observe any colour in a mignonette?
> I will not think of sunset, I crave the dawn,
> With its rose-red light on the wings of a swan,
> And a queen pacing slowly through the Parthenon,
> Her dress a stare of purple between pillars of stone.
>
> (440–41)

This poem, with its beautifully variegated phrasing, alternately drawn out and curtailed, exhibits Amy Lowell's control of cadence. The first stanza hovers in the "feminine" languorousness invoked by the image of the mignonette, which brings to mind the sensuous, romantic diction of Swinburne, the turn-of-the-century favorite for both men and women.

In the contrast between the mignonette and the passion-flower, so Lowellian in its use of color imagery and flora, the poet evokes her commitment to the new poetry with its "hot surprise." The long lines of the first stanza are broken up by short ones in the later verses. Her voice moves from nostalgia to urgency: "I will not think of sunset, I crave the dawn." Lowell's own passion for a future different from the past can be heard in that tone of urgency. It is characteristic of Lowell's late self-positioning that the two choices of poetic styles she imagines are both constructed as female. The two kinds of flowers also suggest two standards of femininity; at this point Lowell can imagine a version of the feminine both powerful and passionate, herself as Eleanora Duse perhaps. In a late poem on the Duse, Lowell describes her in such terms:

> Her voice is vibrant with a thousand things;
> Is sharp with pain or choked with tears,
> Or rich with love and longing.
> Her little inarticulate sounds are sprung
> From depths of inner meaning which embrace
> A life's chaotic, vast experience.
>
> (CP 593)

Though gesturing at a helter-skelter modernity, "Merely Statement" is not really an instance of modernism, however. Its diction remains that of late romanticism or nineteenth-century European symbolism. Compared to the poems of Marianne Moore, of Ezra Pound and T. S. Eliot, which were published in Lowell's lifetime, this poem's pyrotechnics seem tame. It contends with the past even as it incorporates—in the "jumble of papers and books," in the "stare of purple"—images of chaotic, exuberant modern life almost cubist in feeling. Lowell's longing for the "queen" reveals her leanings toward the elitism of an aristocratic order already susceptible to being imaged as "an old bitch gone in the teeth," in Pound's phrase.

Despite its anachronistic elements, however, "Merely Statement" (which is *not* merely statement and thus teases its readers) is an effective poem about the wistful female heritage Lowell had so insistently refused to accept, and the other bolder inheritance she came at last to claim not for herself but for the future. That she had some doubts about the power of the feminine to reshape cultural practice generally is only to be expected. The dress, which is a "stare of purple," is *contained* between the masculine Parthenon's pillars of stone.

For many women poets the difficulty has always been to find a voice which is both "powerful" and "womanly," as Adrienne Rich concludes at the end of her long poem "Sources."[31] In Lowell's case, as in Louise Bogan's, Sylvia Plath's, and many others', the strategy was to acknowledge the strength of previous women's efforts, while subtly denigrating female strategies of individuation. For Lowell, if women poets mined the vein of love, they were deficient in intellectuality. If they were intellectuals, their work was unfertilized and barren. Lowell put women poets in a double bind, with "matrices in body and in brain," as she says in "The Sisters"; she divided head from heart in women and then proclaimed herself a virile poet whose work need not be judged according to the deficiencies of past female efforts.

However, in "La Ronde du Diable" she suspects that attempts to compete with other women for literary primacy in a world still constructed to privilege male contributions were destined to fail. "Therefore, Sisters, it's my belief / We've none of us very much chance at a leaf." In her late poems Amy Lowell seems ready to give up the devil's circle dance in favor of a less alienated form of exercise.

The case of Amy Lowell is significant for the way it illuminates the conflicts suffered by the woman who seeks to be both popular and exceptional. Yet it also must be said that many of Lowell's strategies were both dutiful and daughterly. She eschewed the nightingale tradition and reinstated it. She defied the male prerogative and sought to appease it through imitation. Her contradictions are instructive, for in her work the intersection of culture, psyche, and persona illustrates the mixed messages provided to women artists in a time not so distant nor so different from our own.

3. WOMEN AND SELFHOOD
Sara Teasdale and the Passionate Virgin Persona

If Amy Lowell is rarely read these days, Sara Teasdale is practically forgotten. Routinely excluded from anthologies of American literature, her work doesn't even appear in Gilbert and Gubar's *Norton Anthology of Literature by Women*. It is usually assumed that her poetry, suggestive but chaste in its diction, containing no obscure or arcane language, and absolutely without intellectual complexity or challenge, is better suited to the young girl's romantic calendar with its daily quotation than to assemblages of modernist poets such as Wallace Stevens, Hart Crane, Marianne Moore, and William Carlos Williams. Studies of American culture in the first two decades of this century usually feel they can afford to ignore Sara Teasdale entirely.

Few people now remember that John Berryman had great respect for the dark lyrics Teasdale wrote at the end of her life, or that Sylvia Plath was more than a little influenced by Teasdale's work, or that Louise Bogan—whose work often receives the academic respect refused to Teasdale—made dramatic use of Teasdale's poetry in her own small and carefully edited opus. It has fallen to William Drake, almost alone among contemporary scholars, to give Sara Teasdale the respectful scholarly attention denied her by others. His feminist appreciation of the poet does not overlook the weaknesses in her poems but reminds us that her classic lyrical strengths, reminiscent of Sappho's and Christina Rossetti's, give her poetry a certain staying power in spite of its limitations. In fact, Teasdale's *Collected Poems* remained in print until the mid-seventies.[1]

In our fascination with modernism's pursuit of novelty and intellectual challenge, we tend to overlook the fact that Sara Teasdale was a revolutionary in her own time. True, she was a quiet revolutionary, but she broke new ground for women poets in her particular devotion to what she called "song": a musical poetry based on directness, simplicity, and emotional intensity for which the main model was Sappho. Her first major book, *Helen of Troy and Other Poems*, was published in 1911, before the advent of Edna St. Vincent Millay or H. D., and her particular brand of feminine verse would influence not only Millay but Amy Lowell, Elinor Wylie, and Louise Bogan.

After Teasdale's appearance, it became fashionable for women poets to write poems like hers with short lines of three or four stresses. In fact, the movement away from iambic pentameter in women's poems had begun earlier with the poetesses, with Emily Dickinson and Lizette Woodworth Reese. The ballads of Wordsworth and Coleridge and the later lyrics of A. E. Housman and Thomas Hardy had established the legitimacy within a male tradition of rendering feeling, especially sorrow, in language meant to juxtapose human and natural settings. They too had defied the domination of iambic pentameter. But for women like Teasdale, the language of song was apt to express not only a vision of life controlled by the eternal cycles of birth and death, love and pain, but also the experiences of women speaking, as Carol Gilligan suggests, "in a different voice."[2]

Teasdale's narrow lyrics were principally concerned with emotional life, often with love. Unlike Dickinson and certainly unlike Amy Lowell, Teasdale was seemingly content to mine the territory traditionally conceded to women, what Louise Bogan calls "the line of feeling." In Teasdale's wake a series of women poets followed her pattern of lucid exposition, at times ironic but always intimate in its address to the reader, a poetic practice producing a feminine voice recognized as such and applauded by its generation. As Drake says: "Reviewers found the feminine point of view in her work to be one of its chief points of interest—a revelation of women's emotion."[3] Though the development and proliferation of this kind of poetry cannot be traced entirely to Teasdale, her presence on the literary scene was more influential than is generally recognized. Poets like Aline Kilmer, Hilda and Grace Conkling, Jean Starr Untermeyer, Dorothy Parker, Leonora Speyer, Elizabeth Madox Roberts, and Nathalia Crane emerged in the teens and twenties with "songs" of their own.

To her generation, Teasdale's work was "modern" in the sense that it was virtually stripped of verbal posturing. Though it often relied on metaphors drawn from nature, it epitomized the modern passion for colloquialism and straightforwardness. Beyond this, Sara Teasdale's work represented a tension of considerable interest to her generation and of continuing interest to ours: the modern problem of feminine identity-formation. Put another way, we might describe this as the problem of balancing autonomy with affiliation, freedom with love.

Even Teasdale's verse forms suggest this tension. In her choice of conversational, seemingly spontaneous diction, she appeared to be a free spirit, unconstrained by the affectations of the past. Her poems seem to say, "I am willing to go my own way even at the risk of appearing naive, undereducated, or slight." Though always modest, this poetry was in its own way an indictment of an English tradition which valorized philosophical renderings of "universal" human problems all the while coopting female voices in what Toril Moi has called "the ventriloquism of patriarchy."[4]

However, Teasdale refused the freedoms so ardently proposed by a certain branch of modernism. She was committed to a disciplined art giving full credit to the benefits of traditional meters and rhyme schemes. Like so many modern poets in the nightingale tradition, she admired Sappho, Swinburne, and Yeats. To her their legacy seemed to imply that passion must be restrained and tempered by the discipline of measured cadence, a careful balance between music and silence. Otherwise, it remained mere sentimental indulgence. From this standpoint, her respect for the past was greater than her immersion in the present.

If her verse forms embodied a tension between two commitments—one to independence and the other to conventional proprieties—her themes were even more clearly concerned with the need to balance self-indulgence and self-restraint. In this she captured an undercurrent of her historical moment, in which progressivism struggled with an older Victorianism advocating caution and propriety. One can see these clashing forces represented by the way that women before the First World War were both encouraged to be independent and reminded not to forget their duties. Furthermore, the social revolution of the teens and twenties promised women hitherto unknown opportunities for freedom and self-development while at the same time preserving in its insistence on a romantic love plot many of the assumptions about femininity which had proven so detrimental to women in the past. For women like Sara Teasdale, female identity-formation was likely to be a process fraught with difficulties.

In her choice of the passionate virgin as her most characteristic persona, we can see Teasdale's desire to retain a measure of independence while at the same time insisting upon the importance of living with intensity. By exploring the evolution of Teasdale's persona, we confront more clearly the contradictions of a cultural moment in which the discourses of romantic thralldom and those of feminism both overlapped and converged.[5]

THE PERSONA OF THE PASSIONATE VIRGIN

What is meant by speaking of the passionate virgin as Teasdale's most characteristic persona? Let's begin with the passionate side. As early as her first poems, she identified herself with women like Eleanora Duse, Helen of Troy, and Guinevere, who were notorious for their sexual adventures. Furthermore, her poems about these women do not underplay the power of erotic longing in the dramas of their lives. Duse is epitomized by her lips, upon which hovers the shadow of a kiss. Helen chooses life over death because the dead presumably have no love "to lift their breasts with longing" (10). Guinevere's surrender to Lancelot is recounted as a moment of passion in the garden.

> Quickly he came behind me, caught my arms,
> That ached beneath his touch; and then I swayed,
> My head fell backward and I saw his face.
>
> (18)

One could as easily point to the numerous shorter poems in which the speaker remembers her lover's kiss as the essential, transforming experience, poems like "The Wanderer" and "The Kiss." Surely what the poet implies by her use of the kiss is the larger realm of adult sexuality for which the kiss is a synecdoche. This adult passion does make an appearance. In "After Parting," the poet writes:

> I set my shadow in his sight
> And I have winged it with desire,

That it may be a cloud by day
And in the night a shaft of fire.

(56)

For a virginal poet this is pretty explicit, the only peculiarity being that her shadow rather than his will become the "shaft of fire."

In this peculiarity, however, lies a clue to Teasdale's virginal sensibility. Rarely are her poems concerned with triumphant sensuality unimpeded by the need for psychological distancing or displacement. Just as in "After Parting," where the lovers are no longer together and the speaker must rely on a "shadow" self whose activity is doubly displaced as both masculine and imaginary, so the feminine voice of Teasdale's most typical lyrics is a voice of inhibited longing.[6]

Duse, Helen, and Guinevere are resonant for Teasdale because of their experiences of tragic loss. Beatrice, in another of these early heroine poems, feels remorse for her inability to reach out to Dante. Marianna Alcoforando, the Portuguese nun, finds "lack of love is bitterest of all" (15), and Erinna concludes that she is consecrated to Death, not Love, in the end. All of these women find their lives defined by lack, the very lack embodied in the virgin as a figure who points to a sexual status yet to be achieved. They might be called the expressions of a passionate virgin in the sense that what the poet seems to be interested in is the way their isolated sensibilities mull over the experience of loss or lack in private. Passion most frequently belongs to a temporal or spatial otherness.

The emphasis on lack, however, must be distinguished from a Freudian theory of penis envy and from a Lacanian theory of the Phallus. In Freud the female sense of lack is construed as a covert search for power that can never be fully satisfied since the female can never possess the phallus directly but only through her relations with the male as son or lover. In Lacan the experience of lack defines the human condition since every child comes to consciousness through the experience of differentiation, which is felt as loss.[7]

Though women poets may be read as inscribing the psychic in their preoccupation with lack, such readings must also take account of the intersection of the psychic with the social and cultural. In Sara Teasdale, for instance, we should not neglect the specific cultural power women in the nightingale tradition achieved by exploiting the discourse of frustration in order to achieve a representative voice.[8] Freudian theories leave out of account the way women form bonds with other women (as readers and writers) through their interventions in the cultural conversation. Furthermore, Lacan's universalizing tendency to see all human experience as defined by lack may result in blindness regarding the specific historical positions women occupy when facing the patriarchal Symbolic. In this chapter I will suggest both the resources and power Teasdale found in the persona of the passionate virgin and the inadequacy of this cultural construct as a mode of cultural transformation.

Teasdale repeatedly suggests that within the Feminine, inhibited longing has a ritualized significance. For instance, in "A Maiden" the persona cannot sing to her love but must instead pass him "with downcast eyes."

And since I am a maiden
My love will never know
That I could kiss him with a mouth
More red than roses blow.

(24)

In "Union Square" she envies the prostitutes, who may ask openly for "love." "Central Park at Dusk" reads in the signature of springtime the muted voice of feminine inhibitions: "A hush is over everything— / Silent as women wait for love" (32).

Indeed, silence, in poems too numerous to recount, operates as the double-voiced discourse of feminine desire. Like the silent beauty of an Eleanora Duse, "its longing unappeased through all the years," silence is expressive and full. In "February" the speaker says: "My lips kept silent guard / On all I could not say" (57); in "Night Song for Amalfi" the speaker finds in silence the meaning of nature's restraint but wonders if she can give her lover silence her whole life long.

Wisdom, for the poet, typically means learning the iron rule of not voicing her needs. In the late poem "Wisdom," from *Strange Victory* (1933), she begins, "Oh to relinquish, with no more sound / Than the bent bough's when the bright apples fall;" her music will be "A paean like the cymbals of the foam, / Or silence, level, spacious, without end" (205).

However, "This is my music," the poet says, made "for my need." Thus, it is not a pure renunciation of desire; in its discipline and dignity it offers the speaker a measure of power over circumstance. Furthermore, it connects the poet with other women poets like Emily Dickinson and Christina Rossetti, who have made of silence a resonant theme.

Did Sara Teasdale read the American women poets of the nineteenth century? She certainly knew some of Emily Dickinson and like Dickinson her spirit was torn between pagan and Puritan impulses, both intense. "The Inn of Earth" seems almost a conscious rewriting of two works by Dickinson, #115 and #1406. The first, "What Inn is this," she might well have known from its publication in the 1891 *Poems*, though the second was probably not available to her. In Teasdale's version a story is told of a traveler coming into the inn and asking first for bread and then for sleeping accommodations. At each request the Host goes by "with averted eye" and will not respond to her requests. Finally, she says:

"Since there is neither food nor rest,
I go where I fared before"—
But the Host went by with averted eye
And barred the door.

(64)

Elsewhere, Teasdale's rendering of hunger as simultaneously painful and precious is certainly reminiscent of what Barbara Mossberg calls Dickinson's "aesthetics of anorexia."[9]

Similarly, Teasdale's poem "Desert Pools" reminds one of a nineteenth-century predecessor, this time Maria Brooks. Having concluded that she is "too generous a giver," Teasdale's speaker imagines her lover will turn to desert places in order to escape the intensity of a demanding female presence.

> And there at midnight sick with faring,
>   He will stoop down in his desire
> To slake the thirst grown past all bearing
>   In stagnant water keen as fire.
>
> (55)

The Brooks poem, first published in *Zóphiël; or the Bride of Seven* (1833), also contains the desert landscape and the irrepressible thirst, but for Brooks the drinker is female and the obstacle is the lack of a congenial soul.

> So many a soul, o'er life's drear desert faring,
>   Love's pure, congenial spring unfound, unquaffed,
> Suffers, recoils—then thirsty and despairing
>   Of what it would, descends and sips the nearest draught.[10]

For both Teasdale and her nineteenth-century predecessors, frustration is a fundamental theme. Dickinson found satisfaction in verbal strategies of subversion. Teasdale, like Wylie and Bogan, advocated mental discipline and the conservation of personal resources at the expense of broader sympathies. Despite these differences, however, the mask of the passionate virgin was appealing to all of these women and resulted in many poems in praise of chastity.

The significant point to be made in Teasdale's case is that in spite of the considerable historical changes in women's social opportunities, her rendering of women's experience and her elucidation of what constitutes "wisdom"—a word widely used in her poems—is an extension of the nightingale tradition she thought herself beyond. The best way to assess Teasdale's position with regard to that tradition is to read her introductions to *The Answering Voice*.[11]

In the late teens her publisher asked her to edit a collection of women's love lyrics. The first edition appeared in 1917 and was revised and enlarged ten years later. This collection embodies the contradictions of her cultural moment, for it purports to illustrate the greater freedoms of contemporary women while it reinforces a connection between women and romance not far from Lydia Sigourney's (and Wordsworth's) notion that the soul of woman lives in love. Furthermore, the collection valorizes the relation between women's experience of love and frustration or loss. That Teasdale's formula had considerable staying power may be seen in the fact that this collection was still selling well in 1935.

Though *The Answering Voice* shows only limited knowledge of women's poetry of the more distant past, the second edition does reveal Teasdale's attitude toward the position of the contemporary woman poet. She says:

Though the passion called love has not changed appreciably during recorded time, our ideas about it have changed constantly, and sometimes with great rapidity. The immediate cause of the new attitude can be traced to the growing economic independence of women consequent on education, and to the universal tendency to rationalize all emotion.

Teasdale contrasts the nineteenth-century love poems with their twentieth-century counterparts. Total absorption in the lover is gone.

One finds little, too, of the pathetic despair so often present in the earlier work. To-day there is stated over and over, perhaps a little overstated, the woman's fearlessness, her love of change, her almost cruelly analytical attitude. The strident or flippant notes that occasionally mar the poems, arise from overstating new ideas, a habit that seems unavoidable until through long possession they have become unselfconscious. This is a period of transition. The perfect balance between the heart and the mind, the body and the spirit, is still to be attained.

Teasdale herself experimented with a modern stance toward love, and in "Four Winds," "New Love and Old," and "Winter Night Song" she expresses cynicism or cruelty toward the lover. But her passionate quest was to find that balance between the heart and the mind, the body and the spirit, love and freedom which her contemporary situation did not, in fact, help her to achieve.

Dwelling repeatedly upon these themes, Sara Teasdale found herself looking back to Christina Rossetti, another passionate virgin, for a sense of direction. At her death Teasdale had completed forty pages of a biography of Rossetti that indicated no particular struggle with a strong precursor such as we find in Amy Lowell. William Drake says that her research brought her face to face with many of her own problems, especially "the chain of cause and effect that created the pattern of a life, for she could see clearly how one's supposedly free acts created constantly narrowing limits for the future, imprisoning the will by degrees."[12]

Teasdale ascribes to Rossetti many of her own feelings, including a dislike of doing housework. Concerning marriage she wrote: "I feel [Rossetti's] disinclination to marry [Cayley] sprang chiefly from her disinclination to marriage in general. She wished to be free to follow her own thoughts, to meditate in her own way. She was a born celibate in spite of her impassioned heart."[13] Like Teasdale herself, Rossetti appears in the guise of the passionate virgin.

Much of this material urges us to place Sara Teasdale more firmly in a Victorian nightingale setting than in a modern one. Yet we must not forget that in her day she was an extremely popular poet, whose manipulation of the persona of the passionate virgin gained her a large readership among young women who were themselves uncertain about their role in twentieth-century culture. For them, the passionate virgin seemed to mediate between frustration and fulfillment, silence and voice, marginality and centrality. If we, as late twentieth-century readers, read evidence of continuing oppression in this voice, we must remember that, in an era hardly ready to commit itself to full liberation for women, her ambivalence was widely shared.

THE PARADOXICAL MESSAGE OF "FLAMING YOUTH"

What exactly were young women of this generation finding in the work of Sara Teasdale? My mother, born in 1906, imitated Teasdale in the poetry she published in the *Chicago Tribune*.[14] She admired the delicate passion in these poems. For many members of her generation, poetry was as natural an expression of youthful desires and torments as popular music is today. The women like my mother who wrote such lyrics did not read much nineteenth-century verse by women but they did read Teasdale, Edna St. Vincent Millay, and Elinor Wylie.

One of the reasons they wrote was that they felt their experiences were fresh. Growing up in the postwar world of the late teens and twenties, they saw their position in American culture as unprecedented. As Paula Fass puts it: "In the 1920s, youth appeared suddenly, dramatically, even menacingly on the social scene. Contemporaries quite rightly felt that their presence signalled a social transformation of major proportions."[15]

In many ways, the site of greatest social change was middle-class female behavior among the young. But the flapper image so frequently presented as the emblem of the new American woman was mostly a style rather than a stable conception of identity. The fact that "these modern women" smoked in public, bobbed their hair, stayed out late, and flaunted a kind of hoyden sexuality was less important to the genuine transformation of social norms than it seemed at the time. "Feminist New-Style," as Dorothy Bromley called her in an often-quoted 1927 article, might "have given as few hostages to Fate as it is humanly possible to give" by making comrades of men, by insisting upon "more freedom and honesty in the marriage relation," and by finding "a vital interest in some work of her own,"[16] but marriage remained the ultimate goal of most women's youthful energies and marriage was still an institution hemmed in by tradition.

Premarital sex was far less widespread than it is today. Paula Fass estimates that "probably something less than one-half of all college women in the 1920s experienced coitus prior to marriage, and considerably more than one-half of these had restricted that activity to a serious, marriage-oriented relationship" (276).

Despite the emphasis upon independence characteristic of flapper rhetoric, women were still encouraged to view marriage as their most significant experience. Genevieve Taggard, poet and feminist though she was, wrote: "Marriage is the only profound human experience; all other human angles are its mere rehearsal."[17] The new pressure to marry showed up even in the graduates of women's colleges. This cohort had distinguished itself in the 1890s by choosing career over marriage in relatively large numbers, causing some conservative critics to predict that women's colleges would be the end of the race. Now over 90 percent of the Ivy League women questioned said they wanted to marry and would give up a job if it conflicted with marriage.[18]

It is easy for us to see the inherent contradictions in the picture evoked by Bromley's article and the Ivy League questionnaire. The two great cries of the twenties, love and freedom, could not be easily harmonized. In the first place, young men had radically different expectations than young women concerning the role the wife should play in the marriage, as two social science researchers of this generation, Frank Watson and Clifford Kirkpatrick, discovered. Watson, who studied male students at Haverford College in the early thirties, concluded that only one out of nine men could see themselves accepting a working wife. The sociologist Kirkpatrick, after conducting his survey of the attitudes of college men in the same era, commented: "The abyss of disagreement between the two sexes in regard to the status of women seems to be widening rather than disappearing."[19]

Furthermore, Dorothy Bromley says nothing about who is going to raise the children and how these tasks can be managed while the woman is making herself economically independent. It remains unclear what kind of work she has in mind when she describes the new woman as finding "a vital interest in some work." Most women could not expect to find jobs inspiring a vital interest. She also says that feminist new-style prefers the company of men, "for [men's] methods are more direct and their view larger," without explaining how "feminists" can respect themselves while being contemptuous of other women.

This kind of contradiction was inherent in the new situation in which many women found themselves. Encouraged to take their own needs seriously, they were nevertheless restricted in terms of the options offered for satisfying those needs. As Paula Fass presents the paradoxical message of this generation in transition, women found themselves expecting more of marriage because "it was for them the one arena for expression and the only sphere for personal satisfaction. The stress on rights for women in marriage both symbolized and accelerated this process, as it helped to localize completely female emotions and needs to family life" (82).

If it is hard to imagine the average woman successfully negotiating the bargain feminist new-style has made, it is no less difficult to envision women poets of this period escaping the contradictions of the postwar period. Elaine Showalter's collection of autobiographical essays from the twenties helps us see how Genevieve Taggard and other exceptional women assessed their lives. After calling marriage the only profound human experience, Taggard goes on to add:

> And yet having it, it is not all I want. It is more often, I think, a final experience than a way of life. But I am a poet—love and mutual living are not nearly enough. It is better to work hard than to be married hard. If, at the beginning of middle age, we have not learned some of the perils of the soul, in this double-selved life, we are pure fools. Self-sufficiency is a myth, of course, but after thirty, . . . it becomes more and more necessary. (These Modern Women, 67)

Indeed, the trumpet call to freedom is as frequently a part of the rhetoric of these modern women as is the celebration of marriage. Elizabeth Stuyvesant, a dancer, settlement worker, and birth control campaigner, wrote: "The utmost measure of freedom—economic, intellectual, emotional—is the *sine qua non* of the good life" (97). And Phyllis Blanchard, a distinguished child psychologist, summed up her situation in 1926 again with reference to freedom: "With marriage . . . I am content. It is as if I had accomplished the impossible feat of eating my cake and having it—for I have both love and freedom, which once seemed to me such incompatible bedfellows" (109).

To summarize, then, popular culture supported as intensely as ever the view that heterosexual love was the test situation for assessing a woman's success or failure. However, success in modern terms meant the preservation of a sense of independence along with commitment. Self-gratification, rather than duty or self-sacrifice, was to be the end result of the love relation, freedom the sine qua non of the good life.

In this climate a whole generation of women poets blossomed and the world of publishing turned once again, as it had in the mid-nineteenth century, to considering the nature of women's poetry. Like Amy Lowell, H. L. Davis in *Poetry* (September 1927) felt America was seeing "the transference of poetry from the estate of men to that of women; and the alteration (therefore) in the nature and texture of poetry." Llewellyn Jones, in an article called "The Younger Women Poets" (May 1924), claimed that the younger generation had produced as many major poets in its women as in its men. (He concentrated on Millay, Taggard, Bogan, and Wylie.) Mark Van Doren in the *Nation* (April 26, 1922) felt compelled to state his conviction that "there is such a thing as woman's poetry, that women write differently from men just as they speak differently from men." Virginia Moore echoed his sentiments in July 1930 by saying that "women are forever different from men in mind, heart, and racial experience" and that this difference should be expressed in their poetry. "In America women feel their sex and inadvertently confess it almost every time they write a couplet." Harriet Monroe agreed: "The women poets of our time, in short, have been content to be women; and in thus accepting their destiny they have invaded a field comparatively open to their advance."[20]

In order to have a clearer understanding of the terms in which analysts debated the specific strengths and weaknesses of women poets, we can profitably examine a characteristic exchange on the subject which took place between Elizabeth Breuer and Jean Starr Untermeyer in *The Bookman* in 1923. Breuer's article, entitled "The Flapper's Wild Oats," bemoaned "the lack of flappers of original talents" in poetry. Not exempting herself from the category she is describing, Breuer sorrows over the fact that "we are women first and artists afterwards." Dissenting from much contemporary belief, she says: "There is no younger generation of women [poets] in the same terms in which we deal with a younger generation among the men"; this because women continue to lead sheltered existences protected from the realities of life. "Despite her pretense of weary cynicism," Breuer says, the flapper "graduates from school a confirmed romanticist of the old type, *virginal* in the knowledge or experience that will vitalize her to creative originality" (emphasis mine). Not until thirty does she gain a degree of self-assurance that young men have in sophomore year at college. Breuer maintains that women are far too ready to conform and, echoing popular assumptions about gender, generalizes that "woman's passivity, beginning with her sex functioning, dominates her entire attitude toward experience."

Breuer would much rather see the flappers competing openly with men as innovators instead of following what she saw as their conservative path. "Although negative and positive forces are equally vital to life, the women who have made a dent in the masculine pattern of the arts have always been rakehellers or saints, women who disdained their sex attitude of yielding and waiting. You've got to be a positive force to fight your way up to the top of the particular world you want to own."[21]

In the following issue of *The Bookman*, Jean Starr Untermeyer responded to Breuer's indictment and dissented from it on many points. Whereas Breuer wants women to make a dent "on the masculine pattern of the arts," Untermeyer holds out for feminine verse. Untermeyer demurs:

> I do not assent to Mrs. Breuer's condition that for a woman to be a successful artist she must cast into the discard pile that part of her life that is essentially womanly. . . . Rather there must be a readjustment, not denial. Woman must bring into her art just those qualities that distinguish her as a woman: her intuition, her insight, her adaptability, her feminine ardor and her dream.[22]

With this material as background, Sara Teasdale's work can be seen more clearly as part of the cultural conversation. She emerged as a popular poet precisely at a time when women's roles were under reconsideration, giving voice to the two major preoccupations of this period: love and freedom. In terms of the debate concerning the nature of the poetry women should write, she belongs squarely in the same category as Untermeyer, who was her close friend. Self-representational, as are all the nightingale poets, Teasdale believed that the subject of lyric poetry is always to some degree the sensibility of the poet and said that in writing poetry she was less concerned with communicating with her reader than in finding out about herself. That self was definitely inscribed within the code of femininity that continued to inhibit women in this period, and, unlike Amy Lowell, Teasdale had little desire to compete with men. She wrote: "I have a theory that the only way women can hope to make their work compare with men's work, is not by trying to rival what men say, but by trying to supplement it" (WP 85).

Though essentially nineteenth-century in her sensibility, Teasdale adopts a position ironically close to one some contemporary feminists share: the opinion that women must write out of their "feminine experience" rather than attempt to annex territory traditionally given over to men. Unfortunately, Teasdale's life and the evolution of her persona from virginal passion to passionate virginity suggest that the female experience her work embodies offered little opportunity to create a strong self able to achieve a satisfactory balance between love and freedom. The fact that the social script for women has frequently resulted in such tragic consequences has led some contemporary feminists to advocate drawing upon resources other than social experience for women's art, exploring the pre-oedipal realm, for instance, or "writing the body."[23] For Teasdale, however, such choices were inconceivable. Her story, and the social script that it exemplifies, help to put into perspective our recent troubling history of cultural change and continuity.

HISTORY AS BIOGRAPHY

Sara Teasdale was born in 1884 in St. Louis, the late, unexpected offspring of a couple in their forties. Sara's father was a Baptist, and she was intensely attached to him, calling him unself-consciously "my first lover." But Sara's mother—whose dominant personality affected Sara more directly—was strongly imbued with the Puritan values of her Willard forebears, one of whom founded Concord, Massachusetts. Thus, though Teasdale's Midwestern childhood might seem to exclude her from the company of the thoroughly New England-oriented nightingale poets (like Lowell, Wylie, Bogan, and Millay), she did come into a Puritan legacy through her mother. Writing of her love for the works of Marcel Proust, she would later confess, "All my blood, and all of it is Puritan, more or less, rises against me" (*WP* 235). Like Genevieve Taggard she would find herself more at home in the East than in the landscape of her birth because her sensibility gravitated toward eastern, fundamentally Puritan, values of resistance and restraint.

Nevertheless, she was also a child of her times in which the artistic spirit was inevitably linked to paganism. Her Greek self, the child of Sappho, belonged like H. D.'s to a pre-Christian realm of sensuality. Ambivalent toward these two warring selves, Teasdale was a perfect candidate for the nightingale tradition, in which such ambivalence runs deep. As William Drake explains it in his chapter "Sara Teasdale and the Feminine Tradition": "Sara Teasdale's heritage was the divided self—a personality ready for self-fulfillment, rich in outgoing emotion, sensuous, and keenly sensitive, attuned to esthetic rather than moral imperatives, but stricken with a paralyzing obedience to the rigorous proprieties imposed on her in childhood, mainly by her mother" (*WP* 5).

Growing up lonely and sickly, Sara spent a great deal of time by herself. In compensation, she developed a lively imaginative life that focused upon romance and individual heroism. She read Arthurian romances and particularly loved Richard Hovey's medieval dramas, following the pattern of turn-of-the-century antimodernism outlined by Jackson Lears.

Yet her anti-modernist sympathies did not lead her to androgynous fantasies and nowhere does one hear that Sara Teasdale wished she had been born a boy. In fact, according to one of her friends, "She was not sentimental, but she was extremely romantic. She lived so much in dreams that it was impossible for me to visualize her as a wife or mother. Her spirit remained fixed at the stage of romantic love."[24] Thus, it is possible to say that the persona of the passionate virgin had roots in her psychological makeup as well as in her culture.

During adolescence Teasdale became part of the circle of artistic friends who called themselves the Potters and produced a handmade literary magazine. *The Potter's Wheel* appeared monthly from 1904 to 1907 and finally drew the attention of William Marion Reedy, whom the poet was to call her "literary Godfather."

Sara Teasdale's career began with publication in *Reedy's Mirror*, a St. Louis journal with a national reputation for good critical judgment and for having its finger on the nation's cultural pulse. In fact, it was Reedy who in 1913 gave this era its sobriquet by reading the cultural time as "sex o'clock in America."

Even at this period of her life, Teasdale was writing love poetry. Although she had no male romantic attachment, she created love relationships with her friends, much the way Amy Lowell and Emily Dickinson did. Williamina Parrish, editor of *The Potter's Wheel*, described Teasdale's poetic inclinations during this period as "Pegs for Pegasus."

Nevertheless, Teasdale did have deep and romanticized involvements with women. After her adolescent fixation on one particular childhood friend, Bessie Brey, she transferred her affections to an older, married woman, Marion Cummings Stanley. At the end of her life, when she had become a virtual recluse, her closest link with humanity was Margaret Conklin, though Conklin occupied the role of a daughter rather than a romantic fixation. In her last book Teasdale published a poem to Margaret entitled "To M.":

> Till the last sleep, from the blind waking at birth,
>   Bearing the weight of the years between the two,
> I shall find no better thing upon the earth
>   Than the wilful, noble, faulty thing which is you.
>   (209)

It must be said, however, that Teasdale was not at all in sympathy with the lesbian movements of the 1920s, which counterpointed the dominant ethos like a minor theme, complicated and persistent but hardly heard by most. The poet's friend Zoe Akins seems to have been involved with bohemian lesbianism but Teasdale was appalled by the behavior of the Akins crowd and never accepted, in spite of her references to Sapphic kisses in some poems, that her beloved Sappho was sexually involved with women. Ruth Perry and Maurine Sagoff, in an interesting article entitled "Sara Teasdale's Friendships," argue that Teasdale's relations with women were much more significant than her relations with men, "in part because the relationships were, for her, protected from physical consequences— all heightened sensibility with no physical demands."[25]

Despite her serious ambitions as a poet and her deep affection for other women, Teasdale spent many years underplaying these aspects of her nature and presenting herself as a conventional feminine spirit. This meant denying any undue commitment to a writing career. She wrote to John Myers O'Hara: "Art can never mean to a woman what it does to a man. Love means that" (*WP*, 43).

Many women writers have found the need to underplay their ambitions in order not to appear unfeminine. Sylvia Plath, for instance, echoes Teasdale's self-misrepresentations forty years later as she attempts to win approval for a noncompetitive, conventionally female self. Both women were ambitious but both cloaked their ambitions in rhetoric designed to make light of them. Both assumed marriage and motherhood would resolve emotional problems and deep-seated frustrations brought about by contradictory self-images. In 1914 Teasdale wrote: "I must marry, for at bottom I am a mother more intensely than I am a lover" (*WP*, 137). Both women romanticized marriage in highly unrealistic terms. When Teasdale finally agreed to marry Ernst Filsinger, a cultured businessman, she gave him a very misleading impression of her own needs. Thus, Drake says, Ernst might be forgiven for writing to his parents: "Ever since I knew her she has put the duties of true womanhood (motherhood and wifehood) above any art and would I believe rather be the fond mother of a child than the author of the most glorious poem in the language" (*WP*, 140).

Unlike Plath, however, Teasdale seems to have been unable to take any pleasure in the sexual side of marriage. Marya Zaturenska writes: "Sara Teasdale was extraordinarily virginal, one might say spinsterish. She found the realities of marriage difficult; she was not a domestic type."[26]

The irony that the passionate love poet of "flaming youth" should find celibacy preferable to sex is not so peculiar as it seems at first. Underneath much of the increased emphasis on sex in the 1920s lay continued anxieties on the part of women, many of whom were uncomfortable with intercourse, especially since they had only limited control over their own bodies. Victorian inhibitions persisted, as Amy Lowell notes in "The Sisters."

In "Vox Corporis" Teasdale suggests the power of psychological inhibitions to frustrate even intense sexual desires.

> The beast to the beast is calling,
>   And the mind bends down to wait;
> Like the stealthy lord of the jungle,
>   The man calls to his mate.
>
> The beast to the beast is calling,
>   They rush through the twilight sweet—
> But the mind is a wary hunter;
>   He will not let them meet.
>
>   (38)

Only three decades earlier, Ella Wheeler Wilcox had also written about lust in a hunting poem called "The Tiger." The poet of the 1890s, no doubt influenced by Darwinian naturalism, predicts the triumph of the beast (sex) at the expense of the hunter and "the whole rash world of men" he represents.[27] Here, however, it is the hunter (the mind) who presents the danger, and it is consummation that is threatened. The popular Freudian belief in the importance of sexual release to psychological health hovers in the background, identifying anxieties in terms of a different code. This poet no longer predicts the triumph of passion over reason. In her scenario impulse falls victim to the (interestingly masculine) interference of the mind.

Despite the self-criticism implicit in "Vox Corporis," Teasdale was unable to make her mind more responsive to the needs of the body. Furthermore, she soon felt trapped by the discipline of "true womanhood" she had previously endorsed.

Confronted with a choice between having a baby and continuing to pursue her career, she opted for abortion, relapsing almost immediately into profound self-hatred. As Drake describes it: "Shortly thereafter she admitted herself to the sanitorium at Cromwell, Connecticut, and through the following months sank into a state of physical weakness and severe emotional depression that lasted nearly a year."[28]

Fundamentally, Teasdale found it impossible to negotiate a truce between her Puritan and pagan selves. From 1907 until her death in 1933, she had numerous attacks of what the nineteenth century called neurasthenia. Like Virginia Woolf she was given repeated rest cures, and toward the end of her life she spent more time at various kinds of retreats than she did at home.

Eventually these strains took their toll upon her marriage. By contemporary standards, Ernst Filsinger was a very supportive husband, agreeing to separate hotel rooms and allowing his wife considerable independence for the times. However, his increasing involvement with his work and her increasing disillusionment and depression led her to withdraw further and further into herself. She became the very type of the nineteenth-century woman poet, "a recluse of recluses," as she called herself, plagued by ill health. She now reevaluated the place of romantic love in her life. "No highly developed, thoroughly self-conscious modern woman can really give her soul and be proud of it. I used to always think that I wanted to lose myself in the man I loved. I see now that I can never do that, and that I was foolish to wish that I could," she wrote (*WP*, 148).

Divorce seemed the only solution. Ernst was devastated by her decision, which was forwarded to him by mail while he was out of the country. But her mind was made up. Once the divorce was granted, she briefly enthused: "I'm a free woman. I can do anything I want" (*WP*, 260). However, like so many women of her time and ours, she found it difficult to convert this opportunity to do anything she wanted into a source of real pleasure and stability. Drake absolves Filsinger of any serious misconduct and ascribes Teasdale's unhappiness in the marriage to her belief that a truly successful relationship would inspire her to a slavish devotion.

In the early days with Ernst she had experimented with this vision of their connection. Her poem "Because," from *Love Songs* (1917), clarifies the deep connection she assumed between marriage and female subordination.

> Oh, because you never tried
> To bow my will or break my pride,
> And nothing of the cave-man made
> You want to keep me half afraid,
> . . . .
>
> And since the body's maidenhood
> Alone were neither rare nor good
> Unless with it I gave to you
> A spirit still untrammeled, too,
> Take my dreams and take my mind

That were masterless as wind;
And "Master!" I shall say to you
Since you never asked me to.
(106)

"Because" sums up the progress and regress of early twentieth-century modes of female self-assertion. The speaker announces the importance of her own independence and then surrenders it, voluntarily reinstituting the master/slave relationship so characteristic of romantic thralldom. As an artifact of its time, this poem—with its overlapping discourses of feminism and romantic love—is a classic.

After her divorce from Filsinger, Teasdale never achieved the serenity she so deeply desired. Furthermore, in the maelstrom of her final years, the poet, like Elinor Wylie, Amy Lowell, and Edna Millay, was hit with one death after another. Several of these were suicides. First, Louis and Jean Untermeyer's son, who had been an intimate of Teasdale's group, committed suicide at college. Then Marguerite Wilkinson drowned in ambiguous circumstances. Finally, most shattering of all, Vachel Lindsay, who had once courted Teasdale and was a lifelong friend, swallowed a bottle of Lysol and died in agonizing pain. Within her own world, where she was shut in more and more because of poor health, growing emotional instability, and lack of money, Teasdale herself had been toying with suicide for some time. Her poetry reveals this almost obsessive preoccupation in the late books and this preoccupation may be one reason John Berryman, also "drawn slowly to the foamless weir" of a self-inflicted death, found the late work so moving.

Like many women in the wake of divorce, Teasdale discovered she could not be as delightfully self-sufficient as she had hoped. What did the freedom of a feminist-new style actually mean? Economic realities dictated that few divorced women could be financially independent enough to retain a comfortable middle-class existence. Having grown up with financial security and even indulgence, Teasdale suddenly found herself strapped for funds. She had never enjoyed housekeeping and chose to live in hotels where she was excused from the burdens of cooking and cleaning. Now this life-style was difficult to maintain. Her visits to the sanitarium in Connecticut (which also housed Louise Bogan for a period) also cut into her funds. Though Teasdale was never reduced to poverty, the last years of her life, like the last decades of Bogan's, were plagued by loneliness, depression, and financial anxieties.

There is some evidence that Sara Teasdale was worried about the possibility that she might have a stroke such as had killed her friend Amy Lowell and disabled her brother. When a blood vessel broke in her hand, she took it as a sign of the end. Her circle of friends had also diminished dramatically, and near the end of her life she allowed only Margaret Conklin easy access. Even with Margaret she was sometimes fractious and dismissive.

On January 29, 1933, she took an overdose of sleeping pills and lay down in a warm bath. Her nurse seems to have ignored her duty to watch Teasdale carefully. When she found the poet, she called the doctor. Drake concludes: "The water in the tub was still warm and death had occurred only a short time before, suggesting that Sara might have timed her action in the hope that she would be discovered before it was too late" (WP, 292).

Yet, in many ways Teasdale's death had been coming for a long time. The impassioned voice of "flaming youth" had long since become the voice of a middle-aged woman who had measured the hollowness of her culture's liberationist rhetoric and opted instead for radical autonomy.

FROM VIRGINAL PASSION TO
PASSIONATE VIRGINITY

Examining Sara Teasdale's poetry, we also find the poet evolving from an early preoccupation with passionate love through a period of disillusionment to the late concern with autonomy and death. Helen of Troy, Rivers to the Sea, and Love Songs are the books of virginal passion. Flame and Shadow (1920) announces its position in its title, midway between the books preoccupied with love and those overshadowed by death. Dark of the Moon and Strange Victory offer us a persona whose most recognizable trait is her passionate virginity, a lonely voice "in a darkening garden."

Teasdale's reputation was established in her early phase, however, and her readers and critics continued to associate her with passionate love even after she had ceased to address most of her poems to a lover and began instead to consider her relationship to herself most important. Harriet Monroe's assessment of Sara Teasdale, published in Poets and Their Art (1932), notices that the girlish element found in Teasdale's first three books darkens in Flame and Shadow and after, but even Monroe calls Teasdale "a poet whose songs give the woman's version of the human love-story, or at least as much of it as one of the finer, more sensitive and protected women of our veiled and walled-in civilization may contribute to the whole vast epic of the human race."[29]

If Harriet Monroe, who knew the poet's work very well and had watched Teasdale's progress closely through the years, could miss the profound changes that had occurred in Teasdale's orientation, it is not surprising that other readers continued to categorize her as primarily a love poet. Rivers to the Sea (1915) and Love Songs (1917) had been highly successful volumes in which the passionate persona predominated.

However, in Flame and Shadow Teasdale exhibits considerable frustration with her previous avatar. In the significantly named "Songs for Myself," she longs to be free of herself and to have a heart "as bare / As a tree in December" ("The Tree," 156). In "At Midnight" she claims:

> Even love that I built my spirit's house for,
> Comes like a brooding and a baffled guest,

And music and men's praise and even laughter
Are not so good as rest.

(156)

Though an earlier Teasdale persona sought freedom through love, this later one declares, "Only the lonely are free" ("Morning Song," 141).

Probably the most significant poem from this collection is one called "The Sanctuary," a poem written and rewritten in the nightingale tradition from the nineteenth century onward.

If I could keep my innermost Me
Fearless, aloof and free
Of the least breath of love or hate,
And not disconsolate
At the sick load of sorrow laid on men;
If I could keep a sanctuary there
Free even of prayer,
If I could do this, then,
With quiet candor as I grew more wise
I could look even at God with grave forgiving eyes.

(151)

Sanctuary poems are written by the nineteenth-century poetesses, Louise Imogen Guiney, Amy Lowell, Elinor Wylie, H. D., Edna St. Vincent Millay, and Louise Bogan. Generally it is the burden of emotional demands, feeling too much for others, and "the sick load of sorrow laid on men" that these women seek protection from, though it may also be protection from aggression within and without that fosters the fantasy of a sanctuary. In spite of the psychologically documentable tendency among some women to ground identity and values in relationships with others, poets in the nightingale tradition repeatedly wish for independence in the name of self-preservation. "Fearless, aloof, and free" is what Teasdale wishes to be. Fear and dependence are the problems that, therefore, must threaten her "innermost Me."

Teasdale's repeated longings for freedom and autonomy call into question the universality of what Carol Gilligan has described as woman's "different voice." Though strongly enmeshed in a network of interpersonal relations, Teasdale began as early as 1920 to explore her own need to exist separate from others. What Cora Kaplan has described as "the 'self' that occupies the place-from-which-I-can-write"[30] was vitally important to Teasdale, and that self seems to have been threatened by relationships that became too demanding.

Thus, Sara Teasdale's work exemplifies in the alternation of its moods the two passionate preoccupations of its time—love and freedom—but it does so by suggesting the poet's inability to resolve them into a single program of action. Thus, this work achieves distinction for the way it illuminates the strain between models of identity-formation based on commitment and conflicting models, characterized as masculine by Gilligan and others, based on autonomy.

If *Flame and Shadow* suggests a growing dissatisfaction with passionate love as the primary goal of life, *Dark of the Moon* (1926) seems more than ever designed to create an image of the poet as passionate in her commitment to virginity. No longer is she chaste from lack of experience. Instead, her chastity is a chosen status lifting her above the "people rushing / In restless self-importance to and fro." White is her preferred color in the last books, which no longer tell stories of urban incidents but prefer the polar privacy of stars, desolate seashore, and what Sylvia Plath would call "the light of the mind, cold and planetary."

"The Crystal Gazer" poems insist upon the importance of isolation and self-definition. In the title poem Teasdale writes: "I shall gather myself into myself again, / I shall take my scattered selves and make them one" (179). "The Solitary" advances the vision of this sybil who watches at a distance. She is now "self-complete as a flower or a stone" and, having reached midlife, incurious about others "if I have myself and the drive of my will" (179). "Leisure" finds her "Sharing with no one but myself the frosty / And half-ironic musings of my mind" (181).

"Day's Ending," written in 1921, is probably the clearest rejection of the romantic love plot that informed so many of her earlier poems. Here, in Tucson, watching the mountains and the stars, the speaker claims to have experienced a revelation.

> It was not long I lived there
> But I became a woman
> Under those vehement stars,
> For it was there I heard
> For the first time my spirit
> Forging an iron rule for me,
> As though with slow cold hammers
> Beating out word by word:
>
> "Only yourself can heal you,
> Only yourself can lead you,
> The road is heavy going
> And ends where no man knows;
> Take love when love is given,
> But never think to find it
> A sure escape from sorrow
> Or a complete repose.
>
>   (180)

Earlier the phrase "I became a woman" might have led us to expect as a consequence some reference to romantic passion in the popular sense that one "becomes a woman" when one loses one's virginity. But here Teasdale surprises us by asserting that becoming a woman means growing beyond the expectation that love will save us from having to exist independently. True womanhood means assuming the mantle of the virgin, defined as an autonomous being, "not altered by human activity."[31]

Sara Teasdale's late persona is nowhere more fully embodied than in the particularly lovely and mysterious poem "Effigy of a Nun."

> Infinite gentleness, infinite irony
>   Are in this face with fast-sealed eyes,
> And around this mouth that learned in loneliness
>   How useless their wisdom is to the wise.
>
> In her nun's habit carved, patiently, lovingly,
>   By one who knew the ways of womankind,
> This woman's face still keeps, in its cold wistful calm,
>   All the subtle pride of her mind.
>
> These long patrician hands, clasping the crucifix,
>   Show she had weighed the world, her will was set;
> These pale curving lips of hers, holding their hidden smile,
>   Once having made their choice, knew no regret.
>
> She was of those who hoard their own thoughts carefully,
>   Feeling them far too dear to give away,
> Content to look at life with the high, insolent
>   Air of an audience watching a play.
>
> If she was curious, if she was passionate
>   She must have told herself that love was great,
> But that the lacking it might be as great a thing
>   If she held fast to it, challenging fate.
>
> She who so loved herself and her own warring thoughts,
>   Watching their humorous, tragic rebound,
> In her thick habit's fold, sleeping, sleeping,
>   Is she amused at dreams she has found?
>
> Infinite tenderness, infinite irony
>   Are hidden forever in her closed eyes,
> Who must have learned too well in her long loneliness
>   How empty wisdom is, even to the wise.
>
>   (172)

This poem is written in dactylic tetrameter, though the poet varies the meter in a number of places. Unusual for Teasdale, this meter has the effect of seeming almost effortless, dreamlike, perhaps soporific. The rocking rhythm establishes itself as a retrospective and thoughtful measure in the context of this poem's subject matter.

Dactylic meter is hard to handle successfully since its domination may become enervating. But Teasdale manages it here by alternating feminine with masculine endings and by breaking up the dactyls with trochees and other kinds of metrical feet. Though the immediate effect of the meter is to establish an undulant ease, a sensation of certainty suggested in the notion of time as a dance, the poem's alternation of masculine and feminine rhymes, like its division into opposing versions of the nun's experience (stanzas 2–4 versus 5–7) contradict this effect and provide the mystery which is the poem's most appealing attribute.

In brief, this poem captures both Teasdale's belief in the rewards of autonomy and her lingering doubt as to whether a life lived without romantic connections can be ultimately successful. We recognize, for instance, the sybil from the Crystal Gazer poems in "She was of those who hoard their own thoughts carefully" and in the nun's "high, insolent / Air of an audience watching a play." If it is true that "her will was set" and that once having made her choice, she "knew no regret," then Teasdale asks us to admire this superior virgin whose self-satisfaction resides in "the subtle pride of her mind."

However, stanza 6, beginning "She who so loved herself," breaks the poetic pattern both stylistically and referentially. Already in stanza 5 the poet has introduced hypothetical elements in the nun's character—curiosity and passion—which conflict with what seems earlier to be the dominant interpretation of the nun's self-satisfied and renunciatory nature. In the last three stanzas Teasdale explores possible counter-projections. Perhaps the nun was not so happy after all. Line three of the sixth stanza begins with two dactyls but ends with two trochees, suggesting a pause to reconsider, a pause which results in the question: "Is she amused at dreams she has found?" The phrasing of this question wilfully ignores an opportunity for a dactyl—amused at *the* dreams—in favor of a trochee, again creating the feeling that the speaker is no longer sure how to assess the success of the nun's renunciatory posture.

Though at the beginning the nun's face suggests "How useless their wisdom is to the wise," we cannot know what this means immediately and the context created by the first five stanzas implies that usefulness may not be the highest good. Though the nun's wisdom is useless, it may yet transform her into a creature self-complete as a flower or a stone; such wisdom may be useless only in the sense that it has no telos beyond itself.

Though we may safely say that projection is operating throughout this reading of the effigy, Teasdale only admits to her projections in the last section of the poem, where the *must haves* and the interpretation of the content of *closed* eyes (rather than open faces) alert us that she has dispensed with even the pretense of sculptural criticism in order to tell her own story.

In her own story the persona of the passionate virgin is a dignified and imposing figure, credited with genuine depth and insight. Still, "all the subtle pride of her mind" may not be enough to offset the feeling of emptiness that lack of love produces.

"How I would like to believe in tenderness— / The face of the effigy . . . / Bending, on me in particular, its mild eyes," says Sylvia Plath in "The Moon and the Yew Tree." But both Plath and Teasdale, as suicide approaches, read other meanings than tenderness in the configuration of their circumstances. Teasdale finds in the effigy the irony of an empty wisdom. Plath turns from the effigy to the moon and the yew tree: "And the message of the yew tree is blackness—blackness and silence."[32]

"Every act of individuation, every putting away of childish things and outgrown relationships, every advance involves a concomitant loss that anticipates the ultimate loss of the self," writes Gloria Erlich.[33] Though her reference is to Hawthorne, this is a resonant statement for Sara Teasdale's work. Her passionate virginity, in the end, becomes a script for suicide. Both *Dark of the Moon* and *Strange Victory*, like Plath's *Ariel* and *Winter Trees*, convey a sense of inexorable progress toward death. "Since Death Brushed Past Me," from Teasdale's last book, ends: "My words are said, my way is clear" (213).

Yet, in recognizing that the poet ultimately chose her own death, one need not conclude that she was only and everywhere defeated. Her suicide may be seen also as a way of taking control of her life, her most thoroughly autonomous gesture. In this context, "Strange Victory"—in which two old friends meet on the battlefield—achieves added resonance. The poet seems to have felt grateful at the end of her life for special blessings:

> To this, to this, after my hope was lost,
>   To this strange victory;
> To find you with the living, not the dead,
>   To find you glad of me;
> To find you wounded even less than I,
>   Moving as I across the stricken plain;
> After the battle to have found your voice
>   Lifted above the slain.
>
>   (208)

This poem is poignant because its use of infinitives evokes the rapture of surprise: "to find," "to find," "to find." Yet it is significant that in the end she writes "to have found," as though the moment of elation were past and, in its aftermath, she knows her way lies in another direction.

"Strange Victory" effectively draws upon the classical heritage Teasdale admired in the poems of Sappho. It reads like a fragment found in a sarcophagus. "In a Darkening Garden," which bears close relation to Louise Bogan's "After the Persian," is also classical in its bearing and restraint and deserves quotation here as an example of the way Teasdale associates maturity with an acceptance of death and of the life that continues in spite of it.

> Gather together, against the coming of night,
>   All that we played with here,
> Toys and fruits, the quill from the sea-bird's flight,
>   The small flute, hollow and clear;
> The apple that was not eaten, the grapes untasted—
>   Let them be put away.

> They served for us, I would not have them wasted,
> They lasted out our day.
>
> (209)

In her final assessment of Sara Teasdale almost twenty years after her death, Louise Bogan wrote: "Miss Teasdale's lyrics . . . accompanied her experience of life step by step; they became increasingly lucid and tragic with the passage of time. She expressed not only the simplicities of traditional feminine feeling, but new subtleties of emotional nuance, and her last book, *Strange Victory*, . . . shows classic depth and balance."[34]

Of course, the use of classical techniques does not itself confer value, but in Teasdale's case it seems to offset the more conventional nightingale excesses of her early work and it therefore becomes significant. When Carolyn Kizer writes of "the sad sonneteers, toast-and-teasdales we loved at thirteen; / Middle-aged virgins seducing the puerile anthologists / Through lust of the mind,"[35] she seems to be thinking of the virginal passion of Teasdale's early work. Against this set of condescending references, Teasdale's late dignity and restraint look refreshingly tough-minded.

Yet the persona of the passionate virgin is no more and no less intimately connected with Teasdale's cultural experience as a woman than was her earlier avatar, which Amy Lowell named "the dainty erotic."[36] Her reaction against the modern was also a recapitulation of it. Having initially chosen a persona in tune with popular culture, she ultimately gives us the first extended set of reflections on the burdens of autonomy for a twentieth-century woman poet, a significant feat in itself.

The work of Sara Teasdale embodies in important ways the ideologies of her time, yet it also critiques those ideologies, showing the instability of the attempt to rationalize modes of affiliation and autonomy in a world where such modes were still deeply contaminated with gendered moral imperatives. What we fail to hear in her poetry, the strains of anger and aggression, we will directly encounter in the work of a tougher contemporaneous spirit, Elinor Wylie.

WOMEN AND AGGRESSION

Elinor Wylie and the Woman Warrior Persona

Elinor Wylie shares attributes—poetic and personal—with all the other poets in this study. Like Sara Teasdale, in particular, she was drawn to the life of the nun. Both women were endowed with New England Puritan sensibilities rendering them austere in others' eyes. Both were uncomfortable with sex. Yet no one would confuse the spirit of Elinor Wylie with that of Sara Teasdale.

Wylie's persona is gothic; her intensity causes the manuscripts we read in her name to curl and ignite even now, after all this time, because Elinor Wylie is the angriest woman in the nightingale tradition. "Angry" is not even the right word; "outraged" is more accurate. No one but Wylie could have written "From the Wall," for instance.

> Woman, be steel against loving, enfold and defend you,
> Turn from the innocent look and the arrogant tongue;
> You shall be coppery dross to the purses that spend you;
> Lock up your years like a necklace of emeralds strung.
>
> Lock up your heart like a jewel; be cruel and clever;
> Woman, be strong against loving, be iron, be stone;
> Never and never and never and never and never
> Give for the tears of a lover a tear of your own.
>
> Cover the clutch of your greed with a velvety gloving;
> Take from the good if you can, from the vile if you must;
> Take from the proud and alone, from the cowardly loving;
> Hold out your hands for the pity; accept of the lust.[1]

It is hard to imagine a man reading this poem with the same mingled sense of exhilaration and relief that it still gives me after fifteen years. I associate these feelings, shameful and furtive as they are, with those that women watchers of *Dynasty* confess to in connection with the character of Alexis. There is something cleansing in the white acetyline of the bitch-burn even when we know the purity of that anger to be based on half-truths.

Too often critics ignore the violence in women writers, though recently we have begun to see more attention paid to it in works like Alicia Ostriker's *Stealing the Language*, which includes a chapter entitled "Herr God, Herr Lucifer: Anger, Violence, and Polarization." In literature female capacities for violence appear at least as far back as Euripides' *The Bacchae* and the ruthless Medea, to whom Elinor Wylie compared herself. Much in the culture of our own time caters to this violence, without, however, attempting to explore its deeper ranges and mysteries. In spite of arguments that women are less aggressive than men, Ostriker has noted that at feminist poetry readings the more violent the poem, the more positively the audience responds.[2]

Without paraphrasing the poem of Wylie's just quoted, we might, to begin with, note some basic features of the speaker's position in it. Her anger is violent, her attitude uncompromising, her indictment of men total. Like Claude Lévi-Strauss (and more recently Luce Irigaray), she equates the position of women in society with money which passes from (male) hand to (male) hand in rituals of patriarchal exchange. "You shall be coppery dross to the purses that spend you." The speaker advocates a refusal to be complicitous in this tainted process of circulation: "Lock up your years like a necklace of emeralds strung."

However—and here we move closer to the nexus of this form of female aggression—the speaker at no point indicates a belief in her own capacity to change the rules of the game. Her only strategy is to play shrewdly and defensively: "be cruel and clever." It is taken for granted that woman must live her life within the confines of the male prerogative. Masculine pity will offer her chances for manipulation but she must accept her role as a victim of male lust.

One of the striking features of this poem, of course, is the total absence of masculine pronouns or references to men. One need not read this repression as some strategy of feminist resistance, however. It might more accurately be read as a sign of Wylie's belief in the absolute ability of males to set the terms of social discourse and social exchange. Male presence in the poem may be so massive that it does not need to be noted.

What does this massive male potency, and the comparatively limited female opportunities to resist it, have to do with the aggressiveness of the poem's tone? For it must be said that it is primarily the tone which is belligerent. The speaker advises only *passive* aggression to women; the violence in the poem comes not in the brutality of the deeds recommended but in the extremity of the speaker's emotional "never and never and never and never and never," surely one of the most emphatic uses of dactylic pentameter in the language. Instead of reinforcing the idea of some irreducible level of aggression in the human animal, the kind of aggression Elinor Wylie and others exhibit seems linked indissolubly to a keen sense of impotence. Her angry poems are like the forays of the Maenads in *The Bacchae*: brief reversals of the gender hierarchy not to be taken as permanently altering the structure of patriarchal power.

A second poem worth investigating for its equation of violence with female depredations is "Fable," from Wylie's second book, *Black Armour* (1923). In this poem a white raven preys upon the body of a knight killed at the Battle of Hastings. Despite the fact that the man is actually dead, the poem evokes a set of sadistic sensations whose intensity almost revitalizes him even as it renders him both passive and impotent. The raven drinks his blood and eats out his eyes, finally drinking his brains.

> The old man's beard was ravelled up
> In stiff and webby skeins:
> From his broad skull's broken cup
> The raven sipped his brains.
>
> Insensate with that burning draught
> Her feathers turned to flame:
> Like a cruel silver shaft
> Across the sun she came.
>
> She flew straight into God's house;
> She drank the virtuous air.
> A knight lay dead: his gutted brows
> Gaped hollow under his hair.[3]

This poem redacts the ecstasy of the female ("insensate with that burning draught") who has managed to wrench intellectual power away from male control. Despite the fact that her actions appear as immoral, even criminal, its irony delights in the raven's success at evading punishment, positioning itself against the Law represented by the knight. Nonetheless, the raven never achieves a status beyond that of a scavenger. She is a cruel and clever manipulator, able to make a lucky intervention, rather than a powerful agent capable of redirecting the course of human history.

These two poems serve an important function in introducing Elinor Wylie's place in the nightingale tradition. Despite the superficial similarity with Amy Lowell, who was also known for her aggression and who also occasionally personified the woman warrior, Elinor Wylie must be read as the "borderline personality" in the tradition's closet. Whereas Lowell played with a discourse about madness in her late poems, Wylie affected everyone she met in her last year as living on the edge of hysteria.

On the continuum of masks outrageous and austere, Wylie's are both the most outrageous and the most austere. However, the intensity of Wylie's strongest lyrics derives from the sense we have of her speakers as constrained, backed up "against the wall." Often sadomasochistic, the woman warrior in Elinor Wylie's hands becomes the epitome of both female rage and feminine self-destructiveness.

Wylie's precursors in this mode are the nineteenth-century women poets who wrote "power fantasies," women like Maria Brooks, Frances Osgood, A. R. St. John, and Lucretia Davidson.[4] Yet none of these women was as violent and aggressive in her poems as Wylie. Her followers are Anne Sexton and Sylvia Plath, who in poems like "Speaking Bitterness" and "Daddy" exploit the extremities of discourse sometimes at the expense of their enemies, sometimes at their own expense.

The contemporary poetic climate certainly bears evidence of the sizzling thermodynamics of these women. In fact, Alicia Ostriker comments, "the overwhelming sensation to be gotten from contemporary women's poetry is the smell of camouflage burning, the crackle of spite, free at last, the whirl and rush of flamelike rage that has so often swept the soul, and as often been damped down so that we never thought there could be words for it."[5] Yet Elinor Wylie's poems belong not to Plath's generation but to a world more than fifty years out of date.

The persona of the woman warrior locates Wylie in an earlier time. By the 1950s the woman warrior was out of fashion and neither Anne Sexton nor Sylvia Plath used it much. It belonged to a turn-of-the-century era in which militant women adopted the trappings of military men. For Wylie, the adoption of the warrior persona was also inextricably connected to her personal tragedies and the need for psychic defenses. Thus, like all the masks in this study, the woman warrior persona was an overdetermined choice. The self who "fights" and who wears protective "armor" is produced in part by Wylie's paranoia, in part by her anti-modernist education, and in part by her proximity to the rumblings of the First World War.

In the following sections of this chapter, I will explore the psychic factors in Wylie's biography that kept her emotions at fever pitch, the cultural setting in which she chose to engage her readers as a combatant, and the literary forms of aggression which became her trademark. However, in addition to the aggressive warrior who fights an external enemy, we must recognize the abject in Elinor Wylie as it manifests itself in the war within.

Wylie's choice to make courage, discipline, and will into poetic as well as military virtues laid the groundwork for an antipersonnel maneuver we may call abjection in which the poet's persona is repeatedly attacked and flayed by the poem. The woman warrior brings with her a masochistic squire who is both the double and the opposite of her mistress. As Julia Kristeva has written, "to each ego its object, to each superego its abject."[6] Part of the project of this chapter is to identify the abject in Elinor Wylie's work and to suggest connections between the violence of this kind of woman's aggressive persona and the concomitant intensity of her surrender to abjection, a surrender all too recognizable in the suicidal gestures of Teasdale, Wylie, Virginia Woolf, Sylvia Plath, and Anne Sexton.

BECOMING THE WOMAN WARRIOR

Elinor Morton Hoyt, born in 1885 to a handsome, powerful father and a demanding, sickly mother, knew from her earliest years that women were not in charge. Her father was a lawyer who eventually became solicitor general under Theodore Roosevelt and then counsellor to the State Department. Her mother's ambitions, limited by health and gender, took the familiar distorted form of social climbing and manipulation of her children. Like Amy Lowell's, her family must be considered upper class rather than middle class with its status derived primarily through the male line.

However, unlike Amy Lowell, Elinor Wylie could not really find in her father a role model representing strength and success. Like Lowell's father, he was a remote figure in the household, but his remoteness was also an indication of his inadequacy.

Mr. Hoyt seems to have been emotionally immature, unable to cope with intense feelings, his own or others'. Though prominent in Washington society, he had two nervous breakdowns. Only at the office, where matters remained fairly impersonal, was he able to perform successfully.

Wylie's mother, despite her limitations, was a much more accessible image of efficiency and emotional force, which may be one reason why Elinor Wylie never chose the androgyne, as Amy Lowell conceived it, as her persona. Wylie was always first and foremost a "woman"; though she demonstrated certain attributes not always associated with women of her time, such as resolute courage. She neither wanted to imitate men nor was she in awe of them, writing late in her life, "all men are idiots, only some one loves and some one doesn't."[7]

Elinor Wylie did have an Amy Lowell figure close to home in her aunt, Helen Strong Hoyt (1871–44), whom she may have unconsciously sought to differentiate herself from at an early age. Helen Hoyt never married, taught English at Bryn Mawr, dressed as a man and drove her own coach and four. Such women constituted a small but significant minority at the turn of the century, suggesting the permeability of the boundary between masculine and feminine even in a highly differentiated society.

In contrast, Elinor was in many ways a model "little girl": pretty, precocious, and eager to please. Her first major crisis, however, was a direct result of her malleability. Though for years she had worked hard to impress her mother, memorizing *Hamlet* (as family legend has it) in two weeks and parading her intellectual interests by reading Shelley, Keats, Landor, and Donne, full adolescence found the two women in conflict. Her mother was less interested in intellectual feats of prowess than she was in bringing her daughter "out" as a social debutante. Her aim was to marry Elinor off as soon as possible. Stanley Olson claims that at first "she rebelled against Mama's ambition for her, took up with unsuitable men, and seemed to care very little about marriage" (40). But in the end Elinor succumbed.

She married on very short notice a man who in some ways must have reminded her of her father. Philip Hichborn was also a lawyer, of good family, rather quiet, and intelligent. However, again like her father, he was mentally unstable. Elinor had become pregnant immediately after the wedding and before the year was out, she found herself with a new baby, very little emotional support, and a madman for a husband. Her mother, always conscious of appearances, gave her no encouragement to leave Hichborn, advising her daughter to grit her teeth and bear it. These difficult conditions set the stage for the enactment of Elinor's defiance and the birth of the woman warrior persona.

Horace Wylie came into Elinor's life at a time when she desperately needed someone to understand her predicament, to pay attention to her needs, and to love her. He was a much older man, very wealthy and sophisticated, with a family of his own and a taste for pretty women. Their "affair" probably did not mature into a full-fledged sexual relationship for a long time but Elinor came to depend upon Wylie more and more as her husband's mental state deteriorated. A precipitating event in the progression of her relationship with Wylie was her father's death and Elinor's discovery that he himself had kept a mistress. Rebecca West remembered the effect of this discovery on Elinor in a letter of 1953:

> Elinor described the scene of this discovery with great feeling . . . , and always
> expected me to take it for granted that when you found out that your father had
> been in love with someone not your mother, why, *of course*, you left your own
> husband; you had to, you were so upset. Quite beyond argument. It was something
> she could no more help than her blood pressure. (Olson, 68)

Beyond the humor of this memory, we can see the way Elinor's feelings about
Hichborn were entangled with her relationship to her father. It remains ambiguous,
however, whether she meant West to see her as occupying her mother's role (re-
jecting the offensive husband) or replaying her father's role as the unfaithful spouse.
In any case, on December 16, 1910, Elinor and Horace Wylie left children and
spouses behind and fled to England.

The consequences of this rash act were to haunt Elinor Wylie for the rest of
her life. From this moment on, she saw herself as fighting a hostile world, as
standing alone on a windswept battlefield, sometimes a martyr to a noble cause
and sometimes a fallen woman deserving the world's rebukes. We can hardly imagine from today's perspective the extent and brutality of the reaction to her elopement. Newspapers up and down the East Coast carried front page stories of the
scandal. President Taft actually offered his services in locating the couple. Among
her acquaintances and in the press, Elinor was singled out for portrayal as a monster
for leaving her husband and three-year-old son, though Horace Wylie had more
children and less incentive (since his wife was not vicious and insane). Even her
own family were hostile to Elinor.

During the five years she spent in England with Wylie under an assumed name,
many odd factors in their situation served to make Elinor feel increasingly guilty.
For a brief period it seemed as though Horace and his wife would resume their
marriage, but this attempt failed. A second elopement with Elinor brought the
scandal and its history back into the open. Even newspapers like the *Washington
Post* and *New York Times* carried stories.

Then Philip Hichborn committed suicide. Despite the fact that people close
to him knew that his mental problems predated his life with Elinor, she was once
again vilified in the newspapers as a heartless female, the cause of her husband's
death.

During this period Elinor worried a great deal about her son. She suffered terrible
headaches to which she would be prone all her life. At one point she even underwent shock treatments three times a week. Years later she admitted to Carl Van
Doren: "I left my baby when I ran away. That was the one thing I have ever done
that was bad. Other things, no. I would do all of them over again. But that was
utterly bad. I was a bad woman."[8] Even her happiness with Wylie was a reason
for guilt. In her letters to her mother, Elinor "undercut every declaration of pleasure
and contentment with a poisonous indictment of either her selfishness or villainy"
(Olson, 99).

The years in England would later be remembered as idyllic, but they also had
an edge of desperation. Wylie kept trying to get pregnant in spite of the fact that
the couple was not yet able to marry. Her first pregnancy resulted in stillbirth and

Elinor plunged into hysterical grief, going blind for several weeks. Her doctors advised against pregnancy because of her high blood pressure, but Elinor forged ahead with her plans. A second Wylie baby was born in the United States after a pregnancy of seven months but died a week later.

War had forced the couple to return to America since they could no longer live under assumed names in England once their passports were examined. In 1916 they were finally able to marry but their financial situation was dire. Neither was working and Horace had lost all of his money. Even after six years and marriage, they were still outcasts from polite society. Thus, Elinor Wylie's persona was fired in the furnaces of personal suffering; it now emerged as a rather cold literary figure whose primary virtue was a kind of defiant courage.

Courage Elinor certainly had, indeed had always had. Early in her illicit relationship with Horace in Washington, she had been prone to martyr rituals to "prove her love," like letting matches burn her until the pain became intolerable.[9] Now she had to face straitened financial circumstances, social ostracism, and her continuing inability to have Horace Wylie's child. Elinor had the kind of courage that allowed her to stand firm under attack. However, she lacked another kind of courage, a less glamorous but ultimately more useful kind that might have helped her to adjust to a life of narrowed opportunities with better grace.

Had she been able to accept such a life, of course, she would never have become a poet. In part because she was bored, in part to create a self who could triumph over her circumstances, Wylie turned to writing, singing "off charnel steps," as many women poets had done before her. In 1912 she had had privately printed a volume of juvenilia called *Incidental Numbers*. But her years with Horace Wylie in England had given her more sophistication since Horace was thoroughly cultivated and had taught her both history and literature. Her first serious book, *Nets to Catch the Wind*, was published in 1921 and establishes the literary persona Wylie was to develop and refine in the last seven years of her life: fierce, embattled, proud, chaste, sometimes cruel, sometimes abject, but always disciplined and clever.

By the time this volume was published, Elinor Wylie had turned from Horace Wylie to the man who was to become her third husband, William Rose Benet. Benet, an old friend of her brother's, had seen some of her poems and become committed to the idea of helping her make a career as a writer. The marriage with Horace was suffering from isolation and financial pressures. Benet—who was kind, generous, enthusiastic, and a good literary administrator—offered her a chance to change her situation, move to New York, meet other writers, and, perhaps, start over. These were heady inducements.

Looking back on this time from a later perspective, however, Wylie was once again ashamed of the choice she had made. The year before she died, she wrote to Horace: "I do not admire myself for having fallen in love with the idea of freedom, & poetry, & New York" and, by extension, Bill Benet. She went on to say that the misery of 1919–20 "spoiled what must always seem to me the happiest part of my life—my life with you" (Olson, 149).

Still, in 1920 the world that was opening up to her seemed very alluring indeed. Though she was thirty-five years old, she felt both young and vulnerable. Acquaintances remember her as appearing shy, diffident, withdrawn, not at all the kind of figure who would emerge in her literary persona of the following year. Looking forward to a meeting of the Poetry Society of America, she wrote ingenuously: "It would be wonderful to me to know the younger women who are doing such beautiful works these days, and to feel I was (more or less) one of them" (Olson, 173–74). The most prominent "younger" women of the time were Sara Teasdale and Edna St. Vincent Millay, both of whom she came to know well.

Having spent her life dependent upon the financial support of men, Wylie now looked forward to being self-sufficient for the first time. "I should certainly like to earn my living," she wrote her mother. "Gosh, *how I would love it*" (her emphasis; Olson, 180). Eventually she was to take over Edmund Wilson's position as literary editor of *Vanity Fair* after supporting herself at odd jobs in publishing.

Much went in her favor in New York that had gone against her before. Her scandalous past endeared her to the bohemians who clustered in Greenwich Village, though Frank Crowningshield said of her, she "liked to pretend she was a bohemian, but the sham was at all times apparent."[10] She formed a close friendship with Edna St. Vincent Millay. Her poetry was praised and her style imitated and parodied all over town. There was even a torchlight parade through the streets to celebrate the publication of one of her books, and the Macdowell Colony opened its doors to her.[11] From the outside it often appeared that Wylie had little to complain of, as she graduated from the insecure novice who was eager to please into the powerful, arrogant, and obsessively vain titaness in the silver dress.

But here we must pause to consider the significance of that dress. For many women poets a particular kind of dress suits their personae. There is no real counterpart among male writers because the body and its apparel signify differently for men than for women. Emily Dickinson's white dress figured prominently in her Amherst persona; it announced her as the nun, the poetess, or the Queen of Calvary, a person who had committed herself to lofty projects beyond the world of material life. Edna St. Vincent Millay made a dress out of scarves to declare her bohemian daring and independence. Later she exchanged that costume for a red velvet gown falling to the floor and highlighting her red hair. For her, the important message to convey was passion, particularly sexual passion.

Elinor Wylie's silver dress with its chain-link weave was the costume of the woman warrior, unfailingly connected to armor in the poet's imagination. Sympathetic friends realized its symbolic relationship to Wylie's vulnerability, her *need* to protect herself from the slings and arrows of her enemies. Others found the poet's armored exterior alienating, a deliberate assault upon the liberal values of democratic humanism, a haughty, aristocratic attempt to be distinguished and fine. Louis Untermeyer remembers meeting her for the first time: "I think I expected to see the typical adventuress, dark, passionate, and poisonous. Instead I saw a person made of cold silver whose bearing was puritan-patrician and whose being emanated chastity."[12]

Why did Elinor Wylie need to continue protecting herself when so much was going her way? Part of the answer is that Wylie continued to experience devastating assaults upon her fragile psyche. Her brother Henry, living for a time with her soon-to-be husband Bill Benet, gassed himself in their apartment. Elinor wrote of her admiration for him with the guilt of a survivor in "Heroics." Then her sister Connie committed suicide in Europe. Even her brother Morton, married to Tallulah Bankhead's sister, would make a suicide attempt by jumping ship in mid-Atlantic. (Though Elinor was not to know it, her son Philip Hichborn committed suicide several years after her death, as though unable to withstand the burden of the family legacy.)

There were more miscarriages, more terrible recoveries, more agonizing headaches. When Bill's three children were living with them, Elinor tried desperately and unsuccessfully to be a good stepmother. She was much too nervous and fastidious to be a comfortable mother, but she devoted herself tirelessly to nursing Bill's youngest, who was very ill with diphtheria. Her failures at mothering generated fits of violent crying during which she would smash her head rhythmically against the wall until Bill intervened.

And she was still forced to endure attacks on her moral rectitude, some from unexpected sources. Ellen Glasgow snubbed her when Wylie visited the South. Amy Lowell, in one of her contradictory fits of pomposity, stopped in to congratulate her on her marriage to Benet in 1923, only to add: "But if you marry again, I shall cut you dead—and I warn you all Society will do the same. You will be nobody" (Olson, 225). The League of American Penwomen rescinded an invitation to include her in an Author's Breakfast because of her scandalous past.

So in some ways it is not surprising that the poet felt the necessity to adopt the persona of the woman warrior. She titled her second book *Black Armour*, dividing it into sections like "Gauntlet" and "Helmet" to underscore the importance of the controlling motif. Eunice Tietjens' review provides the following interpretation of the dominant metaphor: "In it [Wylie] has made for herself a breastplate of courage, a helmet of almost ruthless self-knowledge, gauntlets of her own sophistication, and a mocking plume of her very sensitiveness, her happy taut nerves."[13] Among her friends the warrior persona was understood and even considered dramatically useful, but it also concealed darker implications.

In spite of literary success, instability dogged Elinor Wylie's footsteps and she, who had shown so much personal resilience in the face of so many difficulties, spent the last short years of her life on the brink of madness. As her reputation grew, she became more and more convinced that in choosing art she had betrayed her woman-self. She came to see her inability to produce a child as the proof of her guilt, polarizing her situation in terms of motherhood versus writing. In this mood she wrote: "It is, & always will be, the greatest tragedy & complete frustration of my life that I am childless" (Olson, 318). She no longer counted Philip Hichborn III as her son. As the last great depression took hold of her, she began to solicit death in less and less subtle ways, refusing to follow her doctor's orders on diet and plunging into distressing situations, like a soldier taking unnecessary risks in battle.

In the last year of her life, she wrote: "I am, of course, a complete failure, but one mustn't mind that since so many of our best people are failures. I suppose the only way to avoid it is by dying young . . . " (Olson, 319). Like Amy Lowell, Sara Teasdale, and Edna Millay, Elinor Wylie found that popularity provided no insulation from the strains of trying to combine womanhood with the life of an artist. As for them, death began to appear more and more appealing.

In a last desperate emotional volte face, Wylie fell in love with another "forbidden lover," Henry de Clifford Woodhouse, though this time she pledged herself to a romantic abnegation. To one friend she confessed: "I don't want much. I don't expect it. I could be satisfied if I could know that sometime, maybe when we are very old, we could spend the same night under one roof. It would not have to be together. Only under the same roof, peacefully."[14] Cliff Woodhouse was an Englishman with a wife and family who apparently had no intentions of following in Horace Wylie's footsteps, though he was fond of Elinor and took long walks with her through the English countryside, discussing philosophy and literature.

Angels and Earthly Creatures (1929), Wylie's last book, makes effective use of the emotional suffering the writer experienced in this final tormenting passion. Still, many who knew the poet well felt that Wylie had lost her mind. She behaved so strangely, vacillating between violent emotional outbursts and periods of almost superhuman stoicism and restraint. Certainly there are poems from this period that detail the effects of madness, like "O Virtuous Light" and "The Heart's Desire," which will be examined at a later point.

Wylie's physical health also deteriorated. She suffered two strokes; fell down the stairs, severely injuring her back; and woke up one day to find half of her face paralyzed from a nerve in her ear pressing against the bone. Yet she worked carefully and professionally to put the finishing touches on her last book of poems. On December 10, 1928, she died at home of a stroke, having just completed her editorial work. Like her death, hers was a life which had almost too much of a literary shape to it. As the poet wrote in "This Hand," there is something chilling in the figure of Elinor Wylie, something which demands to be reckoned with on its own prearranged terms.

> If I had seen a thorn
> Broken to grape-vine bud;
> If I had ever borne
> Child of our mingled blood;
>
> Elixirs might escape;
> But now, compact as stone,
> My hand preserves a shape
> Too utterly its own.
> (CP, 66)

THE WOMAN WARRIOR IN CULTURAL CONTEXT

Elinor Wylie's troubled career really has no parallel for gothic horrors: the multiple suicides, the abuse she suffered from her immediate family as well as the rest of the world, the progressive disintegration of every intimate relationship, the deaths of her babies and alienation from her son. It is easy to see why she might feel angry and, at the same time, in need of protection.

Yet the woman warrior, a figure of both aggression and defense, belongs not just to Wylie but to the larger cultural moment of her arrival upon the literary scene. We have already looked at the passage from T. J. Jackson Lears's *No Place of Grace: Antimodernism and the Transformation of American Culture 1880–1920* where Lears addresses "the popularity of self-willed chivalric heroines" at the turn of the century, seeing them as representing "liberation from restrictive femininity."

Louise Imogen Guiney, one of those with an appetite for the martial ideal, published her collected poems, *Happy Ending*, in 1909 when Wylie was eagerly reading poetry and very impressionable. We do not know whether Wylie read Guiney but, like Wylie, Guiney was an antimodernist who felt most at home in England. Like Wylie again, she wrote about knights of old. One of her poems, "The Kings," shares profound similarities with the work of Elinor Wylie, both in its attitude toward experience and in its stanzaic pattern. At the end of "The Kings" (1894), Guiney has a Guardian Angel offer advice to her male protagonist:

"While Kings of eternal evil
Yet darken the hills about,
Thy part is with broken sabre
To rise on the last redoubt;

"To fear not sensible failure,
Nor covet the game at all,
But fighting, fighting, fighting,
Die, driven against the wall."[15]

Wylie was also attracted to lost causes (see "Hughie at the Inn," for example) and also identified with figures who made courageous defenses when pushed to their limits. Wylie, like Guiney, created a number of male poetic characters— Peregrine, Lucifer—who were "fighters" in the war for personal authenticity so dear to the hearts of antimodernists threatened by the modern specter of standardization and conformity. Unlike Guiney, however, Elinor Wylie also tried to incorporate elements of the martial ideal into a feminine persona, a figure of female vitality—proud, imperious, self-sufficient, aggressive—whom I have chosen to call the woman warrior.

How did this persona come to fire the imaginations of so many exceptional women at the turn of the century and thereafter? Lears helpfully reminds us that the late nineteenth century set the stage for a vitalist image of the female. "From Rossetti's Blessed Damozel to Baudelaire's Giantess to Henry Adams's Virgin of Chartres, images of female vitality pervaded the Western imagination."[16]

One indication of the pervasiveness of the image is the popularity of the woman warrior as Joan of Arc. We have already seen that Amy Lowell felt the necessity of coming to terms with that figure in her adolescent diary. Sarah Bernhardt's embodiment of this role also brought the Maid of Orleans to the forefront of the popular imagination. In fact, Joan of Arc's image haunted imaginative women in the late-nineteenth and earlier twentieth centuries.

Considerably earlier than the First World War, women were using the image of Joan of Arc and other woman warrior figures to assert their demands for equality and women's suffrage. In the first issue of *Votes for Women* (1907), a women's suffrage periodical, one writer declared: "The founders and leaders of the movement must lead, the non-commissioned officers must carry out their instructions, the rank and file must loyally share the burdens of the fight. For there is no compulsion to come into our ranks, but those who come must come as soldiers ready to march onwards in battle array."[17] On ceremonial occasions, some of the suffragettes dressed as Joan of Arc or Britomart, Spenser's lady knight.

In fact, Joan of Arc continued to have symbolic appeal to certain kinds of women even during the First World War. In *Ladders to Fire* (1946) Anaïs Nin's heroine, Lillian, declares: "All through the last war as a child I felt: if only they would let me be Joan of Arc. Joan of Arc wore a suit of armor, she sat on a horse, she fought side by side with men. She must have gained their strength."[18]

Inez Haynes Irwin (1873–1970), a well-known suffragist, journalist, and novelist, represents the kind of woman who might turn to Joan of Arc as a role model. Fed up with the triviality and blandness of girlhood, she reported:

> I regretted bitterly that I had not been born a man. Like all young things I yearned for romance and adventure. It was not, however, a girl's kind of romance and adventure that I wanted, but a man's. I wanted to run away to sea, to take tramping trips across the country, to go on voyages of discovery and exploration, to try my hand at a dozen different trades and occupations. I wanted to be a sailor, a soldier. I wanted to go to prize-fights; to frequent bar-rooms; even barber-shops and smoking-rooms seemed to offer a brisk, salty taste of life. (*These Modern Women*, 38–39)

Elinor Wylie was not a suffragette, not even a feminist, and few would see an immediate connection between Inez Irwin and the aristocratic poet. However, Wylie created the persona of "Peregrine" as a mask for her own character and preferences. Stanley Olson informs us that she sent a copy of "Peregrine" to Horace Wylie, saying: "This is me, not you" (206). The similarities between the Peregrine character and Inez Haynes Irwin's youthful fantasies is striking. Brief quotations from the lengthy poem can help us to consolidate these cultural connections. Wylie writes:

> Liar and bragger,
> He had no friend
> Except a dagger
> And a candle-end;
> The one he read by;
> The one scared cravens;
> And he was fed by
> The Prophet's ravens.
> . . . .
> He could sit any
> Horse, a rider

Outstripping Cheiron's
Canter and gallop.
Pau's environs
The pubs of Salop,
Wells and Bath inns
Shared his pleasure
With taverns of Athens.
. . . .
His step was martial;
Spent and shabby
He wasn't broken;
A dozen lingoes
He must have spoken.
. . . . . .
He loved a city
And a street's alarums;
Parks were pretty
And so were bar-rooms.
. . . .
His sins were serried,
His virtues garish;
His corpse was buried
In a country parish.
Before he went hence—
God knows where—
He spoke this sentence
With a princely air:
"The noose draws tighter;
This is the end;
I'm a good fighter,
But a bad friend:
I've played the traitor
Over and over;
I'm a good hater,
But a bad lover."
(CP, 57–60)

Wylie would all her life see herself as "a good fighter," a woman warrior, whose capacities to render unselfish devotion were limited: "I'm a good hater, / But a bad lover." In another of her many self-portraits, "Portrait in Black Paint, With a Very Sparing Use of Whitewash," she once again highlights her inadequacies as a friend—"She gives you friendship, but it's such a bother / You'd fancy influenza from another"—and points to her tendency toward violent aggression: "At night she gives you rather the idea / Of mad Ophelia tutored by Medea" (CP, 276–79).

Though Wylie is clearly engaging in self-parody here by exaggerating her antisocial tendencies, she is also presenting a vitalist image of herself. Such images invaded even the most respectable institutions in the early years of the twentieth century. Early editions of the Girl Scout Handbook emphasized the opportunities available through Scouting for girls who wanted "the whole excitement of life in facing difficulties and dangers and apparent impossibilities" such as their male antecedents had faced.[19] Girl Scouts were encouraged to see themselves on the vitalist model of women who could bring their aggressive energies into play against the forces of social deterioration.

THE WOMAN WARRIOR AS ARTIST

Elinor Wylie was in England during the early years of the Girl Guides. She was also in England at the outbreak of the Great War, during which women in large numbers identified themselves with the martial ideal. Martha Vicinus informs us that the suffragist "weekly paper, *Common Cause*, pictured a woman in armor on its front page for over two years (1912–14)."[20] The cumulative effect of these cultural phenomena was to make it possible for Elinor Wylie, who clearly had a taste for danger and certainly could engage her aggressive energies when she wanted to, to assume the role of the woman warrior without alienating herself from her readership. A discourse legitimating the woman warrior was already well established in the culture.

Of course, Wylie also drew upon traditions other than those of popular culture in choosing to adopt the trappings of chivalry for her poetic persona. The title for her second volume of poems, *Black Armour*, comes from Lionel Johnson, whom Wylie greatly admired. Judith Farr usefully reminds us that Wylie was deeply imbued with the spirit of the late-nineteenth-century Aesthetes.[21] The Aesthetic tradition in general and Lionel Johnson in particular harked back to the traditions of chivalry, when knighthood was in flower.

Yet, as a woman, Wylie could not simply take over the masculinist (and sometimes homosexual) traditions of the Decadents. She had to find a way of presenting a female image—"Myself in steel, and helmetted and gloved" (*LP*, 17)—who could embody the particular kind of pain and anger she needed to project. As William Drake phrases it, "The problem for Wylie was to unite her actual female identity with her imaginative projection of a male self who possessed the power to accomplish all that she felt frustrated in doing."[22]

Elinor Wylie's poems were *for her*, though not necessarily for us, a way of constructing and declaring a self powerful enough to address the hostile forces she encountered. One of the genres in which she sought to project the image of the woman warrior was the fable, or mini-allegory. In her essay "Symbols in Literature," she reflects on the artist's need for allegory and mask, revealing that one impetus for employing such devices is "to avoid the bitterness of being understood," when being understood might result in rejection.

Another reason to employ camouflage, she says, is "to avoid the bitterness of understanding; sometimes it is that. And to be able to put a red beard or a lion's skin on your worst enemy, or to seize a rapier or an old-fashioned squirrel rifle, and have at them without explanation or apology."[23] Thus, the literary impulse for her was, by its very nature, both self-protective and aggressive. her "worst enemy" being sometimes an antagonist and sometimes herself.

In presenting herself as an artist, Elinor Wylie was careful to control the suggestions of aggression she reveals here. Many, like Louis Untermeyer, remember her as being particularly professional and detached about her writing, though this was certainly only part of the story. Her literary persona was also designed to convey an impression that the poet was beyond the powerful emotions belonging to aggression. Through it, she emphasized an image of herself as *defensively* armored, disciplined in poetic craft, skillful, sharp-witted, and strong. In "How many faults you might accuse me of," she confesses that as a human being she is weak and faulty. However, her artistic persona is carefully protected from such human frailties.

> But you have hit the invulnerable joint
> In this poor armour patched from desperate fears;
> This is the breastplate that you cannot pierce,
> That turns and breaks your most malicious point;
> This strict ascetic habit of control
> That industry has woven for my soul.
>
>   (CP, 308)

Dayton Kohler's remarks in "Elinor Wylie: Heroic Mask" (1937) indicate how successful Wylie was in projecting the courageous, invulnerable image of herself as an artist. Kohler says: "She was a woman of extraordinary temperament who had known danger and despair and the iron discipline of experience, and she seemed to write with a strict need to reveal her tragic vision of life before the darkness came." According to Kohler, "she had the manner of one whom no disastrous circumstance can subdue."[24]

However, the woman warrior persona, like its shadow self the abject, was obsessive and operated successfully only to the extent that the poet could control the potentially disruptive energies of both her rage and her self-hatred. This she was admirably able to do in her most successful poems. Still, her extraordinary forms of self-discipline, for which Wylie was well known, left room only for what the poet herself would describe as a "little" art: "When I say little, I mean literally diminutive; short lines, clear small stanzas, brilliant and compact. I don't mean inferior or contemptible or negligible. Neither do I mean great."

In "Jewelled Bindings," the curious essay from which this quotation is taken, Elinor Wylie metaphorizes her form of poetic inspiration as a singing bird born in an enameled snuffbox. She declares that if her genius is that of a genuine eagle or nightingale, it will go free of its own accord. Furthermore, "Did I suspect for a moment, as in my own case I have not dared to suspect, that my bird was a live one, I should let him out . . . If he were a real bird he would know his own mind, and his own music."[25]

Most revealing in this short essay are the suggestions of displacement and repression connected with the poet's self-assessment. In the first place, the snuffbox immediately strikes one as much too small a space to house a bird. Both the bird and the space are masculine. Secondly, it is clear that the poet has indeed imagined her bird alive though she coyly refuses to admit it. Finally, the presentation of the two kinds of birds—the eagle, a predatory male image, and the nightingale, a nonpredatory female image—suggests that part of the poet's problem is her inability to find an authentic and powerful poetic voice to use. No poet as ambitious as Wylie has ever been content to practice a "little" art. Though Wylie is no doubt sincere in her remarks, they strike one as self-deceiving. Is she trying "to avoid the bitterness of understanding" when she says, "If he were a real bird he would know his own mind . . . "?

In the end, the woman warrior persona comes across as a compromise, a creation of a spirit hostile to the Law of the Fathers that yet becomes itself a guardian of that Law. This persona suggests that there is no power with which to identify except the power which stigmatizes the female and her "little" art, the power which demands the feminine as abject.

Elinor Wylie's most chilling "fable" about this process is not a poem but a novel. Though we do not have space to consider Wylie's fascinating novels in detail, some discussion of *The Venetian Glass Nephew* (1925) is essential in order to put into perspective the connection Wylie made between the artist, the woman warrior, and psychological repression.

The plot, peculiar as it is, may be briefly summarized. An eighteenth-century Venetian cardinal desiring a nephew (really a son) turns to his friend, the glass-blower Luna, for help. Luna engages the chevalier Chastelneuf (Casanova), whose white magic allows for the construction of Virginio, a triumph of Art. Though perfect, Virginio needs a mate. Rosalba, a young poetess brimming with the vitality of Nature, is chosen but the couple is tormented because the fragility of Virginio is threatened by Rosalba's energy. She literally breaks him into pieces when she touches him. Therefore, Rosalba voluntarily enters the furnaces of Sevres in order to be fired into porcelain. At the end the couple, united on equal terms, no longer lives in fear. Rosalba, fashionable, calm, perfect, has become an eighteenth-century version of a Stepford wife. Only Chastelneuf registers the full consequences of her transformation, though even the simple cardinal is distressed by painful thoughts as he waits at a pub, significantly called "The Silver Bowman."

Several brief observations about Elinor Wylie's relation to her material in *The Venetian Glass Nephew* can be made to begin with. As in almost everything Wylie wrote, the fable transforms elements of Wylie's own experience into a construction at once horrifying and delectable. The tone of this allegory is remarkably light and sophisticated, taking its cues primarily from Chastelneuf, the Casanova figure, who is usually gay, witty, and ironic.

On the other hand, the subjects Wylie deals with here are anything but pleasant. Fourteen-year-old Caterina is raped by a forty-year-old decadent aristocrat while Chastelneuf, who has passed her on after seducing her himself, laughs in the next room with his new mistress. Rosalba is the offspring of this union, and her trans-formation in the fiery furnace is equally horrifying, paralleling as it does the trans-formation of Caterina's rage into her abject acceptance of her rapist. Yet these matters are handled with only the barest frisson of horror. Wylie apparently had little conscious sense either of the social or of the psychological implications of her fable, intending Virginio to be the center, as the worthy representative of Art.[26]

In fact, the two strongest characters in the fable are Chastelneuf and Rosalba, between whom Elinor Wylie has divided her own characteristics. Both bear some relation to the woman warrior persona. Chastelneuf dresses in silver with a white mask. He is a chevalier, a knight, though in the service only of his own passions. He carries a tortoiseshell snuffbox and his is the artistry, the genius rather than the artisan skill, which makes possible the creation of Virginio. He carries the burden of past griefs and guilts though he is remarkably well preserved, as Casanova should be and as Elinor Wylie was.

Rosalba is more immediately recognizable as a mask for Wylie. She has white skin, an ironic mouth, plenty of wit, and writes poetry. Dedicated to Sappho, she is virginal, at times compared to both Diana and Artemis, woman warriors of classical myth. We might profitably speculate about the reasons for Wylie's choice of Artemis. Probably Artemis seemed preferable to Athena as a warrior-goddess since Rosalba is destined for marriage to Virginio. Artemis, Apollo's sister, was terrible in anger and could use her arrows to send either peaceful death or sudden destruction. However, she becomes the goddess of fertility and her cult overlaps with that of the Great Mother; thus she embodies the mixed masculine and feminine attributes so dear to Wylie's heart.[27]

However, Rosalba as vital spirit must die in order to give birth to a second self. Unfortunately, this second self, for whom the first Rosalba is martyred, lacks any emotional affect. She is simply a porcelain mask. Is Virginio worth it? Apparently Wylie hoped so. She describes Rosalba's decision to enter the furnace as "the fabulous chivalry of the girl's devotion" (303). Though Wylie does not put great emphasis on Rosalba's woman warrior characteristics, her pride, her courage, and particularly her capacity for disciplined repression mark Rosalba as a version of the woman warrior persona.

How does Rosalba's decision to be fired into porcelain place the woman warrior and Wylie's conception of art in a late-Victorian, early twentieth-century cultural context? As a conception of art, it shares with the Decadent Aesthetes a sense of the relation between art and artifice, a concern with magic, especially alchemy, scorn for art as a moral instrument, indeed indulging in a certain perversity (suggesting that art is against nature), and an Aesthetic preoccupation with china and porcelain. Max Beerbohm, an Aesthete who often grumbled about creative women, loved *The Venetian Glass Nephew* and Wylie's work in general.

The unstable perspective of the work, however, is more than a little disturbing, reminiscent of a similar inconsistency in nineteenth-century women poets of the nightingale tradition.[28] What are we to make, for instance, of Wylie's comment about the little girl, a feminine form of Virginio, blown from Venetian glass by the incomparable Luna? She is sold "to an elderly senator of atrocious morals and immense wealth. He did not find her fabric durable, and perhaps she had no soul." She, like other "predestined" virgins, is condemned "to eternal violence wrought upon her by the demons of debauch" (241). Is feminine Art, like the female body, subject to rape, dismemberment, even total destruction because of its subjugation to men and the market? Why does Wylie attempt to treat this only lightly, iron-ically?

Furthermore, how are we to respond to the obvious echoes of late-Victorian medical discourse in Chastelneuf's description of the process Rosalba will undergo "whereby young ladies are rendered harmless to the tranquility of others and per-manently deprived of their surplus emotions" (302–3)? Can this process, which fathers force upon their daughters and husbands upon their wives, be understood apart from the nineteenth-century form of female castration, clitoridectomy?[29] Chastelneuf says: "Never, until this hour, have I known a woman to desire the torture of her own free will. It is an agony more incisive than birth or dissolution" (303). Yet Rosalba chooses it voluntarily. As the panels close upon her, we are confronted by two images: "Pan's cruel nonchalance and Medusa's uncomfortable stare" (307).

As readers, we are faced with something truly horrifying in the treatment of women in this novel. It would be reassuring to say that Wylie meant the reader to feel anger. Surely she stokes the fire of that anger with her careful additions of rhetorical fatwood. Yet we should remember that Wylie is also Chastelneuf, who presides over this transformation; Chastelneuf, who takes a certain pleasure in this change, exclaiming to Rosalba with a fey smile that he is glad she has chosen to be fired into Sevres: "Oh, it is undoubtedly your *genre!*" (306).

For women like Elinor Wylie, art generally required the sublimation of rage, the transformation of aggressive emotions through displacement, metaphor, alle-gory, projection. Virginia Woolf, who did not like Elinor Wylie when they met in England, nevertheless shared this view, writing in *A Room of One's Own:* "It is fatal for a woman to lay the least stress on any grievance; to plead even with justice any cause; in any way to speak consciously as a woman."[30]

Elinor Wylie chose instead to practice a "little" art. Yet her work has power even now because one is able to feel the intensity of those fires burning just below the surface.

AGGRESSION AND THE POETRY OF
THE WOMAN WARRIOR

Reading Elinor Wylie's poems, one is invited to feel both the thrill of the poet's courageous display of aggression and the terror which led her to excessive forms of sublimation. In no other woman poet before the contemporary period does the word "hate" appear with such frequency. Like her Simon Gerty, "Who Turned Renegade and Lived with the Indians," Wylie was no doubt thrilled by the power of vengeful cruelty, "Until a beauty came to hallow / Even the bloodiest tomahawk" (CP, 64). And Simon Gerty is a significant choice, because in a sense Wylie herself turned renegade. In order not to be a victim, she was at times willing to identify with the victimizers. Her "Anti-Feminist Song, For My Sister," never reprinted, rings false where she concludes: "It's more fun to be the victims / Than the bloody conquerors."[31] Wylie definitely leaned toward the conquerors in some moods, but like her Indians she was also familiar with victimization.

Of course, this turn, the pretense of preferring the role of victim, is actually quite consistent with the cycle of anger, aggression, and self-recrimination which describes so much of Wylie's behavior, both literary and lived. Just as an angry person often feels powerless in the grip of that anger, so choosing to be powerless can also be (and frequently has been for women) a refuge from the terrors of anger itself. In Wylie's work the tone switches suddenly from externalized hostility to internalized self-disgust.

Wherever one looks in the *Collected Poems*, one comes face to face with examples of intemperance. In "Wild Peaches," for instance, Wylie turns upon her own evocation of the luscious, fertile Eastern Shore to exclaim:

> Down to the Puritan marrow of my bones
> There's something in this richness that I hate.
> I love the look, austere, immaculate,
> Of landscapes drawn in pearly monotones.
> There's something in my very blood that owns
> Bare hills, cold silver on a sky of slate.
>
> (CP, 12)

Yet Wylie's anger, as we have already noted in "Fable" and *The Venetian Glass Nephew*, often reinstates the powerlessness of those with whom she (partially) identifies, notably females. Even her rejection of a fertile landscape here has a kind of masochistic eroticism in it. Her work is particularly fascinating because it captures that familiar feminine interchange between power and powerlessness, playing out in detail all the various roles: repression, rage, self-recrimination.

A classic example of this cycle is "Sea Lullaby," in which Emily Dickinson's somewhat sinister masculine sea-figure from "I started early, took my dog" (*P*, 520) seems reworked as a Devouring Mother. Here is the end of Wylie's poem.

> The sea creeps to pillage,
> She leaps on her prey;
> A child of the village
> Was murdered today.
>
> She came up to meet him
> In a smooth golden cloak,
> She choked him and beat him
> To death, for a joke.
>
> Her bright locks were tangled,
> She shouted for joy,
> With one hand she strangled
> A strong little boy.
>
> Now in silence she lingers
> Beside him all night

> To wash her long fingers
> In silvery light.
>
> (CP, 30)

As in "Fable," one senses a terrible exhilaration in this release of aggression. Like the raven who is described as intoxicated with blood and brains, the sea here, in an otherwise superfluous stanza, is made ecstatic by her own cruelty: "She shouted with joy."

Here, however, the poem takes a sudden turn where the sea, like a madwoman who has killed her baby, now hovers beside the dead child as though filled with love and longing. One feels a certain inevitability in the relapse into guilt, where the sea, like a Lady Macbeth, tries "to wash her long fingers / In silvery light." Likewise, the sudden drop from noise into silence underscores an emotional reversal all too familiar in Elinor Wylie's work.

The dead child is, in fact, a figure for the terrible price Wylie thought women must pay for self-indulgence either in the release of their aggression or (what often comes to the same thing) in the pursuit of their literary ambitions. Confronted by the dead child, the prodigious strength of Wylie's anger seems to buckle and bend. In "Sequence," for instance, the woman warrior who begins "This is the end of all, and yet I strive / To fight," who insists, "And I am barren in a barren land, / But who so breaks me, I shall pierce his hand" (CP, 81), is the same speaker who will in the end resurrect a cruel lover in a kind of masochistic ecstasy both filial and maternal.

> I shall persist, I shall pursue my way
> Believing that his cruelty was fine
> As tempered steel for chastening of clay,
> Impatient of corrosions that were mine;
> He that despised me shall not be forgot;
> He that disparaged me shall be my lord;
> That was a flambeau, half-consumed and hot,
> This was the running light along a sword;
> And though I warmed my fingers at the one,
> The other is my father and my son.
>
> (CP, 83)

It is tempting, knowing what we do about Elinor Wylie's life, to see in the dead child an image of Philip Hichborn III, who outlived Wylie herself but whose loss the poet mourned as one would mourn a death. And this would not be an illegitimate association, since there is considerable evidence that Wylie both resented her son and felt extremely guilty at having deserted him.

However, one must also remember that Wylie was herself just out of childhood when her son was born. The dead child, as more than one poem suggests, is also an image of her own lost innocence, the vulnerable child who had to be killed in order for the armored adult to be born. Wylie repeatedly speaks of a process of transformation that brings into being the woman warrior as a cold creature lacking in human sensitivities. Thus, in "This Hand" the poet explicitly relates her skill as an artist to her inability to become a mother. In "Sequence" she speaks of "having nothing kept / Of loveliness that saved myself alive / Before this killing distillation crept / Numbing my limbs . . . " (CP, 81). "Address to My Soul," which makes the soul a kind of woman warrior, unmoved by "planetary war," brave, masked, "austere and silver-dark," advises that soul (also the soul of poetry) to choose discipline over passion.

> Five-petalled flame, be cold:
> Be firm, dissolving star:
> Accept the stricter mould
> That makes you singular.
>   (CP, 160–61)

And, as the poem that follows this one makes clear, giving birth to art must suffice as a substitution for giving birth to children. "To a Book" uses the imagery of motherhood to describe the poet's feelings about her work.

> In your beloved veins the earthy
> Is mingled with the superhuman
> Since you are mine, and I was worthy
> To suckle you, as very woman.
>   (CP, 162)

Yet, the child thus born is destined to be a "sidereal blossom," in some serious way nonhuman.

The terrible dynamic of Wylie's indulgence of aggression in her poetry is its inevitable rebound. The subsequent dissolution, of self, of hope, of poetic form itself, preserves the violence of the original aggression but turns that violence inward. Thus, one might say with a certain degree of accuracy that all of Elinor Wylie's work moves toward "The Heart's Desire," written late in her life and never chosen by the author to appear in a published book. It appears in the *Collected Poems* among the "Hitherto Uncollected" works and has puzzled critics so much that virtually no one has attempted to interpret it. Nevertheless, it seems to me one of Wylie's most powerful poems.

"The Heart's Desire" is a prose poem, but to say this is to invite an erroneous conception. This poem is really a series of desperate images and cries, covering more than two pages of text, one seemingly endless fragment pausing only long enough for commas until it reaches its final exaltation and despair in "the tongues of inextinguishable fire." Wylie's self-proclaimed commitment to the discipline of art, to short, crafted, metrically correct, rhyming lines—to antimodernism, in fact—here gives way entirely. Repression has been suspended. This is a mad poem and significantly it begins with anger.

> Anger that is not anger, but bubbles and stars of colour, blood in the brain beating
> the nerves into a frenzy of inner light, magnified moons and suns swimming in

the secret understanding that is more the body than the mind, the soul upon the lips for no reason at all, or at the sound of a door or the tinkle of gold and silver money in the street, faces best known and most remembered estranged and a million miles away, and strange greasy faces passing in the dust of evening and now returning illuminated into godhead, cruelty where it cannot be, kindness where hatred is as inevitable as the white rising of a morning where morning may after all never more rise, disintegrate yet exquisite destruction of the heart at the moment of waking, desire for death like the vagueness of a thirst for thin extravagant wine, . . . (CP, 256)

Although the poem seems to unravel as it is being read, each thought superseded by the next, this is a summary poem for Wylie, her "Circus Animals' Desertion." In it she feeds the themes and images of a life's work through the demented mill of a mind no longer willing to make careful distinctions "take shape through patience into grace," as she defines sanity in "O Virtuous Light." In fact, this poem is a kind of companion piece to the antimadness argument made in "O Virtuous Light," where the poet decries the fact that "Sudden excess of light has wrought / Confusion in the secret place" and pleads with the *virtuous* light to "Prevail against this radiance / Which is engendered of its own!" (CP, 199).

In contrast, "The Heart's Desire" seems to surrender utterly to the "frenzy of inner light." This is by no means a completely chaotic poem, however. It is held together by internal rhymes, by repeated images and phrases—the dead heart, the golden head, the towers, "that cruelty which cannot be true"—and by a discernible "plot." When understood against the background of Wylie's other work, this poem emerges as one of the most moving the poet ever wrote.

"The Heart's Desire" would probably have been unimaginable without T. S. Eliot and "The Waste Land," which Wylie reviewed for *Vanity Fair*. She said of Eliot's poem: "This poem trembles and stammers on the very extremity of emotion" (Olson, 210). Unlike Amy Lowell and Edna St. Vincent Millay, Elinor Wylie was deeply moved by Eliot and defended him against his early detractors. "The Heart's Desire" pays tribute to Eliot in its "falling towers," its rock and water imagery, and its disjunctive form.

Still, though Wylie adapted techniques from male poets like her beloved Shelley, Keats, Pope, Yeats, Donne, and Eliot, the final result of this adaptation is a genuine transformation. "The Heart's Desire" is only superficially reminiscent of "The Waste Land." Eliot's fear of women, obvious in this and other poems, limited his usefulness as a model. Furthermore, her intention here is to portray a single mind in the grip of an overwhelming experience. Wylie's poem presents a psychotic episode, brought on by the intrusion into consciousness of forbidden material specifically relevant to Wylie's experience as a woman.

However, the experience Wylie describes does not in the end remain personal and subjective. Though Wylie did what she could to obscure its context by expunging pronouns and neutralizing possessives, it remains embedded in a web of wider female associations. This poem connects in powerful ways with a dynamic of female anger verging on what Catherine Clément describes as the dichotomy of the sorceress and the hysteric. Clément's vision is particularly relevant to Wylie's poem, with its fragmentary form, its climate of aggression, and its antagonism to the armored, formal processes of repression typical of the woman warrior. With oracular intensity Clément writes:

> To break up, to touch the masculine integrity of the body image, is to return to a stage that is scarcely constituted in human development; it is to return to the disordered Imaginary before the mirror stage, of before the rigid and defensive constitution of subjective armor. It is dangerous, for the giant images then shifting along the single axis of aggressivity, that is, turned toward the exterior or the interior, are only strolling pieces endowed with a destructive power: these bits of body attack, burn, shred.[32]

Wylie is here much closer to the hysteric, "caught in the contradiction between cultural restraint and sorcerous repression," than she is to the sorceress. Thus, she cannot experience this breaking apart as pure pleasure but only as pleasure and suffering at the same time. As pure desire, she is assaulted from without (like the "falling towers" repeatedly mentioned in the poem) and also from within, where she becomes "the window of the mirror which looks out into nothing" (*CP*, 257). Her alienation, sometimes seen as heroic, is also a "loneliness and indolence that is forever stigmatized by itself as a spiritual inertia" (*CP*, 256). The dynamics of the poem move the reader back and forth between rage and despair, between screams and quiet weeping, in the "disintegrate yet exquisite destruction of the heart."

At times it seems that the heart longs only "for common sleep among the sounds of a camp or village in which kinsfolk are gathered together for protection." Then "sudden and intolerable perceptions . . . tear the rags from all cradles, marriage beds, and death beds," the stations of life at which women have traditionally presided. Such common sleep cannot be tolerated in the face of one recurrent perception: "that cruelty which cannot be true."

But what is the source of this cruelty? Sometimes it is cast as birds "making ready to devour" the heart "in cruelty, in ecstasy." Are these predatory male birds? Wylie says they are forgivable because this is merely a cruelty of the body. But "that other cruelty" which is cast as a "spiritual exaltation" has something to do with "the golden head for which the dead heart cries." We have seen such spiritual exaltation in "Sea Lullaby," and one tends to wonder: after such knowledge, what forgiveness? The poem provides none. In a curious prolepsis of Sylvia Plath's bell jar, Wylie speaks of "a glass tank full of horror over the eyes" (*CP*, 257). These are surely the eyes of the figure Catherine Clément names "the guilty one," a woman on the edge of a nervous breakdown, perhaps in the midst of one.

What should we make of the golden head? Some clue may be intended in "Madwoman's Miracle," which follows "Heart's Desire" and includes the image of a dead boy wearing a golden crown. (The madwoman's miracle occurs when a sorceress advises an hysteric to dig up the bones of her dead children. The madwoman finds two immaculate dolls untouched by disintegration.) Even without this poem, however, we might guess that the golden head is an image of the lost child or lost innocence. Significantly, "the thing no longer recognizable cast up by a sea full of green ice" (CP, 257) might be the dead heart (her own heart) or the golden head. In other words, the desire may be for something outside the self with which to bond or it may be simply a desire for selfhood. Finally, these two desires become identical.

However, both are destroyed by cruelty, by aggression. The heart's half-sleep is "startled to madness by the sound of the falling towers of Herculaneum and Troy" (CP, 257), reminding us of the destructive force of volcanic action. As in the work of Emily Dickinson and Adrienne Rich, volcanoes suggest anger rising within.[33] Troy, of course, was destroyed by an external assault which reached the inner sanctum. Both images suggest continuity between internal and external assaults.

"The Heart's Desire" ends with a crescendo in which fertility and procreation are overcome by sterility and death.

> . . . the couch in the desert, the grave in the desert, the couch upon the mountainside, the grave under the stars, the rock which will not speak and the water which will not listen, falling, falling down the mountainside over the rock with a noise of voices, the recurrent blow over the heart, the blow over the heart and the bruise turning blue upon the flesh, the arms lifted up to a sky full of screaming birds and stars which are falling, falling over the mountainside upon the towers which house the golden head and the dead heart and the tongues of inextinguishable fire. (CP, 257–58)

At last the dead heart is united with the golden head. Towers here do not refer to Troy and Herculaneum any longer but to "towers of silence," Parsee death structures in which bodies are placed to be devoured by vultures, the bones afterward burned to ash. Significantly, the arms that are lifted at the end toward the screaming birds may be lifted in self-defense, in defiance, or in ecstatic welcome. But in the last image of the "tongues of inextinguishable fire," we have at least a hint of Wylie's hope for purification. The tongues of hellfire may also be Pentecostal tongues of fiery transfiguration.

ELINOR WYLIE AND THE ABJECT

"The Heart's Desire" remains a puzzling poem despite its congruence with themes familiar in Wylie's opus. In addition to seeing the way this poem operates as a culmination of Wylie's cycles of aggression and despair, we can also explore it in the useful context provided by Julia Kristeva's work *Powers of Horror: An Essay on Abjection* (1982).

Kristeva begins her essay with the following reflections.

> There looms, within abjection, one of those violent, dark revolts of being, directed against a threat that seems to emanate from an exorbitant outside or inside,

ejected beyond the scope of the possible, the tolerable, the thinkable. It lies there, quite close, but it cannot be assimilated. It beseeches, worries, and fascinates desire, which, nevertheless, does not let itself be seduced. Apprehensive, desire turns aside; sickened, it rejects. . . . Unflaggingly, like an inescapable boomerang, a vortex of summons and repulsion places the one haunted by it literally beside himself.[34]

In the mode of the abject, there is "neither subject nor object." The abject has only one quality of the object: "that of being opposed to *I*."

"The Heart's Desire," it seems to me, constructs the speaker as the abject: there is neither subject nor object, properly speaking, in the poem. One feels a vortex of summons and repulsion, like "the sword twisted, twisted and turned in the breast unceasingly at the recurrent thought of that cruelty which cannot be true." The poem is desperate, violent, filled with "sudden and intolerable perceptions" (CP, 256) like the realm of abjection. The peculiarities of Elinor Wylie's work have so often been reduced to some sanitizing or delegitimating theory that they now seem to call out for a voice like Kristeva's, willing to explore the forbidden, the horror of self.

In "The Heart's Desire," for example, all the images seem to decay into death's-heads, "dead persons wherever lying, and all graves and altars of the dead" (CP, 256). Kristeva says that the corpse, or cadaver—with its etymological connection to *cadere*, to fall ("falling towers"?)—brings us to consciousness of the abject because "refuse and corpses *show me* what I permanently thrust aside in order to live" (3). In the proximity of these fearful, and usually rejected, images, "I am at the border of my condition as a living being." Wylie seems to cross that border in "The Heart's Desire," hovering like the sadomasochistic sea over just those elements of the psyche that she has previously killed, that have killed her.

Much of what Kristeva says about the mood and spirit of the abject is directly relevant to Elinor Wylie's work. Abjection is a precondition, in the sense of a forestate, of narcissism and is what narcissism can degenerate back into. With the violence of a convulsion, "I expel *myself*, I spit *myself* out, I abject *myself* within the same motion through which 'I' claim to establish *myself*" (3). Nausea and dizziness develop as one is caught "on the edge of non-existence and hallucination" (2). Along with loathing, there is fear. Language must confront this fear. "Discourse will seem tenable only if it ceaselessly confront that otherness, a burden both repellent and repelled, a deep well of memory that is unapproachable and intimate: the abject" (6). For a person who presents herself with her body and ego as the precious though forfeited non-objects, there are the pangs and delights of masochism. The abject exists in the name of one who separates herself, "casts within" the scalpel by which such separations are accomplished.

Kristeva sees abjection as fear producing itself as aggression. When the barrier between subject and object has become an insurmountable wall, abjection of self is "the first approach to a self which would otherwise be walled in" (47). Relief may be sought in the ordering process of narrative, because narrative claims to situate the speaker *between* her desires and their prohibitions. But when location, like subject and object, inside and outside, becomes confused, narrative is threatened. "At a later stage, the unbearable identity of the narrator and of the surroundings that are supposed to sustain [her] can no longer be *narrated* but *cries out* or is *descried* with maximal stylistic intensity (language of violence, of obscenity, or of a rhetoric that relates the text to poetry)" (141). With such analytical tools, we might reexamine "The Heart's Desire."

But well before "The Heart's Desire," we can find a great many suggestions or foretastes of the abject. For instance, in "Sanctuary" the insurmountable wall between subject and object is at first solicited as a form of "fortified castle," to use Kristeva's term. "An ego, wounded to the point of annulment, barricaded and untouchable, cowers somewhere" (47). But as with Kristeva's borderline patient, this situation becomes intolerable.

> Full as a crystal cup with drink
> Is my cell with dreams, and quiet, and cool. . . .
> Stop, old man! You must leave a chink;
> How can I breathe? *You can't, you fool!*
>
> (CP, 14)

This situation sets up the necessity for the first attempt to break down that wall through abjection of self.

Masochism is one obvious mode of that abjection of self, and it is a mode long recognizable in Elinor Wylie's poetry.[35] In "Malediction Upon Myself" Wylie writes:

> Stop up my nostrils in default of breath
> With graveyard powder and compacted death,
> And stuff my mouth with ruin for a gag,
> And break my ankles of a running stag:
>
> (CP, 118)

Wylie does indeed adopt the posture of the one by whom the abject exists, saying here: "Let me dismember me in sacred wrath," using that scalpel to serve the pitiless superego, as she does again in "Felo de Se."

This demand for self-purification reaches its apotheosis in Wylie's last book, where the central sonnet sequence, "One Person," asserts the superiority of the lover and the abject inferiority of the poem's persona: "O now both soul and body are unfit / To apprehend this miracle, my lord!" In this frenzy of self-disgust, Wylie clearly takes pleasure in imagining the breakdown of the self as presently constituted.

> I hereby swear that to uphold your house
> I would lay my bones in quick destroying lime
> Or turn my flesh to timber for all time;
> Cut down my womanhood; lop off the boughs

> Of that perpetual ecstasy that grows
> From the heart's core;
>
> (CP, 187)

For Wylie, as for many women in love, there is a peculiar enticement in what is seen as an opportunity to degrade that very thing which has enslaved her, her womanhood, that so-called self.

So, for Wylie, abjection comes peculiarly close to sexual frigidity. In the very heat of passion, some part of the self becomes closed, alien. Wylie explores this desire for closure in several of her poems. In "Subversive Sonnets" (I) she admits: "Take now the burning question of morality: / I love to keep myself unto myself, / To lock the door with exquisite finality." Yet the poet demonstrates a good deal of self-irony about this process: "Shall I as holy chastity profess / What is mere tidiness and old-maidishness?" (*LP*, 14). Again in "One Person" she admits:

> I have believed me obdurate and blind
> To those sharp ecstasies the pulses give:
> The clever body five times sensitive
> I never have discovered to be kind.
>
> (CP, 177)

Many commentators, including most recently Judith Farr, mention Wylie's sexual frigidity, but until now its connection with self-loathing has remained obscure.

Simone de Beauvoir, however, offers an interesting discussion about the relationship between masochism and sexual frigidity in *The Second Sex*, where she says:

> Frigidity, indeed, as we have seen, would appear to be a punishment that woman imposes as much upon herself as upon her partner: wounded in her vanity, she feels resentment against him and against herself, and she denies herself pleasure. In her masochism she will desperately enslave herself to the male, she will utter words of adoration, she will want to be humiliated, beaten; she will alienate her ego more and more profoundly for rage at having permitted the alienation to start.

Thus, says Beauvoir, "the vicious circle involving frigidity and masochism can be set up permanently, and may then induce sadistic behavior by way of compensation."[36]

Abjection, however, is precisely the other side of that recourse to sadism we see in some of the woman warrior's exploits. It is the moment, the posture, the space in which consciousness occupies being and nonbeing at the same time, challenging the ego's impulse to organize and expel what is dangerous or loathsome. Because it is marginalized, the abject gains in psychic power, drawing us toward forbidden territory with the power and fascination of horror.

One of Wylie's most tantalizing poems, "Village Mystery," provides a potent allegory about both the ego's recourse to sadism and the continued power of the abject.

> The woman in the pointed hood
> And cloak blue-gray like a pigeon's wing,
> Whose orchard climbs to the balsam-wood,
> Has done a cruel thing.
>
> To her back door-step came a ghost,
> A girl who had been ten years dead,
> She stood by the granite hitching-post
> And begged for a piece of bread.
>
> Now why should I, who walk alone,
> Who am ironical and proud,
> Turn, when a woman casts a stone
> At a beggar in a shroud?
>
> I saw the dead girl cringe and whine,
> And cower in the weeping air—
> But, oh, she was no kin of mine,
> And so I did not care!
>
> (CP, 22)

The dead girl who hovers at the periphery, with her intolerable burden of intimate memories, must be rejected. The violence of the rejection measures the pull of the past. It is the "I" in the poem who is torn between identification with the woman who rejects death, fear, powerlessness, and the girl (an earlier self) whose very abjection is the source of her forbidden attraction. In the end, the speaker becomes the abject by producing herself as a mask, a liar. We are specifically invited not to trust her when we are told how she has participated in the cruelty, how she turned her back on her own image: "But, oh, she was no kin of mine. . . . " As Kristeva helpfully suggests: "Essentially different from 'uncanniness,' more violent, too, abjection is elaborated through a failure to recognize its kin; nothing is familiar, not even the shadow of a memory" (5).

In her abject mood, Wylie often attacks herself in her poems. When "Portrait in Black Paint" was published in the Profiles column of the New Yorker, some of Wylie's friends, not knowing that the poet herself had written it, were outraged. Who was this, calling their friend vain, unstable, alcoholic, trifling? Thus the woman warrior, in the blink of an eye, turns from hostile aggressor to abject.

"Miranda's Supper" is a fascinating elaboration of this process. Having established the Southern belle, Miranda, as a woman warrior figure left alone on her plantation at the end of the Civil War, Wylie proceeds to loosen her armor and reveal her as an abject ready to offer herself up. At first, we are impressed by Miranda's superiority to her Northern invaders.

> She never made her anger oral.
> She remained a marble memory

> To the Cambridge Captain Amory.
> She used him like a prince's legate,
> But, oh, her eyes—her eyes were agate!
>   (CP, 127–28)

In this we recognize the familiar coldness and rigidity of the woman warrior, who establishes herself through the dynamics of repression. Like the warrior women Wylie has described before, Miranda is "secure in silver mail envestured." But the pillars and roofs of Peacock's Landing are equally affected by this arrogant aesthetic. "Calm, austere, aloof, commanding," they share with Miranda an exterior defensiveness that hides an interior vulnerability.

In this "unbearable identity" between the narrative persona and the surroundings that are supposed to sustain her, we begin to feel a sinister echo like the desolation streaming from the mansion and the slave quarters.

> Where are all the souls that filled them?
> Who has killed them? Who has killed them?
> For a moment's space the lady
> Feels her pulse's beat unsteady.
>   (CP, 130)

How will she calm herself and restore order to these structures threatened with dissolution? In a very peculiar move, Wylie has Miranda dig up her buried china and silver and, at a ceremony of ritualized self-sacrifice, offer herself as abject.

> Here, prepared within an upper
> Chamber, is Miranda's supper.
> Now partake; it is her body;
> And the carven cup is bloody
> Where her fingers drew it forth
> From mortality of earth.
> Every broken crust and crumb
> Savours of your coming home,
> And the berries she has gathered
> By divinity are fathered.
> Eat the bread she is adoring,
> Drink the water she is pouring;
>
> Now approach, both man and ghost;
> Nothing is lost! Nothing is lost!
>   (CP, 133)

To engage in a vital way with this poem is likely to induce some sense of literary vertigo not unlike that which disorients one in *The Venetian Glass Nephew*. Miranda is, on the one hand, carefully designed as a self-portrait: she wears silver, loves porcelain, and is proud though preyed-upon both by destabilizing memories and by enemy forces. On the other hand, Miranda is mocked by the poem, which also plays off of Pope's satire "The Rape of the Lock." Like Belinda, Pope's mock heroine, Miranda is preoccupied with her appearance and demonstrates an unhealthy degree of interest in her material possessions. She is insensitive to the cost to others of her aristocratic privileges: "Three novices went blind at Brussels / To weave the enigma of her scarf" (CP, 127). Surely there is something satirical in Wylie's suggestion that "All the miracles of Cana / May be performed by painted china" (CP, 132)?

Yet in other places Miranda's emotional traumas are rendered sympathetically. The threat of poverty and starvation, the murderous memories are real. When "Miranda buckles on her courage," when she kneels and digs in the ground, we tend to see in her another Scarlett O'Hara summoning strength to face another day. But the questions the poem asks—"What is the thing that her hands have found? / Is it horror, or beautiful?"—reverberate with the ambiguity of the abject. We feel we are on the verge of discovering a cadaver. And when Miranda's supper turns out to be a cannibalistic orgy that reverses the sublimation of the communion mass, we know we are in the realm not of the either/or but of what is both horror and beauty, both mandrake and skull, both crucifix and pistol, the abject realm lying, as Kristeva says, at the border of the sacred.

The poem engages in a kind of sorcerous solicitation of death: "Every broken crust and crumb / Savours of your coming home." Why should we suddenly interest ourselves in "man and ghost" when Miranda (alive not dead) has been our focus until now? The poem's ending, with its shift in orientation and its weird, whispering effects, is apt to inspire the nausea consequent upon vertigo.

One of the causes of this sense of vertigo is that the time frame of this last section of "Miranda's Supper" seems displaced, as though we are being asked suddenly to step out of our common circumstances. In this mystical moment of oblivion and revelation, familiar time disappears, the time of "civil war," of men and women, of the Law of the Fathers and the abject feminine. In a newly opened space, entered only by passing through the abject, we seem to be released from both Miranda's narcissism and the assaults upon it by Captain Amory and his crew. Only here, only now does it become possible to say "Nothing is lost! Nothing is lost!" In every previous attempt to establish the ego, something is lost, something is abject.

Elinor Wylie's poetry remains of interest because it is both of its time and of ours. By turns hostile, aggressive, abject, coy, solicitous, Wylie establishes only an uneasy intimacy with her readers and yet we might say of her work what Julia Kristeva says of the literature of abjection, that it "represents the ultimate coding of our crises, of our most intimate and serious apocalypses" (208).

Yet Wylie's work is not beyond gender, does not undo the terms of sexual identity, as Kristeva claims her artists of abjection do. Instead, Wylie's work clarifies the way those crises are experienced in the nexus of gender and history. Not all women are caught in the particular vicious cycle of rage and self-recrimination that afflicted Wylie. Yet this cycle does have descriptive potential for many women; my discussion of it here is meant to contribute to the ongoing debates within feminist studies about women and violence, women and narcissism, women and rage.[37]

Wylie is certainly not the only angry poet in the nightingale tradition. Amy Lowell had plenty of angry literary moments. H. D.'s "Calypso" and "Eurydice" are very angry poems. Stoic Louise Bogan shares with Elinor Wylie a certain waspish irony. And Lowell, H. D., and Bogan were also afflicted with a tendency to surrender to abjection. But none of these other women highlights to the same extent the connection between ruthlessness and self-torment. None presents herself so strikingly in the guise of kamikaze woman warrior.

If there is one conclusion to be reached from reading Elinor Wylie's poems, it is the futility of attempting to locate a "true self" among the representations of selfhood, the numerous self-portraits Wylie furnishes her readers. More fruitful than the attempt to locate such a "true self" is the effort to connect Wylie's oddities with materials situating them in broader perspectives about culture and gender. Rather than leaving us with the thought that her poetry would have been better had she been able to be more "honest," Wylie's work strongly implies that literature gains in power when the psyche struggling for expression in it happens to be in a position to feel certain kinds of representative stresses, but prefers to avoid both "the bitterness of being understood" and "the bitterness of understanding." What kind of novel would Elinor Wylie have produced had she actually set out to make *The Venetian Glass Nephew* a novel about patriarchal oppression? And yet this novel has something approaching a mythic feminist plot, full of dark resonance and mystery.

Though we may be perversely grateful that Wylie was not a more reasonable and integrated human being, we cannot leave her without acknowledging that her lack of integration and autonomy had severely negative consequences. Reading her work, we can appreciate the greater degree of independence contemporary women have. To the end, Elinor Wylie was still soliciting male approval, still caught in the struggle to usurp male privileges. "And the berries she has gathered / By divinity are fathered." More an Athena than an Artemis, Wylie directed her primary emotional and intellectual energies toward men, and her work illustrates both the possibilities and the limitations of that stance. In the next chapter, we will consider a poet whose reconciliation with her father-self set her free to summon those energies in a very different cause.

1. Amy Lowell   Courtesy of the Houghton Library, Harvard Library

2. Sara Teasdale   Courtesy of the Yale University Library

3. Elinor Wylie   Courtesy of the Yale University Library

4. H. D.   Courtesy of the Yale University Library

5. Edna St. Vincent Millay   Courtesy of the Vassar College Library

6. Louise Bogan   Courtesy of Rollie McKenna

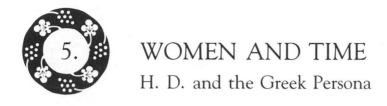

WOMEN AND TIME
H. D. and the Greek Persona

Hilda Doolittle, or—as she is now known—H. D., is the only true modernist among the nightingale women. Though by temperament she shares many person-ality traits with Elinor Wylie, including austere preferences, psychological intensity, aristocratic tastes, and a desire to "burn with a hard, gemlike flame,"[1] her poetry was from the beginning more imagistic than even Amy Lowell's. Though H. D. also frequently had recourse to images of silver and crystal, though like Wylie she was ready to identify herself with Artemis, her temperament was altered by intense relationships with modernist men: Ezra Pound, D. H. Lawrence, T. S. Eliot, Rich-ard Aldington. When the First World War started, Elinor and Horace Wylie left England for America, whereas H. D. stayed on, experiencing firsthand the dev-astation of war and its aftermath.[2]

H. D. used the Greek persona to help her cope with chaos within and without. Her preoccupation with Greece, and the search for authentic experience wrapped up with it, might easily have made H. D. into an antimodernist. Even her early imagist poems struck some readers as recapitulating modes of the past. As David Perkins relates: "To such readers, her Imagist 'hardness' of style was not impressively 'Greek,' neither was it especially 'modern,' for except that the diction was idio-syncratic and the verse was free, it recalled the familiar 'sculpture of rhyme' of the 1890s." Just as Elinor Wylie took her cues from the Aesthetes and dipped back in time, H. D. seemed to some to follow Aesthetic tendencies in her escape from the present. Perkins says: "It was obvious that her art, like that of the [A]esthetes, had limited itself by retreating from the world of actual experience."[3]

Yet, what seemed at first like echoes of an older aesthetic soon resolved them-selves into a pattern clearly endowed with contemporary resonance. The important problem needing immediate attention was historical. What connections, if any, linked past and present? How could one refuse a linear logic that foreshadowed serious destruction?

Not all the modernists would resolve the problem of history in the same way, but for some, like Yeats, Mann, Pound, and H. D., the surface of temporal linearity would give way to a mythic vision of larger coherence such as Nietzsche had suggested in his theory of eternal return. As Ricardo Quinones sees it, in *Mapping Literary Modernism: Time and Development* (1985):

Against the worn-down homogeneity of experience they would look for and
present the freedom of difference, discrepancies based on qualitative intensities
rather than linear sameness. They would look for the permeable presence of the
past, undying and strangely reappearing in the unthinking moments of the present,
and, finally, rather than the smoothly running machine they would look for
something that had, in [Henri] Bergson's words, 'the bite of time' in it.[4]

What led H. D. to identify her deepest concerns with this modernist movement?
How did the choice of the Greek persona reflect both her particular cultural position
and her gender-related alienation from her own time? How is H. D.'s relation to
time representative of the concerns of many twentieth-century women, and how
does H. D.'s resolution of the problem of time as history reveal her story to be one
of the most positive, in its larger implications, of all those within the nightingale
tradition? These are the questions we will address in the subsequent sections of
this chapter, which will look first at the adoption of the Greek persona, second
at the cultural context which made that persona an available choice, and finally
at the way H. D. develops and modifies the Greek voice in her renegotiation with
her own father and with Father Time.

H. D. AND THE GREEK *KATHARSIS*

In 1905, the year Hilda Doolittle entered Bryn Mawr College, there was little
expectation that her signature, later shortened to H. D. by Ezra Pound, was destined
to become a hieroglyph. The woman we now think of as the high priestess of
literary modernism was drifting, out of step with her generation, anonymous. Like
so many other writers of that period, like Edwin Arlington Robinson and Hart
Crane to name but two, she would find her coterie among those at odds with
American progressivism. Like Robinson, Crane, Amy Lowell, Elinor Wylie, and
Louise Bogan, her career would begin with a significant sense of failure. She left
Bryn Mawr in her sophomore year, did not find a job, muffed and muffled her
engagement to Ezra Pound, and surrendered to despair. Later, she described herself
as "a disappointment to her father, an odd duckling to her mother, an importunate
overgrown unincarnated entity that had no place here."[5]

Yet, in this same year, she began to imagine a way out of that sense of failure
through the adoption of a different set of values, a different locale where, as a
newly reincarnated entity, she might live and work and have her being on more
successful terms. According to Barbara Guest, in her biography of H. D. called
Herself Defined: The Poet and Her World, the poet awakened to the Greeks and to
Greek culture in 1905 when she went to a production of *Iphigenia in Aulis* in which
Ezra Pound performed. This was also the period in which Pound was courting
H. D., writing her poems in which he called her "dryad."

Why was the Greek persona so appealing and in what way did it promise to
liberate H. D. from the difficulties of an unacceptable temporal and cultural position? In order to address these questions, it is useful to know both what H. D.
intended, what she herself understood about her choice, and also what was beyond

intention, what we can reconstruct with hindsight about the intersection of culture, psyche, and persona.

In pursuing H. D.'s intentions, it is useful to examine some of her prose writings where H. D. repeatedly returned to her past to try to make sense out of the events of personal as well as cultural history. This autobiographical impulse would also infiltrate her poetry. In fact, according to Barbara Guest, all of H. D.'s writing was autobiographical, since one of the motives behind the writing was her need to put together what she felt to be the significant fragments of her experience, not in order to create a wholly integrated persona with a single project but in order to see the lines of patterning and stress more clearly. Yet, the novels, with their lack of linear plot, their postmodern collation of homologies and linguistic echoes, are especially revealing as reworkings of the traumatic events of H. D.'s life. Guest says: "Unlike her contemporaries, Eliot, Pound, and Stevens, who used historical fragments in their efforts to construe an impersonal and, to them, necessary order, H. D. assembled those compulsive word associations, hieratic images, hallucinatory landscapes as frames for the documentation of her own history."[6]

Thus, the novels provide vital frames in which to place elements as tantalizing as H. D.'s choice of a Greek persona. In *HERmione* (1927), H. D. reviews the prewar period of her engagement to Pound and her lesbian relation with Frances Gregg, called Fayne Rabb in the novel. It is clear that the Pound character, George Lowndes, appeals to H. D. because of his flamboyance and his independence from the bourgeois world of H. D.'s Pennsylvania upbringing. (Her parents were quite opposed to the engagement.) As a disappointment to her father, an odd duckling to her mother, H. D. / Hermione is looking for a new way of seeing herself. "Almost, almost she heard words, almost, almost she discerned the whirr of arrows . . . almost, for a moment, George had made it come right, saying, 'You are a Greek,' saying, 'You are a goddess' " (*H*, 67).

Hermione, like her creator, is an academic failure; she has flunked conic sections. She is also shut out of the fraternal brotherhood of science which links her brother, Bertrand, and her father, Carl Gart. She wants to join the men in the world of intellectual power and vision but she finds the way barred. "Celestial Mechanics proved a barrier. She had failed, even the beginning, Conic Sections. She had failed to reach Bertrand. She had failed, though she could not have then defined it, to attain the anesthesia her odd brain sought for" (*H*, 18).

It is important to remember that H. D.'s father was a famous astronomer. Her brother followed in his footsteps. Against this male alliance of mind and science (and of an arrogant assumption of superiority shared by Lowndes/Pound), Hermione places the sisterhood of women and words. She reads *Jane Eyre*, she unites with Fayne Rabb in the spirit of Philomela and Procne, she pays tribute to her mother's strengths: "Words of Eugenia [her mother] had more power than textbooks, than geometry, than all of Carl Gart and brilliant 'Bertie Gart' as people called him. Bertrand wasn't brilliant, not like mama. Carl Gart wasn't brilliant like Eugenia" (*H*, 89).

The Greek world becomes appealing because its union of intellect and spirit challenges the smug progressivism of the patriarchal present. It defies the world which has humiliated Hermione. "Dealing with terms of antiquity became a sort of ritual. It was all out of reality. I mean reality was out of it precisely. The very centre of spark of the divinity was in a Greek boy praying" (H, 211). The Greek world of antiquity provides "the anesthesia her odd brain sought for."

All of these issues become more complicated as H. D. views them through the lens of her experience during World War I. *Bid Me to Live*, a novel that considers this period, again takes up the importance of the Greek persona as an escape. It also situates its heroine in another world of betrayal (as father, mother, brother, lover, and friend all betray Hermione). Again what H. D. will call "the Greek *katharsis*" will come to her rescue.

In *Bid Me to Live* Julia, a poet and translator, is translating a Greek choral sequence as the war moves closer and her husband, based on H. D.'s husband Richard Aldington, has an affair with a woman who lives upstairs. Once again the heroine looks to words and to a spiritual dimension outside of time to save her from the potentially destructive consequences of masculine arrogance and aggression. "I would get something out of this war," an older Julia reflects. Her Greek coldness, dedication, and purity allow her to take refuge in the Greek dictionary lying open at her elbow. "Inside she was clear, the old Greek *katharsis* was at work here, as in the stone-ledged theatre benches of fifth-century Greece."[7]

How did H. D.'s experiences as a child, adolescent, and young wife lead her to equate linear temporality with a destructive masculinity and Greek time with a literary escape from patriarchal oppression? Some of the answers to these questions are suggested in a late novel by H. D. called *The Gift*, written between 1941 and 1943.

This memoir reflects on H. D.'s childhood and the conflicted feelings the poet struggled with as she considered the priority given her father the astronomer ("everything revolved around him") and the secondary position accepted by the women of the household who were actually, from H. D.'s point of view, more talented. The book is about a childhood trauma and the gift of transcendence provided by Mamalie, the grandmother, through her vision of spiritual redemption.

Because the book is written almost entirely from a child's point of view, it is difficult to understand clearly all the connections H. D. is making. However, one receives the distinct impression that time is something that men control and something that victimizes women. The story begins with a female victim, a girl who has been burnt to death, and then moves directly to a powerful grandfather and the grandfather clock with which he is associated. This grandfather clock hovers over the action like Rafe's watch in *Bid Me to Live*, both suggesting the way time became gendered in H. D.'s mind.

The central incident in *The Gift*, however, concerns the father, who stumbles in late one night, incoherent, bleeding from a head wound, and who the little girl fears may die. The guilt she seems to feel suggests that this incident is an externalization of previously experienced and repressed feelings of anger against the father, a suspicion which is confirmed by the confusion in the little girl's mind between her father and Bluebeard and her father and nightmare.

Like Bluebeard her father has had more than one wife. "There was a man called *Bluebeard*, and he murdered his wives. How was it that Edith and Alice and the Lady [her father's first wife] (the mother of Alfred and Eric) all belonged to Papa and were there in the graveyard?"[8] Though her father is perceived as kind, he becomes associated in the little girl's mind with female deaths. He is a version of nightmare because he "neighs like a horse" when he laughs and he goes out at night to study the stars. He is also a scientist, and nightmare is conflated with science in the girl's book, *Simple Science*:

> It was like an old witch on a broomstick, it was a horrible old woman with her hair streaming out and she was riding on a stick, it was a witch on a broomstick, but the book was science, they said it was to explain real things. Then a witch was real; in Grimm it was a fairy tale but a witch in a book called *Simple Science* that someone gave us must be real because Ida said that was what science was. Papa and Papalie [the grandfather] were working at real things, called science; the old witch was riding straight at the girl who was asleep. (G, 51)

As in *HERmione* science becomes a source of terror to the H. D. character, who must find a way of eluding its strength in order to give birth to a new and stronger self. Time, as the subject of scientific investigation here, emerges in the dark as nightmare, an inexorable force carrying the vulnerable female psyche toward death. "A nightmare is a mare in the night, it is a dream, it is something terrible with hooves rushing out to trample you to death. It is death" (G, 51–52).

All of these associations are provoked by the traumatic vision of the father wounded. The father is a servant of time, himself a wounded victim. But he is also a perpetuator of a destructive heritage which has brought and will again bring about war, the First World War, in which H. D.'s brother Gilbert will be killed. "Gilbert must go to France, for Gilbert must inherit the pistol from Papa who was in our Civil War" (G, 66).

In H. D.'s mind, time becomes confused with the time of political history carrying the world toward destruction and death in the two world wars H. D. would experience firsthand in Europe. Historical time she sees as directed, until the present, by men. Thus, time as history becomes male-identified, leaving H. D. no choice but to turn to a different conception of time linked in her mind to the female.

The framing device of *The Gift* is a bombing raid during the Second World War. Her longtime friend and lover Winifred Ellerman (Bryher) is a resource for her during the raid just as her grandmother Mammalie, in the traumatic incident during her childhood, helps H. D. to understand "the gift" as her true inheritance.

Like Greece as an alternative to present-day reality, women and the linguistic magic they represent to H. D. provide an alternative to the destructive time of the fathers. Thus, Mama in *The Gift* plays with anagrams. "It was a game, it was a way of making words out of words, but what it was was a way of spelling words, in fact it was a *spell*. The cuckoo clock would not strike; it could not because the world had stopped. . . . It was a drop of living and eternal life, perfected there" (G, 10).

In a similar fashion, Mamalie's chosen band of initiates brings a message of human connectedness which transcends time and geography, linking the American Indians with the Moravians, Hilda Doolittle with an early Moravian visionary, and a twentieth-century world at war with *Wunden Eiland*, where a Moravian love feast was celebrated. H. D. finds a central role for herself in this set of female and familial relations, becoming the exponent of a mystery that reinterprets the meaning of time.

But to be able to face up to the challenge represented by her father, men in general, and history—which appears to be in the control of men—would take H. D. many years. As she describes it in *The Gift*, her experience of childhood trauma would result in years of self-alienation. "I cannot date the time of the thing that happened, that happened to me personally, because I forgot it. I mean it was walled over and I was buried with it. I, the child was incarcerated as a nun might be, who for some sin—which I did not then understand—is walled up alive in her own cell" (G, 85). Looking back from the perspective of a woman almost sixty years old, H. D. describes the journey which would eventually set her free. "I must go on, I must go into the darkness that was my own darkness and the face that was my own terrible inheritance, but it was Papa, it was my own Papa's face, . . . " (G, 100).

Until that confrontation with the meaning for her of Papa's legacy, H. D. would look to literary time and particularly to Greek culture as an escape from the terrifying, violent, and destructive aspects of patriarchal history. During the First World War, H. D. reexperienced that sense of imprisonment and female oppression in time most poignantly. Now married to the writer Richard Aldington, she found herself acting as his secretary, spending long hours typing up drafts of his manuscripts. When she lost her first baby, she retreated from conjugal relations out of a sense of terror while Aldington went out to find solace in other women.

In *Bid Me to Live* all of these events are overshadowed by Rafe's watch, which he gives to "Julia" in order to keep her psychologically tied to him. Linear, historical "clock time" seems once again in the hands of men. Julia, in the classic submissive posture of a woman, must simply wait: until Rafe comes back from his war training, until he finishes having sex with his mistress upstairs, until he tires of the body and returns to her as his spiritual mistress. Julia ponders the way Rafe's watch symbolically shapes her experience. "Its disc was covered with round woven wire, a tiny basket, bottom side up, or a fencer's mask. Time, in prison, that time" (BML, 19).

But Rico (based on D. H. Lawrence) offers her entry into a different world, beyond the grasp of Rafe, outside of historical time, protected from the threat of war and death. "And just opposite her, if she could find a second in eternity, that was out of time, out of this time, was a series of brightly coloured magic-lantern slides, Rico and herself in another dimension, but a dimension so starkly separate from this room, this city, this war, that it actually seemed to be taking place somewhere else" (*BML*, 87).

This timeless realm will be most clearly articulated in the Greek world of H. D.'s early poetry. Though not a matriarchal world, the Greek universe H. D. envisioned was not patriarchal in the same sense that her present-day reality was patriarchal. This antique space was brought to life through words and in art, which H. D. inevitably associated with a feminine spirit. It was a world of intellectual camaraderie in which gender divisions could be dissolved.[9]

Thus, the Greek persona seemed to offer H. D. a number of precious possibilities. It provided escape from a humiliating time in which male pretensions to superiority—her father's, Ezra Pound's, Richard Aldington's—resulted in female silencing and victimization—her mother's, her friends', women poets', her own. Furthermore, the Greek persona connected her to a time in which a woman, Sappho, was supreme in the art of poetry. It liberated H. D. from derogatory associations with a female tradition of poetesses. Finally, the Greek persona was an austere mask behind which H. D. could safely express various problematic passions: lust, anger, ambition, lesbian love.

For a woman like H. D., who wanted to challenge patriarchal authority and set herself up as principal progenitor, the Greek persona seemed the most appealing device. Thus, it did indeed offer H. D. a form of Greek katharsis: purging the negative feelings aroused by her own time, redeeming through ritual a contaminated reality by expelling the problematic elements in symbolic form, and bringing about a new temporal order just as ritual sacrifice, in the original Greek katharsis, was undertaken in order to begin a new and more productive era.

In *Bid Me to Live* the H. D. character, Julia, pledges herself to "coin new words," to adopt a new persona in order to transcend the humiliations of the present. "I will find a new name. I will be someone" (*BML*, 176), Julia thinks. Even more dramatically, Hermione determines to find herself a mythic identity which will displace male authority, science, and the determining aspects of both clock time and sidereal time.

> Words may be my heritage and with words I will prove conic sections a falsity and the very stars that wheel and frame concentric pattern as mere very-stars, gems put up there, a gift, a diadem, a crown, a chair, a cart or a mere lady. A lady will be set back in the sky. It will be no longer Arcturus and Vega but stray star-spume, stars sprinkling from a wild river, it will be myth; mythopoeic mind (mine) will disprove science and biological-mathematical definition. (*H*, 76)

THE GREEK PERSONA AS CULTURAL CONSTRUCT

Though H. D. was not consistent in her commitment to the Greek persona, sometimes relinquishing it in favor of others and at no time limiting it absolutely to a certain set of qualities, we can, with reasonable accuracy, pinpoint the aspects of the Greek persona which typically appealed to H. D. From the early days in

London, when the poet thought of herself as a Greek statue come to life, to her epitaph—"Greek flower; Greek ecstasy"—the Greek persona represented qualities she desired: aloofness, inner strength, mental superiority, physical boyishness, courage, freedom, and wildness; a psychological landscape comparable to the physical landscape of the New England coastline which she—like the nightingale women generally—would forever remember and admire.

Roughly, the figure of Artemis emerges as her preferred version of the Greek persona, and, in fact, in her memoirs, called *The Heart to Artemis*, Bryher glosses the Artemis figure as a version of both herself and H. D.[10] Hippolyta, whom H. D. would use as a mask for her own struggles, is a follower of Artemis. At the end of her life, the poet would once again imagine herself as Artemis in her writing of *Tribute to Freud*, Artemis who is strong enough to take on the Professor, Artemis "the tough goddess of the hunt" (Guest, 305).

It is easy to see the particular attraction of the Greek persona for a woman like H. D. In addition, we can also see the overlap between it and aspects of the personae chosen by other women poets in the nightingale tradition. Like Amy Lowell's androgynous persona, it blended "male" and "female" characteristics, helping to free the poet from derogatory assumptions about sentimental women poets. Like Sara Teasdale's passionate virgin, which also had connections to Greek culture, H. D.'s Artemis persona was associated with chastity and personal autonomy as well as passion. In fact, according to Barbara Guest, John Gould Fletcher remarked "that Teasdale's fragile appearance and her tendency to seclude herself from society reminded him of H. D." (43). Like Elinor Wylie, who also dressed in Greek fashions and identified herself with Artemis, H. D.'s Greek self was a woman warrior of sorts, both vulnerable and aggressive, the kind of woman who never forgot a slight.

One might say, therefore, that there is some convergence in the problems faced by these women because of the cultural moment in which they lived. However, the intersection between psyche and culture was just different enough to make each choose a distinctive persona capable of being analyzed in slightly different terms.

H. D. herself traced the beginning of her interest in Greek myth to her childhood reading: Hawthorne's *Tanglewood Tales*, Gilbert Murray, Bulwer-Lytton, Oscar Wilde, Walter Pater.[11] The world of Hawthorne's youth was a world dominated by neoclassical images like Hiram Powers's statue, *The Greek Slave*, and Washington D.C.'s Greek architectural monstrosities. However, for H. D.'s generation, the lost world of Greek culture was more distinctly pagan, a combination of elegance, sensuality, and carefree joy.

The appeal of the Greek spirit to turn-of-the-century artists expressed itself in the performances of Eleanora Duse and Isadora Duncan, in the poetry of Sappho, and in the lush lyricism of Swinburne. In 1907 Wallace Stevens wrote to his fiancée that he was reading about Greece. Like H. D. and her friends, he felt personally enthralled by "a pagan world of passion and love of beauty and life. It is a white world under a blue sky, still standing erect in blue sunshine" (quoted in Guest, 222).

What was Greek was, by this time, specifically *not* the domain of official architecture or moralistic statuary. It was, in fact, frequently associated with forbidden impulses such as plagued Sara Teasdale when she was in her pagan moods. Just as classical Greek was traditionally denied to women scholars, so institutions like Bryn Mawr insisted upon Greek as part of their entrance requirements precisely in order to demonstrate a complete break with the past.

Still, we must recognize that without one final move, H. D.'s development might not have culminated so absolutely in the adoption of the Greek persona. That move was her decision in 1911 to travel to England and the subsequent entanglements that led her to remain in Europe, except for brief intervals, for most of the rest of her life. When H. D. arrived in London, she discovered a city much more congenial to her temperament than Philadelphia or New York. And in 1911 London, as Barbara Guest tells us, "*Greekness* was everywhere."

> People, not only those just down from university, were quoting Samuel Butcher and Andrew Lang's Homer. Sculpture by contemporaries was made with Greek curls. Sandaled or bare feet marked a complete break from buttoned boots. Gone were the curves and boned collars. Fashion switched to Poiret of France and Fortuny of Venice. Fortuny dresses were cut straight from the shoulder to flow unimpeded, with just a hint of chiton. Poiret, the new French dressmaker everyone took up, introduced dresses cut to resemble the maidens on Greek vases, a loose overblouse falling over a long skirt. Hair was also loosely knotted and worn with a band across the forehead a la grecque. The body should be long, lean, and willowy—very Hildaish. (33)

Here at last H. D. found boldly represented what was in America a minor theme. By finding a culture which approved those features and preoccupations H. D. already possessed, by adopting the Greek persona, the "unincarnated entity" had found a form. In the following sections of this chapter, we will see how that form established H. D.'s specifically female orientation to modernism and how it came to mediate her relations with Father Time.

TIME AND THE GREEK PERSONA BEFORE FREUD

Having specified the relationship between the Greek persona and H. D.'s discomfort with patriarchal time through a brief examination of her prose, we are left to consider how her poetry deepens our sense of women's art as a rich engagement with the cultural issues of modernity. It is important to state at the outset that H. D. changed her relationship to the Greek persona over time just as she changed her conception of time itself. Whereas the Greek "katharsis," as she called it, allowed her to escape the detrimental aspects of her own historical moment in the early years, in her later work she returned to use the Greek persona as an agent of vision and change, potent to redirect the energies of history. In her late epics she gave her poetry the scope to deal with both personal and cultural issues on a grand scale.

In this movement toward relating the psyche to historical forces of time and change, H. D. goes beyond the nightingale tradition, and her late work does not really belong within a discussion of the traditional modes. However, for this very reason it is useful to ponder that trajectory. Like all the other women in this tradition, she begins by feeling alienated from the historical present, sensing that history is, in fact, "his story."

However, by recovering some of the structural properties of H. D.'s development, we can see the possibility of a change in women's relationship to history come into focus. At the end of her life, the poet has accepted both her place in time and her responsibility to work for change. Therefore, unlike the closing up so characteristic of Lowell, Teasdale, Wylie, Millay, and Bogan, H. D.'s last years provide us with the most optimistic and visionary moments of her work. In spite of enduring pain and personal suffering that would bring her to the brink of madness several times in her life, H. D.'s story remains the one true success story in this study, and it is a success story in part because of H. D.'s ability to expand her conception of the nature of "women's time."

What kind of temporal mode do we find representative of H. D.'s early poetry? In *Sea Garden* (1916) temporal references are almost nonexistent though, in what Alicia Ostriker calls H. D.'s "encoding of active desire,"[12] one does feel a certain conception of temporality at work. It is, however, much closer to what Julia Kristeva describes as the time of female subjectivity than the narrative succession of beginning, middle, and end some critics have associated with the coding of masculine phallic desire. The second section of "Sea Gods" is a characteristic moment in H. D.'s early work.

> But we bring violets,
> great masses—single-sweet,
> wood-violets, stream-violets,
> violets from a wet marsh.
>
> Violets in clumps from hills,
> tufts with earth at the roots,
> violets tugged from rocks,
> blue violets, moss, cliff, river-violets.
>
> Yellow violets' gold,
> burnt with a rare tint—
> We bring deep-purple
> bird-foot violets.
>
> We bring the hyacinth-violet,
> sweet, bare, chill to the touch—
> and violets whiter than the in-rush
> of your own white surf.[13]

This poem does have the quick succession of images allowed for by the rules of imagism, but it suggests something very different from linear temporality or even from Pound's famous "In a Station of the Metro," in which the speed of modern time is reflected: "The apparition of these faces in the crowd; / Petals on a wet, black bough."[14] The urgency of the train on its way somewhere else is reflected in the way the faces blur into petals. For Pound the image of imagism is "that which presents an intellectual and emotional complex in an instant of time."

Though H. D. was deeply influenced by Pound in some respects, her temporal sense in this poem is much closer to what Kristeva has described as one phase of "women's time" than it is to Pound's instant. Kristeva writes:

> As for time, female subjectivity would seem to provide a specific measure that essentially retains *repetition* and *eternity* from among the multiple modalities of time known through the history of civilizations. On the one hand, there are cycles, gestation, the eternal recurrence of a biological rhythm which conforms to that of nature and imposes a temporality whose stereotyping may shock, but whose regularity and unison with what is experienced as extrasubjective time, cosmic time, occasion vertiginous visions and unnameable *jouissance*. On the other hand, and perhaps as a consequence there is the massive temporality, without cleavage or escape, which has so little to do with linear time (which passes) that the very word "temporality" hardly fits: All-encompassing and infinite like imaginary space, this temporality reminds one of Kronos in Hesiod's mythology, the incestuous son whose massive presence covered all of Gea in order to separate her from Ouranos, the father.[15]

In Kristeva's taxonomy, we can find a number of qualities that directly pertain to H. D.'s early work. "Sea Gods," in particular, confronts us with "vertiginous visions," on the one hand, and the massive presence of something eternal, a landscape, on the other. The speaker becomes the landscape with its precipitous cliffs, its thundering shores, its flowers of serenity; as though Gea were being separated by an act of will from Ouranos, the father.

But what of *jouissance*? Ecstasy is there but principally in an erotic form, subject to loss, despair, and so subject (again) to time. While furnishing us with an important part of H. D.'s temporal orientation, Kristeva's description, then, only begins the process of elucidating our experience of these poems. The undertow is the reified presence of the father, the antagonist and the representative of another form of time. He is the presence who freezes the speaker and upon whose "frozen altars," as D. H. Lawrence called them, H. D. sometimes seems to pile her poems. He is the repressed desire.

Despite the lack of a linear plot in *Sea Garden*, I am struck by the subtle presence of narrative as one moves from poem to poem. The narrative is certainly not history; it is something closer to positionality, as though the theme of pursuit were being explored in order to assert and reassert legitimacy, to take the status of an outsider and turn it into that of an insider. There are hardly any particular counters to label the presiding consciousness a "persona" and, in this sense, the poems appear "extrasubjective." But the Greek spirit presides almost *as* the force of legitimation itself.

More than "I" this book speaks of "you," the god, the daemon, the lover, the one inspired and inspiring, among all the dull, extinguishing spirits. In "The Shrine" H. D. writes:

> O but stay tender, enchanted
> where wave-lengths cut you
> apart from all the rest—
> for we have found you.
>   (CP, 8)

In "Loss" we have: "We were hemmed in this place, / so few of us, so few of us to fight" and "only we were left, / the four of us—somehow shut off" (CP, 22). This poetry praises and shelters "the scattered remnant," the special few who, as in Mamalie's story, are initiates into a timeless world of mystery and superior wisdom.

Yet conflict underlies poems like "The Gift."

> Life is a scavenger's pit—I escape—
> I only, rejecting it,
> lying on this couch.
>   . . . .
> Sleepless nights,
> I remember the initiates,
> their gestures, their calm glance.
> I have heard now in rapt thought,
> in vision, they speak
> with another race,
> more beautiful, more intense than this.
> I could laugh—
> more beautiful, more intense?
>
> Perhaps that other life
> is contrast always to this.
> I reason:
> I have lived as they
> in their inmost rites—
> they endure the tense nerves
> through the moment of ritual.
> I endure from moment to moment—
> days pass all alike,
> tortured, intense.
>   . . . .
> I reason:
> another life holds what this lacks,
> a sea, unmoving, quiet—
>   (CP, 15–18)

The struggle in poems such as these suggests connection to two sorts of time: one fractured, intense, on edge, modern, and the other serene, ritualized, antique. Yet, when the serenity of the poppy dream triumphs, H. D. does not seem entirely content to leave the more tortured world of the present behind. Poems like "Sheltered Garden," which begins "I have had enough. / I gasp for breath," remind us of Elinor Wylie's "Sanctuary" in their presentation of the dangers of escapism.

If H. D.'s early poetry illustrates her desire to escape the dead hand of the fathers with its temporal signature as history, it also relinquishes the present with some sadness, as though the speaker were a prodigal daughter, longing to return home but pessimistic about her welcome. In *The God* (1917) a much angrier voice speaks. Artemis is "poisoned with the rage of song" in "Orion Dead" (CP, 56–57). In "Eurydice" the speaker breaks with her group identity to assert the value of autonomy.

> At least I have the flowers of myself,
> and my thoughts, no god
> can take that;
> I have the fervour of myself for a presence
> and my own spirit for light.
>
> (CP, 51–55)

Yet the group is still invoked as a means of legitimation existing outside the historical present. "We," who seem to be mostly male, remain as a scattered remnant in "The Tribute," which evokes a timeless time as the only hope for future regeneration.

> We are veiled as the bud of the poppy
> in the poppy-sheath
> and our hearts will break from their bondage
> and spread as the poppy-leaf—
> leaf by leaf, radiant and perfect
> at last in the summer heat.
>
> (CP, 59–68)

Beauty here, though a female presence, is timeless and immortal, for "could beauty be done to death, / they had struck her dead / in ages and ages past." It is as though the female, when subject to time, is lost, dismembered. Only in a timeless realm, in which male-female bonding may occur without conflict and almost without gender, is there a chance for a female voice.

Between *The God* and *Hymen* (1921), H. D.'s life was torn apart and reassembled. Her marriage broke up; she almost died of pneumonia; she had a child by a man whom she would have little to do with for the rest of her life (Cecil Gray); the war took its devastating toll and ended; her brother died in it and her father never recovered from the loss and died soon after; but Bryher, whom H. D. called "the child," was a strong, fierce child—pure in spirit and associated in H. D.'s mind with intellect and whiteness. Bryher saved her "when all her hope was dead" (CP, 122–24).

In one of her darkest moments, when she was suffering from influenza and almost died, H. D. was introduced to the wealthy and spirited Bryher, who quickly intervened in H. D.'s life and became her nurse, financial supporter, and eventually her lover. Bryher knew the Greek anthology well, knew H. D.'s early poems by heart; and though she herself was thoroughly bound up with time, politics, and history as the daughter of one of the wealthiest men in England, Bryher kept H. D. to her original Greek spirit. The force of Bryher in H. D.'s life as friend, lover, inspiration and support can be felt throughout *Hymen*.

Yet the marriage celebrated in the title of this book is a commitment to holding certain uneasy alliances together—lesbian and heterosexual eroticism, art and life, mind and body, death in time, and life in a "white world" of passion and art. The lovers cannot escape the burdens of time, either as memory or as disruptive present. Like Amy Lowell's fantasy of Neron and the king, H. D.'s "Phaedra" (CP, 135–36) admits that all is not well.

> For art undreamt in Crete,
> strange art and dire,
> in counter-charm prevents my charm
> limits my power.

In the same poem, the poppy that once signified a genderless, timeless union of opposing forces cannot transcend the present.

> The poppy that my heart was,
> formed to bind all mortals,
> made to strike and gather hearts
> like flame upon an altar,
> fades and shrinks, a red leaf
> drenched and torn in the cold rain.

Whereas earlier the Greek world was remote from the present, safe, genderless, timeless, unscathed, now it appears vulnerable. "What is Greece if you draw back," the speaker asks in "The Islands" (CP, 124–27). One might also say that in this book Greekness has become synonymous with female victimization, as though H. D. were beginning to confront the implications of that covert male identification in her earlier works. *Hymen* is full of the stories of women in Greek mythology who were tormented or betrayed: "Demeter," "Circe," "Hippolyta," "Phaedra." Thus it also draws closer to the issues of male domination of women that H. D. associated with Father Time.

Yet the poet is still committed to trying to find terms of reconciliation. In "Egypt," for instance, she pairs Egypt (female mystical power) with Greece (male intellectual power):

> We pray you, Egypt,
> by what perverse fate,

has poison brought with knowledge,
given us this—
not days of trance,
shadow, fore-doom of death,
but passionate grave thought, belief enhanced,
ritual returned and magic.

(CP, 140–41)

From this reconciliation is "Hellas re-born from death."

In the period of her middle work, one feels H. D. struggling to hold that marriage together and failing. Her relationship with Bryher was never unproblematic and included affairs with other women and with men, including Bryher's husband (married for respectability's sake), Kenneth Macpherson. Furthermore, having found the world of Greek antiquity—that timeless world of escape from the present—vulnerable, H. D. must confront what Julia Kristeva describes as the limitation of female subjective time. "Female subjectivity as it gives itself up to intuition," Kristeva writes, "becomes a problem with respect to a certain conception of time: time as project, teleology, linear and prospective time as departure, progression, and arrival—in other words, the time of history" (192).

From the mid-1920s through the 1930s, this problem was one the poet began to feel more and more acutely. In the poetry she seems to be struggling with a sense of stultification as she bemoans the loss of her poetic power, vacillates between free verse and a dismal, plodding bondage to rhyme (as in many poems in *Heliodora*), or finds refuge in the terrible repetitions of *Red Roses for Bronze* (1931).

The persona seems to be literally unraveling in the repetitious lines of the poems in *Red Roses*. At the other extreme, she is a statue or a marble mask as in "Trance," where she says: "my eye-balls are glass, / my limbs marble, / my face fixed / in its marble mask;" (CP, 244–45). The poet is half in love with easeful death. Does she belong to the realm of the Greeks, or, as in "Halcyon," to the thinly disguised world of contemporary civilization? The Greek is synonymous, as often as not, with death, and in this we may read the return of the repressed. If time as death was what H. D. originally sought to escape through the Greek persona, here she has been brought face to face with her fears, as we can see in the "translation" called "Sea Choros":

I am dead
whether I thread the shuttle for Pallas
or praise the huntress,
the flower of my days
is stricken,
is broken,
is gone
with my fathers,
my child
and my home;
wind,

wind,
we have found an end
in the sword of the Greek
and his fire-brand.
                                    (CP, 237–41)

The poet longs to return to her poppy dream (in the "Choros Sequence" from *Morpheus*) but even the breath of Artemis can no longer enchant her reality. Like Elinor Wylie in "The Heart's Desire" we can see her "slip / out of the borderland of consciousness" (CP, 263). Self-division becomes more and more extreme and, again like Wylie, H. D. seems in constant dialogue with herself. "Let Zeus Record" even finds her putting together a Wylie-esque self-portrait, including the "chiselled and frigid lips" so frequent in Wylie's work. The stable sense of self she longs for reminds one of Wylie's "Let No Charitable Hope" in its desired superiority to the depredations of time and fortune:

yet disenchanted, cold, imperious face,
when all the others, blighted, reel and fall,
your star, steel-set, keeps lone and frigid tryst
to freighted ships, baffled in wind and blast.
                                    (CP, 281–84)

In such a state of mind, H. D. was driven to seek professional help. In 1933 and 1934 she underwent analysis with Sigmund Freud out of a need to overcome stagnation. As she saw it: "I wanted to free myself of repetitive thoughts and experiences—my own and those of many of my contemporaries."[16] Freud made her write "history" and reactivated her struggle with her father, thus bringing her back to time and repositioning her Greek persona.

H. D.'s *Tribute to Freud* (written in 1954 and 1955) cannot be taken as a completely reliable account of her relations with the "Professor," as she called him, and raises as many issues as it resolves. Nevertheless, in H. D.'s associations of her father with "Papa" Freud and of men with time, we can see in this text the form of the struggle that had remained inchoate until this moment.

Professor Freud and Professor Doolittle shared important characteristics in H. D.'s mind. Distrusting astrology and the occult, they tended to place more faith in scientistic explanations, preserving what Susan Stanford Friedman calls "Enlightenment presuppositions" about the linear nature of temporality. Against their views, H. D. held fast to her sense of a fourth dimension, a feminine supplement making possible spiritual transformation of the other three (male) dimensions.

The actuality of the present, its bearing on the past, their bearing on the future. Past, present, future, these three—but there is another time-element, popularly called the fourth-dimensional. The room has four sides. There are four seasons to a year. This fourth dimension, though it appears variously disguised and under different subtitles, described and elaborately tabulated in the Professor's vol-

umes. . . . is yet very simple. It is as simple and inevitable in the building of a
time-sequence as the fourth wall to a room. (*TF*, 23)

Yet what was disturbing to H. D. at this time in her life was the very fact of
history, the destructive force of time which presented itself in war and suffering.
"My sessions with the Professor were barely under way, before there were prelim-
inary signs and symbols of the approaching ordeal. And the thing I primarily wanted
to fight in the open, war, its cause and effect, with its inevitable aftermath of
neurotic breakdown and related nerve disorders, was driven deeper" (*TF*, 93–94).

H. D.'s analysis with Freud represented a coming to terms with time and the
father that allowed the poet to see the four temporal dimensions in different relationship. If the maternal was associated in her mind with the fourth dimension
and the paternal with the other three, H. D. was able through analysis to reunite
the introjected father and mother, time and timelessness. "I am on the fringes or
in the penumbra of the light of my father's science and my mother's art—the
psychology or philosophy of Sigmund Freud. I must find new words as the Professor
found or coined new words to explain certain as yet unrecorded states of mind or
being" (*TF*, 145). This also means a reorientation to time. "There is a formula
for Time that has not yet been computed" (*TF*, 145).

A number of H. D.'s best readers, such as Susan Stanford Friedman and Rachel
Blau DuPlessis, have pointed to H. D.'s lifelong interest in comprehending the
meaning of history according to a theory of palimpsest, in which earlier and later
eras belong to a single pattern, one layer superimposed over the other. DuPlessis
explains: "The technique of aligning different eras so that certain 'points' coincide,
H. D. calls 'a correlation of entities.' It is a way of establishing thick fictional
networks among her friends and of transferring emotional charges across long-
separated eras."[17]

Susan Stanford Friedman is even clearer about the implications of this view of
history.

> From her earliest to her latest work, however, H. D. never portrayed time as
> evolutionary. She returned many times to the image of palimpsest to embody her
> essentialist view of history. For H. D., the superposition of new writings upon
> the old in a 'palimpsest' paralleled history as a 'palimpsest' of repeated events
> whose essential meaning is embodied in the various forms of chronological time.[18]

Joseph Riddel sums up the main thrust of these views by saying, "History for
H. D. is not progressive; each age lives its variation on the Ur-pattern."[19]

Though these statements are not wholly inaccurate, they tend to obscure what
may now be seen as a crucial change in H. D.'s orientation to time after her analysis
with Freud, and this change has to do with the position occupied in her thinking
by the present. According to this perspective, H. D. felt frozen out of time until
she learned how to "place" her father, his positive and his negative influence. At
first, only the Greek world of antiquity offered freedom, but that world became
increasingly unsatisfactory as H. D.'s Greek persona began to merge more and more

with her present life and self. Through her analysis with Freud, H. D. came back to Father Time and recuperated the present, a move which allowed her to engage with history on different and much more significant terms, terms not entirely adequately represented by the palimpsest.

If we look at her 1926 (pre-Freudian) novel *Palimpsest*, we can see in its juxtaposition of three time periods—War Rome 75 B.C., Postwar London 1916–26, and Excavator's Egypt 1925—H. D.'s belief in the eternal cycles present in specific experiences in history. She clearly sees the fourth dimension operating in present-day experience. However, the emphasis in the novel is on antiquity as "the real" and modernity as illusion.

> Antiquity showed through the semi-transparence of shallow modernity like blue flame through the texture of some jelly-fish-like deep-sea creature [the murex]. Modernity was unfamiliar and semi-transparent and it obscured antiquity while it let a little show through, falsified by the nervous movement of its transparent surface.[20]

Present-day reality has much more validity for H. D. after her analysis with Freud, when history begins to make an appearance as the record of change as well as continuity. It may not be progressive, as Friedman rightly says, but it ushers in situations which have not necessarily been confronted before. In *Tribute to Freud*, therefore, H. D. insists upon the importance of confronting that present reality rather than taking flight into a Greek world of timelessness. She says: "But we are here today in a city of ruin, a world ruined, it might seem, almost past redemption. We must forego a flight from reality into the green pastures or the cool recesses of the Academe; though those pastures and those gardens have outlasted many ruined cities and threat of world ruin; we are not ready for discussion of the Absolute . . . " (*TF*, 84–85).

Her insistence upon the present after her analysis involves a renegotiation with time. As she phrases it in the private jottings she made in 1949–50 called "Notes on Recent Writing": "I am trying to pin down my map, to plot the course of my journey, to circumscribe my own world or simply to put a frame around my clock-face."[21]

This also meant a different role for the Greek persona. The poet did not abandon the Greek as she might have done but instead decided to reformulate the Greek project. As she wrote to Bryher at the end of 1934: "My work is creative and reconstructive, war or no war, if I can get across the Greek spirit at its highest I am helping the world, and the future. It is the highest spiritual neutrality. . . . The Greek will hold me to my center" (Guest, 218–19). As H. D. reformulated the usefulness of her Greek persona, she saw that it could operate better in the service of time and history than as an escape from them.

TIME AND THE GREEK PERSONA AFTER FREUD

Though H. D.'s most significant encounters with temporal issues would not come until the Second World War, we can already see in the poems of the late

1930s a changed form of the Greek persona and a new orientation to time. In *The Dead Priestess Speaks*, for instance, Artemis (who was from Delos) returns in the figure of "Delia." (Apollo was called Delius for the same reason.) Of these poems Louis Martz says: "The Greek mask is here quite transparent: the prophetess is a modern woman speaking modern thoughts about herself and her psychic resurrection—presumably after the consultation with Freud."[22]

In the title poem H. D. as Delia rebukes her past self but in a different way from that of the "she" who rebukes Hippolyta. Both question the purity of their mythic personae, but the new Delia is now ashamed that she did not bring purity to cope "with the world's lost hope," that she "never made a song of war." Her revised vision encompasses a broader spectrum of individuals: "I knew the poor, / I knew the hideous death they die, / when famine lays its bleak hand on the door" (CP, 369–77). Thus, she is no longer determined to chronicle only an elite, a special group of superior individuals like herself who know the way. Delia is ashamed of the fact that she has been so self-preoccupied. Instead of gathering herbs for a new medicine to soothe "the after-ravages of the plague," as the community assumes its priestess has been doing, she has actually spent the night with a lover. Thus, she (like H. D.) has been wrongly stereotyped as pure; now (after death) she wishes she had used her arts for more socially reconstructive purposes.

Though her special task as interpreter returns as an element in "Sigil," she accepts her role as a servant of time. "Now let the cycle sweep us here and there, / we will not struggle." Time is concentrated in the present moment.

> There is no sign-post to say
> the future is there,
> the past lies the other way,
> there is no lock, no key;
>
> . . . .
>
> there is one mystery, "take, eat,"
> I have found the clue,
> there is no old nor new:
>
> wine, bread, grape and sweet
> honey; Galilee, Delphi, to-day.
>   (CP, 411–18)

Thus, H. D. comes close to the layering of temporal consciousness she will offer in the late poems, bringing time-out-of-time (*kairos*) into time (*kronos*) with "today."

In "The Master" (CP, 451–61), also contained in A *Dead Priestess Speaks*—a book H. D. hesitated to publish because she felt it was too transparently autobiographical—the poet meditates upon her relationship with Freud: "It was he himself, he who set me free / to prophesy," she insists. Yet even this poem maintains the fiction of the Greek persona. The analysis in Vienna is transposed in time: "When I travelled to Miletus / to get wisdom, / I left all else behind," "Delia" says.

Nevertheless, this is a key poem in understanding the connection between time and the father that was resolved by H. D.'s analysis with Freud. In it we feel the strength of H. D.'s earlier resistance to her father's arrogance in her transferred resistance to Freud: "his tyranny was absolute" is reminiscent of "everything revolved around him." We can also comprehend the way both fathers, Papa Freud and Dr. Doolittle, made her feel inferior as a woman. Much of this material has been analyzed from helpful feminist perspectives by Friedman and DuPlessis, so I won't do more here than say that Freud's theory of penis envy, like her father's exclusion of her from the world of science, seemed to marginalize her in a world of women denied respect. In "The Master" H. D. counters this masculine impulse by insisting on the independent perfection of woman.

> for she needs no man,
> herself
> is that dart and pulse of the male,
> hands, feet, thighs,
> herself, perfect.

Freud may have told her that the psychic problems she had to confront concerned the triangulated relations of mother, brother, self, but father and father-transference are much more potently the issues of "The Master."

This poem is particularly interesting for the way it counterbalances the reaction formation so obvious in *Tribute*. Here we are much more aware of H. D.'s anger at the fathers. Equally important to a resolution of H. D.'s blockage, however, is her acknowledgment of love and her ability through the release of that love to use her father's legacy positively.

Ambivalence is allowed to surface and express itself.

> Let the old man lie in the earth,
> (he has troubled men's thought long enough)
> let the old man die,
> let the old man be of the earth,
> he is earth,
> Father,
> O beloved
> you are earth,
> he is the earth, Saturn, wisdom,
> rock, (O his bones are hard, he is strong, that old man.)

In addition to the obvious and poignant ambivalences ("let the old man die / . . . O beloved"), we find the association of the father with power, fear, rock, intellectual "wisdom," and death. We should also remember that the god Saturn was alternately known as Kronos, the same as the Greek word for time. However, in H. D.'s summoning of these varied associations, she exorcises both the fearful side of the father and his absolute dominion over those elements of her own experience she now wishes to take under her own control: time, wisdom, regeneration.

However, the Freud figure here is not only masculine. Because Freud was committed to a maternal, nurturing function with his patients, H. D. seems to have
experienced him as both male and female. Though Freud is sometimes equated
with Father Time, he is also earth. The violent dichotomy Kristeva describes in
which Gea is wrenched by Kronos from Ouranos, the Father, seems to have given
way here as the father merges with the mother and becomes nurturing as well as
terrifying, spatial as well as temporal, female as well as male.

In addition to breaking down the old dichotomies, H. D. here prescribes a role
for herself as her father's daughter, a role impossible for her to envision before.
The poem concludes with a vision of female rites where Freud, alone among men,
also participates. Except for Freud:

> no man will be present in those mysteries,
> yet all men will kneel,
> no man will be potent,
> important,
> yet all men will feel
> what it is to be a woman

Thus H. D. turns a male legacy into a female triumph. In her salute to Rhodocleia ("bride of the sun") at the end, she prophesies her own ascent over the
fathers, her own apotheosis: "you are that Lord become woman." She also suggests
the complication of the Greek persona by other elements. Rhodocleia is not only
Greek, she is also imbued with Christian resonance (the woman clothed with the
sun from Revelation) and evocative in the context of Egyptian mysteries (Isis, "that
Lord become woman"). From now on we will see a Greek persona who mediates
between various time periods and traditions as Helen does in *Helen in Egypt*.

Though the thirties were an important time of intellectual growth for H. D.,
it was not until the Second World War that the poet was able to convert her
tremendous gains into poetry of enduring value. World War II catapulted H. D.
into a phase of heightened creativity, only the more extraordinary when we consider
her complete mental breakdown at its end.

Trilogy was written in the years 1942–44 and is certainly one of H. D.'s most
impressive poems, an epic of book-length proportions which keeps alive a vision
of rebirth during the darkest days of the London bombing. *Trilogy* is also a poetic
reencounter with history and time such as H. D. had never undertaken before.
"This search for historical parallels"—as she names it in "The Walls Do Not Fall"—
was not just an exercise but a way of preserving sanity and restoring hope for
civilization. Living amidst the falling bombs meant real terror, the heritage of the
fathers come home to roost in war, but it also meant for H. D. a curious exhilaration
easier to understand when we consider the need she had to try her courage and
her art in the fires of the worst onslaught of patriarchal power.

Though the speaker is Psyche, able to transcend the destructive effects of war,
we should remember that her vision here is an epiphany experienced *in time*, a

revelation she hopes to pass on to illuminate her readers, much as Mary opens the eyes of the ordinary servant Kaspar. Like us, Kaspar is designated to receive the gift. As H. D. describes his transformation, first he is lost in the experience of revelation, "out of time completely," but ultimately he is returned to his present-day existence: "Or rather a *point* in time," (CP, 608) to integrate what he has learned.

Similarly, at the end of *The Gift*, written in the same period, the narrator says: "I seem to be sitting here motionless, not frozen into another dimension but here in time, in clock-time" (G, 140). One way of interpreting this is to say that trauma breaks through our normal sense of things and shows us the fourth dimension, but we must return to our ordinary reality to use that expanded consciousness productively.

Though *Trilogy* is a fascinating work, and has recently received a great deal of attention, for our purposes *Helen in Egypt* (written in the early fifties) is the best measure of the way H. D. transformed her relationship to time. This is the poem that recapitulates her relations with all the various father/lover figures in her life through a renewed vision of the Greek persona. In writing about the poem, Albert Gelpi captures the spirit which motivated H. D. to respond to the terrible events of war with this form of self-exploration: "Divine decree requires that we submit ourselves to Life, for all the war wounds and deathblows, so that, providentially, in comprehending the train of temporal events, we can accept and transcend them in an earned identity through participation in the design ordained for time."[23]

Helen in Egypt is both a memoir and a prophecy, a hymn to her mother and a chronicle of her reconciliation with her father, a personal autobiography and a work dedicated to the process of cultural repair. In it H. D. also preserves her admiration for the timeless realm of *kairos* and insists on the importance of coming to terms with *kronos*, the world of the fathers she had earlier sought to escape. As Horace Gregory writes in his introduction to the poem, "Without mentioning parallels between them, the situations in *Helen in Egypt* contain timeless references to our own times. It is as though the poem were infused with the action and memory of an ancient past that exist within the mutations of the present tense."[24]

In *Helen in Egypt* H. D. uses Stesichorus's revised version of Helen's story, in which the Greeks and Trojans fought for an illusion at the Trojan War, while another Helen, more complex and more substantial, sat out the war in Egypt. In H. D.'s poem this Helen struggles to take responsibility for the confusions of a history which she both mysteriously shares with her avatar and transcends. In what follows I will not attempt to analyze the whole book-length poem, especially since it has received very detailed attention from a number of contemporary critics.[25] Instead, I will focus upon its coding of H. D.'s theories of time.

Helen in Egypt is divided into three sections. The first, "Pallinode," takes place in Egypt in a timeless realm of the Amen-temple. Here there is "only space and leisure / and long corridors of lotus bud" where Helen and Achilles can meet on something like equal footing.[26] He is now "dead," wounded in the heel, and thus ready to learn the vulnerability of his power, his Time. However, he is still capable of making Helen fearful. Like her father in *The Gift* and Freud in "The Master," "though wounded, he carries with him the threat of autocracy" (*HE*, 15).

They meet here, however, under the aegis of the mother-goddess, Isis or Thetis. "This is no death-symbol but a life-symbol" (*HE*, 13). Here "Helen achieves the difficult task of translating a symbol in time, into time-less time or hieroglyph or ancient Egyptian time," the prose notes tell us (*HE*, 13). Thus, the first section of the poem represents H. D.'s first approach to the problem of time through evasion, escape into a timeless realm. One can read *Helen in Egypt* as a kind of temporal autobiography, moving through all the stages of H. D.'s thinking about the relative values of synchronic and diachronic descriptions of reality.

The central problem of the poem—the relation between Love and Death, L'Amour and La Mort—is also translatable into the conflict between female power (love) and male power (aggression), between kairos (timeless wisdom) and kronos (linear time). Achilles introduces the problem of male hostility against women as he lashes out against Helen, whom he at first holds responsible not only for his own death but for the death of "the flower of all-time, all-history," his warriors. Helen ponders the meaning of this hostility throughout the rest of "Pallinode"; in an early section she addresses Horus, the child symbol, asking: "O child, must it be forever, / that your father destroys you, / that you may find your father?" (*HE*, 28). And it is clear that Achilles is for Helen a father/lover figure who brings with him the whole burden of time activated by the fathers as a linear progression toward death: "the purely masculine 'iron-ring whom Death made stronger' " she calls it in Book IV (*HE*, 55).

Though it takes place in the timeless Amen-temple of Egypt, "Pallinode" regresses toward history, especially in Book IV, where Achilles remembers the Trojan War. Here the prose voice "explains" some peculiar negotiations undertaken by Odysseus which sound remarkably like the history of World War II: "If Odysseus succeeds in his designs, Achilles will be given Helen and world-leadership. This is contrary to the first agreement of the allies" (*HE*, 51).

Of course, this never happens because Achilles fails the "Command" and is killed. The Command, with its fascist aura, is comparable to the iron ring of patriarchy; utterly powerful in time, the Command represents a male bonding that Achilles betrays by his interest in Helen. He now wonders whether he has betrayed himself by breaking his connection to linear time:

> The Command was bequest from the past,
> from father to son,
> the Command bound past to present
>
> and the present to aeons to come,
> the Command was my father, my brother,
> my lover, my God;
>
> (*HE*, 61)

In response to this, Helen seeks "an intermediate dimension or plane" in which she asserts her loyalty to women: "I am not happy without her, Clytemnestra, my sister." However, this further links her to female victims like Iphigenia, whom Achilles "as well as her own father would have sacrificed" (*HE*, 84). This seems a dilation of the Bluebeard passage in *The Gift*, where H. D.'s "kind father" is

associated with the sacrifice of female victims. It is also comparable to the exploration of female victimization in *Hymen*. However, here Achilles is exonerated.
Like the father in *The Gift*, he was subject to the Command himself. But, more
importantly, Achilles has broken with the heritage of his fathers for love, for
women, his mother and Helen.

At the end of this section, Helena is redeemed by time and in time (a cult has
been established in her honor): "Helena has withstood / the rancour of time and
hate" (*HE*, 96). However, she must leave Egypt in the second section and return
to Greek time to continue her quest. "Obviously, Helen has walked through time
into another dimension," the prose tells us. "But the timeless, hieratic symbols
can be paralleled with symbols in-time" (*HE*, 107).

"Leuke," the second section of *Helen in Egypt*, chronicles Helen's return to
Greek time. She awakens from the dream of Egypt and encounters Paris, a repressed
memory of passion representing many of H. D.'s male lovers. Paris also narrates
the fall of Troy, the triumph of death, in terms which again evoke the devastation
H. D. saw during the Second World War: "the stairs were blasted away, / The
Wall was black, / the court-yard empty" (*HE*, 129). Paris wants Helen to forget
the past and her I-cons and live in the present. But she cannot forget either them
or Achilles. So she comes to Theseus, just as H. D. came to Freud when she feared
she was obsessed with her past. Her decision predicts her reconciliation with time:
"I found perfection in the Mysteries / but I was homesick for familiar trees" (*HE*,
154). She wants to return to ordinary reality and the present tense without for-
getting what she has learned.

Theseus guides her, helps her unstrap the heavy burden of the past (her sandal)
and heal her wounds. Calling her "beloved Child," he says he too is "weary of
war, / only the Quest remains" (*HE*, 158). Claiming that myth, "the one reality,"
dwells here, he advocates returning to Paris and the present time, as Freud advocated reconstituting the self in the present by confronting "the myth" as the
buried structural pattern of her past.

Helen experiences a revelation through Theseus's help (Book VI, 8) but does
not accept all his interpretations. She returns greatly disturbed to Leuke, a sanctuary
in a timeless realm ruled by Artemis, in preparation for her return to Egypt and
Achilles. This self-enclosure within "a white shell" parallels H. D.'s temporary
rejection of the burden of time, her breakdown after World War II and incarceration
at the clinic at Kusnacht in Switzerland. Throughout her life she would periodically
need such places but she would also need to leave them, as Helen asks: "is it Death
to know / this immaculate purity, / security?" (*HE*, 194).

A strengthened Helen must now return to Egypt to bring time to timelessness
and timelessness to time. "Leuke" ends with Helen finding that a new task awaits
her. "She will encompass infinity by intense concentration on the moment" (*HE*,
200). This represents the last of the three stages of H. D.'s relationship to time.
Like the H. D. who wishes to reecounter her father and her own personal history
through myth, Helen decides to measure "time-in-time (personal time)" as well as
"star-time (the eternal)" (*HE*, 202) by returning to Achilles and "the writing"
which is "herself": "I will encompass the infinite / in time, in the crystal, / in my
thought here" (*HE*, 201).

"Eidolon," the third section, begins with an acknowledgment of the centrality of time to Helen's quest. H. D. says: "Now after the reconciliation with time, Greek time, (through the council and guidance of Theseus), Helen is called back to Egypt" (*HE*, 208). But why Egypt again? H. D. herself poses this question in Book II of "Eidolon." It appears that Achilles also seeks in Helen a way into Love, not erotic love but rather mystical love under the sign of his mother, Thetis, whose eidolon—or avatar, or image—frees him from his anger against the historical Helen and reminds him of the larger vision of acceptance and wholeness represented by the sea, her element: "She fought for the Greeks, they said, / Achilles' mother, but Thetis mourned / like Hecuba, for Hector dead" (*HE*, 296). In order to be fully human, H. D. seems to say, one must accept both the realm of personal love, of war and history, and the realm of transcendental Love, of Egyptian mysteries, and divine forgiveness. Refusing to choose one or the other, Helen seeks a third answer. So, in returning to Egypt, "this third Helen, for the moment, rejects both the transcendental Helen and the intellectual or inspired Helen" (*HE*, 258) created by Theseus and his Greek wisdom.

Most readers are convinced that in the end Helen finds a third way, resolving the contradiction represented by Paris-Achilles and situating herself in what Frank Kermode describes as the *aevum*. According to Kermode, "The concept of *aevum* provides a way of talking about this unusual variety of duration—neither temporal nor eternal, but, as Aquinas said, participating in both the temporal and eternal. It does not abolish time or spatialize it; it coexists with time, and is a mode in which things can be perpetual without being eternal."[27] Albert Gelpi, responding to a similar model, also quotes Aquinas and sees Helen "between time and eternity and participating in both." He compares H. D.'s vision with T. S. Eliot's "still point of the turning world" and Ezra Pound's "SPLENDOUR, / IT ALL COH-ERES." As Gelpi (and other readers) read the poem, "everything [is] caught up in the resolution."[28]

Despite its neatness and persuasiveness, I would like to dissent from this widely held view concerning H. D.'s temporal resolution at the end of *Helen in Egypt*. For such readers it is often Theseus/Freud's vision which sums up such a resolution: "all myth, the one reality dwells here" (*HE*, 297), a phrase suggesting the persistence of structural patterns available in the past but impinging on the present moment and thus establishing history as both palimpsest and fate.

However, Helen has carefully separated herself from Theseus at several crucial moments in the last section of the poem. In Book II, Section 2 of "Eidolon," she insists on a separation between psychological reality and historical reality. She also acknowledges the value of *not* resolving all dichotomies: "Perhaps it is the very force of opposition that creates the dynamic intensity of 'the high-altar, [her] couch here' " (*HE*, 225).

Furthermore, very close to the end of the poem, in Book VI, section 5, Helen challenges the value of Eliot's still point.

In the beginning of this sequence, the voices of Achilles and Paris seemed to argue, unreconciled. Helen woke to struggle with the problem, in the human dimension, "my mind goes on, spinning the infinite thread." Helen is "awake,

no trance." In a trance, "on the gold-burning sands of Egypt," she may have
solved the problem. And Theseus, wholly intellectual and inspirational, resolved
it with his "all myth, the one reality dwells here." But Helen says, "did I challenge
the Fates when I said to Theseus, 'the Wheel is still?' " (HE, 297)

The implicit answer to this question seems to be "yes" because in human time the
Wheel is never still. Thus, the divine resolution of opposites in Egypt and the
psychological myth of Theseus do not answer all problems, resolve all dualities,
make everything cohere. Achilles and Paris are not made one at the end; they
retain their oppositional force.[29]
    In the last section before the Coda, the prose notes insist that "one greater
than Helen" provides an answer to the problem of reconciling different forms of
time.

> there is no before and no after,
> there is one finite moment
> that no infinite joy can disperse
>
> or thought of past happiness
> tempt from or dissipate
> now I know the best and the worst;
>
> the seasons revolve around
> a pause in the infinite rhythm
> of the heart and of heaven.
>   (HE, 303–4)

But is this "one greater than Helen" meant to be H. D. herself and is this the
wisdom we are to absorb?
    The poem as a whole suggests otherwise. Although "there is no refutation of
her final decision or choice" (HE, 301), the one finite moment is soon displaced
by the final section, "Eidolon," in which Helen returns to her longing for Achilles.
Achilles represents not the aevum but H. D.'s old love, kairos, the fullness of
synchronicity outside of linear temporality.
    In choosing for Achilles at the end, she does not simply resurrect the tran-
scendentalism of her first anti-historical vision in Egypt. Yet she does diminish the
importance of historical time and of the present moment in favor of those images
of eternal return, the sea and the sand, "the infinite loneliness" of a quest for other
shores than those upon which one is born mortal and mundane.
    In Helen in Egypt she has brought time to timelessness and timelessness to time.
She has attempted a reconciliation with her own past and an interpretation of the
history of her era. But she has also made it clear that "the snare of Apollo" means
that the poet must step outside of history in order to hear "the rhythm as yet
unheard" (compare HE, 229–32). H. D.'s reconciliation with time would never
be the same as that of her friend, the historical Ezra Pound, whose Cantos were
one of the inspirations for Helen in Egypt. Her unification of opposites in the artistic

realm here means abandoning any political attempt to alter the course of history; it means an acceptance of fate.

As Susan Stanford Friedman has noted, however, the end of one quest is often sufficiently ambiguous in H. D.'s work to allow for the beginning of a new quest.[30] *Hermetic Definition*, H. D.'s last major work, is the most personal and least transcendental, in the old sense, of all H. D.'s volumes. Its temporal code, rather than *Helen in Egypt*'s, shows the real integration of body and spirit, time and timelessness, as the poet acknowledges her imminent death and rejoices in the persistence of her work as an artist. Perhaps the most poignant aspect of this sequence's treatment of time is the fact that in it the poet does allow a resolution, suggesting her surrender of life construed as ongoing dialectic. There is "the sense of an ending" here, a sadness and surrender we don't feel in H. D.'s earlier work.

The poems in *Hermetic Definition* were all written between 1957 and 1961, the year H. D. died. Though the collection does not have the scope and visionary appeal of *Trilogy* and *Helen in Egypt*, it does indicate how far the poet had come from the poppy-seed ecstasy of her early imagism. As she says here: "I need no rosary / of sesame / only the days' trial, / reality."[31]

The title sequence of poems takes its inspiration from H. D.'s last infatuation, with the much younger Haitian journalist, Lionel Durand. The fact that she fell in love with a journalist is, in itself, significant. He suddenly died nine months after their encounter in Switzerland and the poet uses this strange coincidence to envision her literary role as giving birth to the spirit of Durand and once again to herself. She sees the whole project of her life's work as a quest "to recover identity." Art is the child, salvaging the best of the past and giving hope to the future: "the writing was the un-born / the conception" (*HD*, 54).

Nevertheless, art is not simply an escape from the tedium and triviality of the present but a way of reconceptualizing the present in the interest of suggesting new possibilities. In "Grove of Academe," for instance, she pays tribute to St. John Perse, whom she has been reading with great appreciation for his classical art: "this retreat from the world, / that yet holds the world, past, present, / in the mind's closed recess" (*HD*, 27). But at this stage of her life, she can no longer find this pause an ultimate refuge; the future, for instance, is absent.

> you showed me how I could cling
> to a Greek rock and how I could slide away,
> but did you show me how I could come back
>
> to ordinary time-sequence?
>
> (*HD*, 44)

This is what she finds important now, not the timeless myth but the human equation embodied in it, providing hope for the future.

The second sequence, "Sagesse," further emphasizes H. D.'s interest in present-day reality with its cockney dialogue and its connection to a newspaper account of an owl at the London Zoo. However, it is the third sequence, "Winter Love," which is most interesting for our purposes, since it offers a final vision of the Greek persona we have traced through so many avatars.

Written as a coda to *Helen in Egypt*, "Winter Love" divides H. D.'s characteristics between the Helen persona and the *sage-femme*, midwife, Grande Dame "with faded hair" whom Helen accompanies so gratefully. Wisdom, the midwife, brings to birth a child, *Espérance*, who is also a symbol of the artistic creation. Helen sees this child as "the past made perfect" and, having given her life's blood for its creation, is willing to be transfigured, used up, as it thrives: "*Espérance*, O golden bee, / take life afresh and if you must, / so slay me" (*HD*, 117).

Time in these last poems conforms to both kronos and kairos, as the birth of this child, of H. D. as art, achieves *pleroma*, the fullness of time as meaning.

> Hermione lived her life and lives in history;
> Euphorion, *Espérance*, the infinite bliss,
> lives in the hope of something that will be,
>
> the past made perfect;
> this is the tangible
> this is reality.
>
> (*HD*, 112)

In the assertion that the book, the child *Espérance*, is the reality, one fails to see in these lines any desire to escape the terrible recognition that chronological time means mortality. History too is reality: "Hermione [both H. D.'s earlier persona and, perhaps, her child Perdita] lived her life and lives in history." But this reality is imperfect, fragmented, ungraspable. As a poet deeply imbued with modernism, H. D. says that what we can grasp and make perfect is art, art which carries with it the hope of transforming the future and enclosing the past. Toward the end of the poem, "Helen" wishes to escape the child's grip as she longs to preserve her physical being from time's ravages. But she cannot and H. D. knows that. All she can do is "*write, write or die*" (*HD*, 49).

The Greek persona in this volume has reached a new level in its relations with history and thus it approaches what Julia Kristeva describes as the third stage of feminism in Europe: "*insertion* into history and the radical *refusal* of the subjective limitations imposed by this history's time" (195). But, unlike what Kristeva criticizes about this movement, H. D.'s experiment is not carried out "in the name of an irreducible difference" between the sexes. Her reconciliation with father and mother does not mean a surrender to either one and it does open up possibilities for acknowledging continuities.

In the end the Greek persona "dissolves" like a cinematic image into history. Helen gives birth to time, both as implacable diachrony and as visionary synchrony, conceiving of hope for the future—that is, for real historical change—by dedicating herself to an art created in the name of that change.

The last phase of H. D.'s work corresponds to the visionary project Kristeva advocates in "Women's Time" as "the demassification of the problematic of *dif-*

ference." By this Kristeva means "showing what is irreducible and even deadly in the social contract" (209), but in the interest of seeing where difference is not irreducible, where the evolution of civilization may require a sense of continuity as well as divergence in the experience of the two sexes. Kristeva advocates doing this "in such a way that the habitual and increasingly explicit attempt to fabricate a scapegoat victim as foundress of a society or counter-society may be replaced by the analysis of the potentialities of *victim/executioner* which characterize each identity, each subject, each sex" (210). This is what H. D. has undertaken in *Helen in Egypt.*

In spite of her commitment at one level to detailing the battle formations in the war between the sexes, H. D. was ever ready to see the male as a friend and ally as well as an enemy. In fact, much of H. D.'s struggle with the meaning of time shows her to be playing the sister to a group of male modernists who were also struggling with some of the same issues.

For instance, H. D. was deeply impressed by Pound's *Pisan Cantos* and said that her *Helen in Egypt* was written as a kind of companion piece to them. In both works the poets find persistent echoes from the past that have mythic potential in understanding the present. Pound, H. D., and other modernists like Thomas Mann, shared a belief in a higher truth pervading the seeming superficialities of present experience. Their confidence in an ultimate unity binding lives together in meaningful patterns cannot be seen as specifically male or female.

However, H. D.'s relationship to Father Time was affected by her gender. We must call it daughterly rather than filial. She brought to her explorations a series of insights that derived in important ways from her female position. She understood that historical change for her would require a renegotiation of the relations between the sexes, that the future must not simply repeat old patterns. Unlike Pound, whose work would increasingly concentrate on virile heroes of the past whose wisdom was civic and economic, H. D. had to project visionary heroines, women of the future who might transform history into something more than "his story."

Even in *Hermetic Definition* the future is envisioned as linked to the past. Still, the presence of history establishes the value of material reality over against a merely abstract vision of that linkage. In the title poem, for instance, H. D. thinks of the metonymy of three men of color in her life: Paul Robeson (with whom she starred in the film *Borderline* and to whom she dedicates several passages in "Red Roses for Bronze"), Lionel Durand (the Haitian journalist), and Rafer Johnson (the decathalon star she admired). However, here the metonymy does not simply confirm the timeless realm such metonymies suggested before.

> the Red-Roses-for-Bronze
> roses were for an abstraction;
>
> now with like fervour, with fever,
> I offer them to a reality;
> the ecstasy comes through you [Durand]

but goes on;
the torch was lit from another before you,
and another and another before that . . .
                              (*HD*, 14)

Here the revelation of temporal connectedness is not only a way of linking the past with the present, as it was for H. D. in the 1920s. Now there is a future and it is a future which we cannot yet know. It may be terrifying since it will mean the poet's death and may also mean the death of civilization. (H. D. was haunted by the possibility of nuclear holocaust.) But this future will in any case be *different* as the organic process of fate unfolding is always providing us with surprises. The only "unalterable law" (*HD*, 9) is that "the reddest rose unfolds" in time.

Significantly, the H. D. of *Hermetic Definition* is comfortable with all the various forms of time. She no longer tries to elude the grasp of the present, the burden of the past, or the threat of the future.

So my *Red Roses for Bronze* (1930)
bring me to-day, a prophecy,
so these lyrics that would only embarrass you,

perhaps reach further into the future;
if it took 30 years for my *Red Roses for Bronze*
to find the exact image,

perhaps in 30 years,
life's whole complexity will be annulled,
when this *reddest rose unfolds*;

I won't be here,
probably you won't either;
in the meantime, there is beauty and valour

in these contests and passionate excitement as well,
and who was I to shrug and pass them by?
                              (*HD*, 16)

Thus H. D. concludes, as she looks back over her life and considers how her relation to the meaning of time has changed. We can also see that, as a woman poet, she has engaged with problems of large significance to women and to contemporary culture. Her persona has mediated in important ways between psychic and cultural strains. In her desire to help others, in her reconciliation with historical time, in her recuperation of the present, in her de-dramatization of gender conflict, H. D. has moved beyond her early and middle phases. Her Greek persona is now dedicated to an unknowable future as well as to a reunderstood past. The child of her art, *Espérance*, a male child with a female inheritance, combats the earlier forces of her despair. Though it is not a materialist analysis of history, in all these ways her visionary work (like Julia Kristeva's) offers useful imaginings to a world afflicted by the specter of loss. *Espérance* is H. D.'s gift to a barren time.

WOMEN ON THE MARKET

Edna St. Vincent Millay's Body Language

Though born only six years after H. D. (1892 versus 1886), Edna St. Vincent Millay seems to belong to a different era. H. D.'s persona, often an elegant form of Artemis, surely has little in common with the flapper image of early Millay. One gives the impression of timelessness; the other strikes us as dated. This may be due to the fact that whereas H. D. toys with the endless displacements necessary to representations of Desire, Millay wishes above all to present herself as Desire incarnate. Her most recognizable mode is demonstrative rather than restrained.

For examples of the demonstrative mode we need only turn to Millay's early letters, in which she sounds at moments eerily like the voice of Emily Dickinson. Writing to Edith Wynne Matthison in 1917, Millay exhibits her manifest hunger for attachment. Having showered Matthison with professions of devotion ("love me, please; I love you"), she insists: "I am not a tentative person. Whatever I do, I give my whole self up to it." One wonders what Matthison thought of sentiments like: "enormity does not frighten me; it is only among tremendous things that I feel happy and at ease; I would not say this, perhaps, except that, as I told you, I do not trouble to lie to you."[1] The echoes of Emily Dickinson in this are also both prominent and troubling.

For the earlier poet would voice such feelings only in her letters. Her poems were far more calculating and coy. Edna St. Vincent Millay, on the other hand, staked her reputation on just such dramatic announcements. She was seemingly unaffected by the social forces of repression which resulted in Dickinson's reluctance, for instance, to use the word *leg* in any of her more than 1,700 poems. Whereas Emily Dickinson was given to explore the realm of sexuality by writing of snakes, bees, and boats mooring, Edna Millay refused such circumspection, announcing: "I too beneath your moon, almighty Sex, / Go forth at nightfall crying like a cat."[2]

It is tempting to a feminist to feel that Millay's stance is much healthier, less tormented by internalized prohibitions against explorations of physical experience. And, indeed, in Edna Millay's poems we can find not only arms and legs but chins, ears, tongues, shoulders, and bellies; in fact, a full panoply of references to the body.

However, the career of Edna St. Vincent Millay does not seem to justify the temptation to celebrate such "liberation." The projection of her earliest persona as a creature of appetite made her famous but ephemeral. A brief survey of responses to Millay's self-presentation suggests that her demonstrative persona had only limited viability. If it inspired a number of romantic tributes in the early years to Millay as "a New England Nun; a chorus girl on holiday; the Botticelli Venus" or "a sensitive spirit on a romantic pilgrimage through an over-sophisticated civilization"[3]—by the late 1930s her public was becoming less enthusiastic about what seemed to be an adolescence prolonged into middle age.

In 1939 Louise Bogan wrote a mixed review of *Huntsman, What Quarry*, asking whether or not a woman poet "as she grows older" shouldn't give up posturing. "Is it not possible for a woman to come to terms with herself, if not with the world; to withdraw more and more, as time goes on, her own personality from her productions; to stop childish fears of death and eschew charming rebellions against facts?" Bogan surely had herself in mind as much as Millay but after 1940 others were also inclined to grumble. In 1957 Bette Richart categorized Millay's persona as "a haunting and persuasive portrait of neurosis." Maureen Howard, in *Women, the Arts, and the 1920s in Paris and New York* (1982), comments that Millay's "spirit of the modern with its promiscuity and smart cynicism now seems dated."[4]

Though some critics like Jane Stanbrough, Nancy Milford, and Walter Minot have attempted to provide new and sympathetic views, a more typical response to Millay in the period since World War II is Elizabeth Perlmutter Frank's. Frank plays Millay off against Louise Bogan, focusing on the maturity of Bogan at the expense of Millay, who remained "the fragile girl." Frank is charmed neither by Millay's mood swings nor by her physicality. "Indeed, Millay's Girl was essentially a theatrical persona, a medium for the expression of sudden shifts in tone and implied bodily gestures."[5]

To be fair to Millay, however, we must recognize that her work represents a genuine breakthrough for the nightingale poets because it makes the female body more than a set of implied gestures. Though in the end Millay's exploitation of the body betrayed her, it is possible to understand this failure less as a result of personal weakness than as the consequence of women's continuing commodification, as bodies "on the market."

In the following sections of this chapter, I will consider Millay's body language both as a genuine departure from women's poetry of the past and as an unconscious recuperation of oppressive patriarchal attitudes. In order to understand both why she was once so popular and why late-twentieth-century women have been so uncomfortable with her, we must see Millay's poetry as a point of intersection at which culture, psyche, and gender come together in significant ways. Millay's work may indeed strike us as dated compared to H. D.'s. But from another point of view, it remains topical for its exploitation and critique of the ideology of sexual liberation, which we now see as far from simply "liberating."

EDNA MILLAY AND LOVE'S BODY

Edna St. Vincent Millay was something of a phenomenon when the persona she adopted in *A Few Figs from Thistles* became the symbol of Greenwich Village bohemianism. Allen Churchill, in *Improper Bohemians: A Re-Creation of Greenwich Village in Its Heyday*, claims that when *A Few Figs* apppeared in the early twenties, Greenwich Village found its voice.[6]

In addition to her liberal attitudes about sex and politics, Millay brought a wider range of physical experiences to women's poetry than the nightingale tradition had previously allowed. Her poems do not simply *imply* bodily gestures, as Elizabeth Frank says, but actually describe the movements of bodies—both male and female—in some muscular detail. A characteristic moment occurs in "Sonnets from an Ungrafted Tree" where Millay writes of her female protagonist: "She filled her arms with wood, and set her chin / Forward, to hold the highest stick in place," (CP, 608). This is a poet who pays attention to the way poetry thrives on physical experience. In acknowledgment of this, Carl Van Doren wrote: "What sets Miss Millay's poems apart from all those written in English by women is the full pulse which beats through them."[7]

This statement in all of its ambiguity, of course, also suggests the erotic aura that persistently surrounded Millay's persona. Though extremely reticent about the identities of her lovers, Edna Millay was perfectly open about her unconventional attitude about sex. She simply felt that women as well as men should be allowed to indulge their instincts at will, as long as both parties were consenting adults. Though hardly a new idea, this view made her notorious at a time when some Americans were looking for just that combination of the bourgeois and the demimonde that middle-class, Vassar-educated, theatrical, and outré "Vincent" Millay sought to embody.

Millay's most famous poem, "First Fig," is a case in point.

> My candle burns at both ends;
>   It will not last the night;
> But ah, my foes, and oh, my friends—
>   It gives a lovely light!
>
>   (CP, 127)

Elizabeth Atkins claims that when this poem appeared, there was hardly a literate young person who did not have it memorized in short order. Atkins remembers: "Edna St. Vincent Millay became, in effect, the unrivaled embodiment of sex appeal, the It-girl of the hour, the Miss America of 1920."[8]

Given the extreme popularity of this work, we can be sure no one thought it was a poem about candles. Like the nursery rhyme about little Nanny Etticoat ("the longer she stands / the shorter she grows"), this poem makes an implicit connection between a candle and a female body. For many, Millay's own diminutive figure was part of the poem's evocative potential.

This aspect of the candle poem, however, signals the darker side of Millay's use of body language. In "First Fig" Millay exploits her body as the site of pleasure and the locus of metaphor while at the same time acknowledging that the resource whose energy she consumes must also consume her. The candle is a sign of her rebellion against conventional limits, a magic lantern designed to make us imagine her late-night escapades, her ability to take pleasure in the body, and yet it is also a memento mori, as so much in her poetry is. Taken literally, the candle that burns at both ends is a stick of dynamite.

Thus, this poem may be read as part of the drama of consumption we can see operating in Edna St. Vincent Millay's work. On the one hand, this drama involves controlled self-exposure, packaging the body in certain ways for consumption by her large and enthusiastic public. On the other hand, her persona often envisions herself as depleted, brutalized, objectified at the cost of some genuine sense of self-worth. She presents herself as a victim who is sometimes also guilty of wanting to hide her body or kill it off.

In her day the bright side of Millay's body-consciousness was more evident in her self-presentation. She expressed a confidence in her physical presence also reflected in the privately circulated self-portrait Allan Macdougall published in his selection of Millay's letters:

> Hair which she still devoutly trusts is red.
> Colorless eyes, employing
> A childish wonder
> To which they have no statistic
> Title.
> A large mouth,
> Lascivious,
> Aceticized [sic] by blasphemies.
> A long throat,
> Which will someday
> Be strangled.
> Thin arms,
> In the summer-time leopard
> With freckles.
> A small body,
> Unexclamatory,
> But which,
> Were it the fashion to wear no clothes,
> Would be as well-dressed
> As any.[9]
>
>   (L, 99–100)

Given the problems of alienation from their flesh that Amy Lowell, Gertrude Stein, Sara Teasdale, Elinor Wylie, and H. D. all struggled with, Millay's positive body-consciousness at first seems a cause for celebration.[10]

However, there are two peculiar aspects to this self-portrait. One is the imagined violence, the throat which will one day "be strangled." Though Millay undoubtedly intended this as self-irony, when placed beside her other fantasies of enduring similar acts of violence, this element comes to seem significant, a dark indication of the vulnerability of women under patriarchy which links her to Amy Lowell, Elinor Wylie, and H. D.[11]

The other peculiarity is more subtle but equally significant. There is something almost clinical about Millay's description, as though her body were part of a department store inventory. One disturbing implication of Millay's body language is that it often suggests that women are "on the market," objects to be scrutinized in what Luce Irigaray calls "a scopic economy" where the value that is attached to women's bodies is prescribed by the male gaze.[12]

How should we interpret these contradictions in terms of Millay's individual experience and psyche? One prominent feature of biographical accounts of Millay's life is the poet's vacillation between "good girl" and "bad girl" identities. When she was at Vassar, for instance, she almost did not graduate with her class because she broke the rules concerning "overnights" away from the college. However, instead of taking a stand against the rules themselves, she resorted to tears and pleas, getting others to insist upon her reinstatement and eventually winning the college over through "girlish" charm.

Similarly, as a single woman living a bohemian life in Greenwich Village, Millay became the epitome of sophisticated independence. Nevertheless, her letters to her mother and sister are often written in baby talk. As soon as she could, she brought them to New York to live with her and her frequently passionate declarations of love to her mother led the poet to speculate that in future someone might publish *The Love Letters of Edna St. Vincent Millay & Her Mother* (L, 120). Clearly she had great dependency needs that kept her iconoclastic energies within certain bounds.

Nevertheless, Edna St. Vincent Millay thought of herself as a fighter and a feminist. She is the single poet in this group who was politically engaged: a friend to the conscientious objector during World War I, vitally involved with the trial of Sacco and Vanzetti, an outspoken advocate of women's rights, and defender of Elinor Wylie against the snubs of the League of American Penwomen. She fought with her editors, she argued with her friends, she offended her public, and she certainly was not a submissive wife. Yet, temperamental to an extreme, she was also generous and loyal, and she would have been horrified to hear that for all her courage and feistiness, her life text and her work nevertheless illustrate John Berger's remark that "to be born a woman has been to be born, within an allotted and confined space, into the keeping of men."[13]

Yet this is surely one way of explaining the bad girl/good girl syndrome. Millay actually wanted desperately to please the public and this meant, in a significant way, pleasing a masculine-centered culture enthralled with the white female body as tabloid image. Even poets got their pictures in the papers and became "stars." Edna St. Vincent Millay enjoyed this kind of notoriety at one level. Yet her psychological history suggests hidden conflicts that took a serious toll upon her health.

From her thirties until her death at the age of fifty-eight (1950), Millay was plagued with physical complaints: intestinal problems, severe headaches like Wylie's that lasted for months, bursitis, and nerve disorders, among others. Some of these were diagnosed as psychosomatic and certainly in the 1940s she appeared to fit the definition of the hysteric whose body becomes the theater of deformed or frustrated desire. Her lesbian connections, her stable marriage, her many affairs: none of these was able to relieve the suffering for which she adamantly refused to seek psychological treatment except when hospitalized for nervous collapse.[14]

In spite of her health problems, Millay continued to promote her public presence for more than twenty years, going on reading tours which boosted the sales of her books and expanded her readership. Her reading presence was notorious: clad in a long red velvet dress or diaphanous veils, she purposefully projected a sense of being the poet in the flesh, of the flesh; the poet whose flesh was somehow the very material of her material.

Even her marriage at the age of thirty to Eugen Boissevain, a free-thinking Dutch coffee importer, did not revise her girlish, eroticized image, still often connected to the poems in A Few Figs from Thistles, which Millay had originally intended as a book of light verse. Though Millay grumbled about the continuing demand for the poet of A Few Figs, she was herself distinctly aware of her physical presence as a commodity. Her letters mention both wanting to be sculpted and being etched; she describes her dirty fingernails, her need to throw up, her refusal to be seen in a disheveled state. The language she uses to evoke her feelings about giving readings is particularly revealing: "If I ever felt like a prostitute it was last night" (L, 181), she says about one such occasion. And of another, "Once a day my keepers come & drag me forth 'with all my silken flanks in garlands dressed,' to the miniature sacrifice" (L, 184). Thus, Millay with intentional irony describes her public appearances as a form of alienated labor while at the same time allowing her body to be used as a means of generating income. She also tended to think of publishing itself as physical exposure, insisting sardonically to her mother: "A person who publishes a book wilfully appears before the populace with his pants down" (L, 220).

Yet, from our perspective fifty years later, Millay's conversion of the private act of writing into a modern, market-oriented performance has particular significance in the context Millay here suppresses, the context of gender. John Berger's remarks about the spectacle of the female body within bourgeois culture are illuminating in this regard. Berger says that

> men act and women appear. Men look at women. Women watch themselves being looked at. This determines not only relations between men and women but also the relation of women to themselves. The surveyor of woman in herself is male: the surveyed female. Thus she turns herself into an object—and most particularly an object of vision: a sight.[15]

In Millay's era women were only beginning to be widely accepted as public personalities and thus Berger's remarks have even greater relevance to that period than to our own. The presentation of the white female body for public consumption had a freshness then which it lacks today. But what Millay unconsciously reveals in her letters is that, in some real way, her body was not her own but an object inscribed in a cultural context dangerous to its health.

In the forties Millay's health broke down completely. With the advent of the Second World War, she—like many who had opposed U.S. entry into World War I—reversed her position on pacifism and became an ardent supporter of the war effort. As a poet this meant that she wrote propaganda poetry, risking her reputation in the process. In 1941 she confessed her anxieties as well as her patriotism in a letter to a friend worried about her sons.

> . . . though I have no sons to be caught in this war, if we are caught in it, I have one thing to give in the service of my country,—my reputation as a poet. How many more books of propaganda poetry containing as much bad verse as this one does, that reputation can withstand without falling under the weight of it and without becoming irretrievably lost, I do not know—probably not more than one. But I have enlisted for the duration. (*L*, 311–12)

In this letter Millay reveals how much her public persona meant to her. "Have you the slightest conception of what this reputation means to me, who have been building it carefully for more than twenty years . . . ?" She calls it "the dearest thing in life I possess."

Of course, one could say that a literary reputation is different from a public persona, except in Millay's case the distinction is tenuous. As a "personal" poet, her cultural role was under constant pressure. Thus, her decisions to give radio broadcasts in support of the war and to publish *Make Bright the Arrows* were especially risky and likely to bring about the effect they, in fact, created: the destruction of her credibility as a literary force.

Millay was certainly sincere in her support of the war effort. However, consciously or not, she was also engaged in an attempt to change the character of her persona. No longer presentable as a flapper coquette, she hoped to become something closer to Elinor Wylie's "woman warrior." In fact, *Make Bright the Arrows* contains a typical woman-warrior motif, a tribute to Joan of Arc.

However, this gambit was not successful. Having lost her ability to negotiate with the literary world, Millay had a nervous breakdown at the end of the war. Jean Starr Untermeyer remembers a public appearance Millay made during the dark years of the 1940s.

> She was a travesty of the girl I had known. Her hair, which she wore in a long pageboy cut, was now shades lighter than the red-gold locks of her girlhood. It seems to me now . . . that she was attired in a long, straight gown of dark red velvet, but the face under the thatch of yellow hair had changed, almost unbelievably: it had aged but not ripened. With its flushed cheeks it reminded me of a wizened apple.[16]

One senses that Millay never found a way to revise her earlier persona successfully and thus, unlike H. D., whose Greek persona was not designed to represent
girlish appeal, she could not grow old with grace. When Edmund Wilson and his
wife, Elena, visited Millay and her husband at their upstate New York estate
"Steepletop" in 1948, the Wilsons found a very shaky and frightened "Ednah,"
whom Eugen treated with the patience of an adult caring for a child. It is significant
that on this occasion Millay gave a reading of "The Poet and His Book," a poem
she had published in *Second April* in 1921. She could not read the poem now
without breaking down.

In this poem Millay makes explicit the connection between the physical text
and the poet's "real self." Millay juxtaposes the decay of the poet's body with the
survival of the book of poems that contains "All that once was I!" She here glories
in the belief that workers, farmers, women, lovers, and even children will mix her
with their work and play, long after her death. Thus the text becomes a new body
and that body becomes the text of survival. Millay demands:

> Bear me to the light,
>   Flat upon your bellies
> By the webby window lie,
>   Where the little flies are crawling,
>   Read me, margin me with scrawling,
> Do not let me die!
>
> (CP, 87)

As Joan Dash remarks of the poem, "in the particular turn of phrase she has chosen,
'margin me with scrawling,' is the echo of an almost physical intimacy, as if it were
her very body she offers up to be scrawled upon."[17]

We can, in fact, link up Millay's connection of her physical body with her art
to similar connections made by other women, especially in the modern period.
Wylie's "Miranda's Supper" sets the metaphorical table for a communal meal between writer and reader, offering for our delectation "Miranda's," also Wylie's,
flesh: "Now partake; it is her body" the poet says. H. D. links the physical presence
of Helen in *Helen in Egypt* to the Amen-script, saying: "She herself is the writing."
In *Hermetic Definition*, art—in the image of the infant *Espérance*—is kept alive by
feeding off the flesh of the woman writer who may be used up in the process, dying
into art.

Addressing these issues of the relation between the modern woman writer and
her body as text, Susan Gubar writes: "Many women experience their own bodies
as the only available medium for their art, with the result that the distance between
the woman artist and her art is often radically diminished; second, . . . cultural
forms of creativity are often experienced as a painful wounding."[18] Edna St. Vincent
Millay records that painful wounding in a number of famous poems alluding to the
way the female body must be violated and then transformed in the production of
a (woman) poet's art. Thus with typical personal reference Millay writes in "Burial":

"Mine is a body that should die at sea!" As in "The Poet and His Book," she once again imagines her body recycled in an economy of exchange, with

> . . . terrible fishes to seize my flesh,
> Such as a living man might fear,
> And eat me while I am firm and fresh,—
> Not wait till I've been dead for a year!
> (CP, 98)

"Firm and fresh" were terms of praise used about her poems as well as her (young) flesh. Millay wanted her readers to get the juice out of her poetry, to consume it (and her) in order to keep her spirit "in circulation."

LOVE'S BODY ON THE MARKET

The fact that Millay is a particularly good illustration of the way that women tend to become objectified in androcentric American culture should not blind us to the fact that her popularity also reflected a genuine loosening of restrictions on female behavior. Unlike her nineteenth-century sisters, she could and did travel alone, control her own money, smoke and drink without apology, attend lesbian and interracial parties, and sleep with a number of partners; and none of these facts about her reduced her popularity. In fact, such publicity contributed to her allure.

From another point of view, however, this "liberation" meant the loss of some earlier supports in forming a stable identity. In this way Edna Millay had to confront a new set of confusing choices. By examining some of the cultural components of these choices, we can see the way Millay's treatment of the body in her poetry emerges out of a context which affected many other women of her time and ours.

T. J. Jackson Lears has suggested that the emergence of a market-oriented economy in America went hand in hand with a destabilized conception of the self. Though the older ethic had been repressive in some ways, the newer one was confusing, tending to produce a self without stable outlines, manipulated to suit the expectations of others and the needs of the moment. As a result the modern person might end up with nothing more vital to sustain him or her than "a set of social masks."[19]

Though this destabilization affected both men and women, women were the targets of a particular kind of socioeconomic engineering which encouraged them to participate in "making a spectacle of" themselves. Mary Ryan has noted that the habits of consumption inculcated by the advertising media strengthened sexual stereotypes and reinforced images of women "not only as lovers, mothers, and housewives, but as narcissists and masochists as well." As we have already seen in the chapter on Sara Teasdale, popular culture of this period elevated romantic love to a position of increased importance in the lives of women. Ryan claims that in both advertising and psychological theory, "narcissism merged with masochism" as women were encouraged to think of themselves as sex objects whose bodies needed constant modification in order to protect their value on the market. In this way "love's body" became a commodity of particular importance in an economic realm where a great variety of new products were competing for female attention: for example, cosmetics, deodorants, and cleansers. Ryan concludes: "Female sexuality once again led to work and anxiety rather than the simple pleasures of the body."[20]

An interesting poem to consider in light of these factors is Millay's sonnet "Oh, oh, you will be sorry for that word!" (1923).

> Oh, oh, you will be sorry for that word!
> Give back my book and take my kiss instead.
> Was it my enemy or my friend I heard,
> "What a big book for such a little head!"
> Come, I will show you now my newest hat,
> And you may watch me purse my mouth and prink!
> Oh, I shall love you still, and all of that.
> I never again shall tell you what I think.
> I shall be sweet and crafty, soft and sly;
> You will not catch me reading any more:
> I shall be called a wife to pattern by;
> And some day when you knock and push the door,
> Some sane day, not too bright and not too stormy,
> I shall be gone, and you may whistle for me.
>
> (CP, 591)

This poem sets up an opposition between mind and body in which the speaker, "sweet and crafty, soft and sly," is willing to appear to adopt a conventionally "feminine" persona, substituting for intellectual exchanges sexual signals of devotion: "Give back my book and take my kiss instead."

Reassuring her patronizing husband with images of herself as a well-trained consumer engaging in the conventional rituals of consumption certified by his gaze—"you may watch me purse my mouth and prink"—this speaker is actually plotting revenge. Her revenge involves a particular kind of duplicity in which she will appear to be "a wife to pattern by," that is, a visible spectacle of female submission and consumerism. Only at the end does she reveal what she has decided to do. Typically, her revenge involves no open confrontation but instead a devious escape: "I shall be gone, and you may whistle for me."

In this poem Millay gives us an insight into the way many women conceived of the requirements of their social role. Without the stabilizing components of an older model of social identity based on family, geography, age group, and marital connection, the newer woman often had to make her body her main resource. This involved establishing a different relationship with *things*. Instead of regarding them as tools or even as background effects against which to appear to greatest advantage, women came instead to see themselves as things, commodities on the market. Rachel Bowlby sums up the effect of consumer culture on women in the modern era.

Seducer and seduced, possessor and possessed of one another, women and commodities flaunt their images at one another in an amorous regard which both
extends and reinforces the classical picture of the young girl gazing into the mirror
in love with herself. The private, solipsistic fascination of the lady at home in
her boudoir, . . . moves out into the worldly, public allure of *publicité*, the outside
world of advertising.[21]

Perhaps it should not surprise us, then, that a woman like Edna Millay should
conceive of her poetic role as including spectacle and publicity. As early as the
publication of *Second April* (1921), she was inclined to take a hardheaded view of
success. In a letter from this period, she confessed: "I think, personally, [the critics]
are giving it more than it deserves. But I am glad, as long as I myself am not taken
in, that it is selling, and pleasing, and that I shall not be in disfavor at the time
of the appearance of my next book" (L, 129). Even the use of the word "appearance"
has a suggestive ambiguity here.

At the end of her life Millay was still talking about literary spectacle, using
the imagery of currying and braiding her poems, "for the Fair (to say nothing of
the Market)" (L, 361). Her outrage in 1950 that the American Cancer Society
was refusing to exploit modern methods of advertising is very revealing, as it shows
the extent to which Millay herself saw the use of such methods as expedient.[22]

Given the particular features of modern culture outlined above, *and given Millay's particular susceptibility* to the temptations of participating in a capitalistic literary
marketplace, elements of her persona that have previously perplexed readers now
become more comprehensible. Edna St. Vincent Millay was a poet of the body
who presented the text and her own flesh as mirroring one another. However,
since a female body in her culture was an unstable commodity whose value was
certain to diminish in time and whose connection to mind and spirit was at best
undefined and at worst dismissed, Millay's success at exploiting her body-consciousness in her early work provided no stable persona for the poet but simply
involved her in a drama of consumption. Seen from this angle, her vacillation
between spirited self-dramatizing and dispirited lament, her lack of any one consistent image of self, makes a good deal of sense. She was not simply neurotic or
immature; she was confused by mixed cultural voices which invited her to reveal
herself in certain ways and then grew tired of the very vision of flapper femininity
they had solicited. Examining her career reminds us that too often the nightingale
poets who begin in gladness, come in the end (as Wordsworth said) to despondency
and madness.

THE BODY AS SPECTACLE IN
MILLAY'S EARLY WORK

"Renascence" is probably Millay's best-known and best-loved serious poem. Its
publishing history is often rehearsed in Millay scholarship: the fact that she sub-
mitted it at her mother's urging to a contest volume called *The Lyric Year*, her
twenty-year-old hopes prematurely raised by Ferdinand Earle, one of the judges;

her subsequent failure to win one of the three prizes, but the enormous outpouring of praise for the poem and her instant rise to prominence in literary circles; all of this before she had done her four years of college at Vassar, financed in part through the attention this poem received.

Typically missed in readings of the poem is the way "Renascence" mythologizes female creativity in terms of an assault upon the body.[23] For "Renascence" is a deeply strange and disturbing work which, in its capacity to allegorize a certain version of women's experience, can come to seem not only powerful but uncanny.

In the course of the plot of "Renascence," the first-person speaker begins by experiencing herself and her world as bounded. "All I could see from where I stood / Was three long mountains and a wood" (CP, 3). She then aspires to touch the sky, for which she is brutally punished. She suffers the sins of all, the torments of guilt, tortures unbearable in her body; she craves death, dies, but mourns the loss of beauty and the pleasures of the senses. Having been chastened, she is returned to life where, like Emily Dickinson in "Behind me dips eternity," she experiences herself as "the term between" who must keep coded sets of binary oppositions carefully separated: "East and West will pinch the heart / That cannot keep them pushed apart" (CP, 13).

The ending of the poem is moralistic and dutiful, the speaker reciting her lesson: "he whose soul is flat—the sky / Will cave in on him by and by." This seems an eerie rejoinder to Dickinson's open-ended conclusion, where the female soul is left with "Midnight to the North of Her— / And Midnight to the South of Her— / And Maelstrom—in the Sky" (P, 721). It is as though Millay, refusing the destabilizing vision of the earlier poet, has opted for life at the expense of her original courageous ambitions.

And does the poem make its conclusion seem appropriate? Are we left to agree that the speaker's initial longings and terrifying experiences have been satisfactorily resolved in the concluding implication that her soul was previously inadequate, her innocence (like Eve's) the ground of her guilt?

In the end the poem comes to seem "uncanny" in a Freudian sense of combining the familiar and the strange within the circle of fear. In his essay on "The 'Uncanny,' " Freud says: "It may be true that the uncanny is nothing else than a hidden familiar thing that has undergone repression and then emerged from it, and that everything that is uncanny fulfills this condition."[24] Part of the continuing appeal of this poem—an appeal to which even an adolescent Audre Lorde succumbed in the forties—is its ability to suggest two familiar elements of our history: the connection between the female body and feminine creativity and the capacity of patriarchy both to injure the aspiring female and then to insist upon repression of the memory of injury as payment for entry into the realm of the empyrean.

In a real way the events of this poem take place in the speaker's body. When she reaches up to touch the sky in a metaphorical attempt to satisfy her ambition, her self-assertion is greeted by initial success. But this success is soon met with physical opposition.

> I screamed, and—lo!—Infinity
> Came down and settled over me;

Forced back my scream into my chest;
Bent back my arm upon my breast;
And, pressing of the Undefined
The definition on my mind,
Held up before my eyes a glass
                                                    (CP, 4)

Her punishment for indulging her desire is a kind of rape where Desire is literally
forced back into her body and the speaker learns the Law by first passing through
a mirror stage and then encountering Logos: Immensity is "made manifold," unity
is dismembered, and the Law (here named "Infinity") "whispered to me a word
whose sound / Deafened the air for worlds around" (CP, 5). (We are never told
what this word is if not the Word, Logos itself.)

Familiar in many accounts of creative women is the sense of frustration that
governs the initial struggle in the poem. Though the speaker is never precisely
denominated female, she has (like Michelet's sorceress) a woman's craving. Craving
for what? For everything.[25] Like the Sorceress she also takes all of life into her
body and experiences no distinction between herself and the world about her. But
Millay's vision is fundamentally disturbing because the "dream" is both painful and
graphic:

I saw and heard, and knew at last
The How and Why of all things, past,
And present, and forevermore.
The Universe, cleft to the core,
Lay open to my probing sense,
That, sickening, I would fain pluck thence
But could not,—nay! but needs must suck
At the great wound, and could not pluck
My lips away till I had drawn
All venom out.—Ah, fearful pawn:

For my omniscience paid I toll
In infinite remorse of soul
                                                    (CP, 5)

The "great wound" is suggestive of multiple interpretations. It reminds us of
Susan Gubar's statement that women experience the influx of creativity as a wounding. Like H. D. in *The Gift*, the speaker is herself wounded, but in the process of
learning the limits of her subjectivity, she must also externalize the wound. This
will help her return to "health" but at the expense of certain kinds of knowledge.
She is allowed to learn about the world but she must forget the rape which ushered
in this knowledge. Like Christina Rossetti's *Goblin Market*, in which sucking imagery is also prominent, this poetic vision equates the access to knowledge with
rape, desire with guilt, and release with renewed repression.

Yet, unlike Lizzie's in "Goblin Market," there is something strangely liberating
about this speaker's experience. She has entered a liminal realm in which the
division between herself and the powerful forces at work in the world is momentarily

suspended: "All suffering mine, and mine its rod; / Mine, pity like the pity of God" (*CP*, 7). Her body is no longer hers but becomes the theater for reenacting the sufferings of humanity, a demonic festival in which the marginal are given voice: "A thousand screams the heavens smote; / And every scream tore through my throat" (*CP*, 7). This scene, drenched as it is with female significance, invites us to turn to French feminism for an analysis of comparable mythic images of the feminine.

In *The Newly-Born Woman*, Catherine Clément describes this kind of experience as a "return to the disordered Imaginary before the mirror stage."[26] In this statement Clément is appropriating the terms of Jacques Lacan in distinguishing between the Real and the Imaginary. For Lacan, the child leaves the realm of the Imaginary and enters the mirror stage when it becomes preoccupied with its own image in the mirror. "This represents, for the child, usually for the first time, the image of itself as a unified controllable body; it is an image which will govern [his/ her] relations with other children, turning them frequently into games of master and slave, actor and spectator."[27] Lacan sees subsequent experience for both sexes as governed by the Law of the Father, bounded by the Symbolic or linguistic, and darkened by the inability to adjust the world to Desire.

While the speaker in Millay's poem enters the world of her fantasy through the mirror, in Lacanian terms her journey seems to be leading her back toward the pre-oedipal Imaginary rather than forward into the Law. (Though it is never possible in Lacan to leave the Symbolic realm entirely once one has passed over, elements of the Imaginary remain available in dream and some irrational states.) How is this return to the Imaginary coded feminine in Millay's poem?

In the first place, though the speaker is herself a victim of violence, she also seems to cross a dangerous boundary where aggression and seduction constantly change places. This is the realm of the sorceress familiar from our analysis of Elinor Wylie's poems. Because of the aggression flying free in this realm, Clément finds the sorceress in paradox: there is "hell and pleasure at the same time, suffering and a tacit paradise that is secret, hidden in a little implicit smile through even the most intense pain" (*NW*, 34).

In the second place, in a manner recognizably female, Desire appears alienated and reformed in the image of another's demand. Thus, what started out as a lament over inadequate opportunities ("All I could see from where I stood / Was three long mountains and a wood") becomes a recognition of the seemingly more legitimate demands of others.

> A man was starving in Capri;
> He moved his eyes and looked at me;
> I felt his gaze, I heard his moan,
> And knew his hunger as my own.
> (*CP*, 6)

In the end, what Clément calls "sorcerous repression" takes over and the speaker returns, through the intervention of Logos, to the Symbolic realm governed by the Law of the Father. She who had longed to touch the sky now acknowledges that the sky belongs to a power she cannot share: "O God, I cried, no dark disguise / Can e'er hereafter hide from me / Thy radiant identity." A world of binary oppositions has been explicitly brought back into play, and the speaker becomes a self because she is no longer like God. She is simply the intermediary term that allows phallogocentrism to assert itself:

> The soul can split the sky in two,
> And let the face of God shine through.
> But East and West will pinch the heart
> That can not keep them pushed apart;
> And he whose soul is flat—the sky
> Will cave in on him by and by.
>
> (CP, 13)

As in "The Suicide," also from Millay's first book, a life of a sort is purchased through repression of the anger associated with the memory of injury. In each of these poems, one feels the interference of the male gaze causing the speaker to revise her original demand for recognition of what is not only a lack but, especially in "The Suicide," a form of abuse: "Thou hast mocked me, starved me, beat my body sore" (CP, 25).

It is, in fact, not difficult to find places where Millay acknowledges her preoccupation with the male gaze. In Sonnet IV, the speaker imagines that if her lover had not grown tired of her resistance, she would have flung aside her "pretty follies": " . . . , and beneath your gaze, / Naked of reticence and shorn of pride, / Spread like a chart my little wicked ways" (CP, 569). A more ironic view of the internalized male gaze emerges in the first of "Three Songs of Shattering":

> Grief of grief has drained me clean;
>   Still it seems a pity
> No one saw,—it must have been
>   Very pretty.
>
> (CP, 40)

In order to see how the self-critical and revisionary effect of the male gaze is connected to the poet's time and place, however, we might look at a poem—"I, being born a woman" (CP, 601)—where the persona adopts a self-consciously modern pose. Like "Oh, think not I am faithful to a vow," "I shall forget you presently, my dear," and "What lips my lips have kissed and where and why," this poem purports to defy the masculine sexual prerogative by asserting the female speaker's independence and lack of sentimentality regarding sex. For these reasons it became something of a battle cry for modern women who could now say, in effect, I am a free woman, or, as Millay more delicately puts it: "I find this frenzy insufficient reason / For conversation when we meet again."

However, if we look more carefully at this poem—and at others like it—we can see that it does not really transcend the strictures of the male prerogative. It begins:

> I, being born a woman and distressed
> By all the needs and notions of my kind,
> Am urged by your propinquity to find
> Your person fair, and feel a certain zest
> To bear your body's weight upon my breast:
> So subtly is the fume of life designed,
> To clarify the pulse and cloud the mind,
> And leave me once again undone, possessed.

Though the sestet will recoil—"Think not for this, however, the poor treason / Of my stout blood against my staggering brain, / I shall remember you with love"— we have already seen that, for all her defiance, the speaker has accepted her passivity in relation to "the fume of life" which will leave her "once again undone, *possessed*."

What this fume of life is we cannot be sure, but Millay's reference to it seems quite close to a biological determinism she repeats elsewhere in "Whether or not we find what we are seeking / Is idle, biologically speaking" (CP, 571). Still, biology does not explain why she should present herself as "undone, possessed," instead of gratified and possessing. Suddenly, in a typical exterioration of her desire, she sees herself as the property of the male. Like many contemporary women trying out "sexual liberation," she is unable to feel herself to be the one seeking and satisfying the body's desires. For an explanation of this, we need to turn not to biology but to culture, which controls the way sex is experienced. In fact, as we now know, it is often experienced differently by the two sexes, women tending to see themselves as *giving* something, men as taking.

Here, as in Millay's "Witch-Wife," the fantasy of independence must exist side by side with the intervention of interpretive models derived from culture. The body is never simply a "given." Even the witch-wife "learned her hands in a fairy-tale, / And her mouth on a valentine" (CP, 46).

We should remember, however, that Millay, unlike the witch-wife, did not consistently exploit the imagery of femininity in her self-presentation. Photographed in masculine clothes in the twenties, widely known by and preferring her second name, "Vincent," to Edna, the poet sometimes adopted a masculine persona and always spoke of "the poet" in the masculine gender. One poem that captures the unstable androgyny of Millay's masculinized persona is "The Bean-Stalk" (CP, 71–73). "Ho, Giant! This is I! / I have built me a bean-stalk into your sky!" the poem begins.

Another work extremely popular with the public, this poem like "Renascence" teases us with indications about the way Millay saw her own ambitions. Here the poet imagines herself as Jack, climbing. It is difficult to resist the invitation to connect Jack's "climbing" with her own ascension up the literary ladder, and, in fact, the poem speaks openly of her sense of Jack as an artist/craftsman, not just a thrill-seeker.

One of the first benefits of Jack's increasing distance from the ground is the transformation of his perspective on that showplace of American capitalism, the city.

> Till the little dirty city
> In the light so sheer and sunny
> Shone as dazzling bright and pretty
> As the money that you find
> In a dream of finding money—

It seems odd but also significant that a poem about the perils and pleasures of ambition should so quickly become connected to "a dream of finding money."

In her imagination she is able to transform real money, little and dirty like the city, into dream money—"bright and pretty"—but once again her vision of agency, her attempt to be Jack (or "jack," money valuable in a privileged economy), gives way to images of her body being acted upon from without.

> And the wind was like a whip
> Cracking past my icy ears,
> And my hair stood out behind,
> And my eyes were full of tears,
>
> Wide open and cold,
> . . . .
> And my teeth were in a row,
> Dry and grinning,
> And I felt my foot slip,

From being the one with the gaze herself ("When I shot a glance below"), she becomes someone looked at (by the giant?). For she cannot see how her hair "stood out behind"; the dry and grinning teeth again remind us of the memento mori. Her cheerful (and childish) remarks to the giant at the end indicate that she must make her peace as a "pliant" being, maker of bean-stalks rather than giant killer, and thus the pretense of assuming a masculine persona eventually gives way to clear indications that we are listening to a feminine speaker.

> Your broad sky, Giant,
> Is the shelf of a cupboard;
> I make bean-stalks, I'm
> A builder, like yourself,
> But bean-stalks is my trade,
> I couldn't make a shelf,

> Don't know how they're made,
> Now, a bean-stalk is more pliant—
> La, what a climb!
>   (CP, 71–73)

If the sky is the space of freedom, the giant has contained it (in the cupboard). She retreats to a separate space of freedom, the phallic bean-stalk feminized, since competition with the giant on his own ground is fraught with peril. The poet cajoles the giant by telling him she is not in the same business he is, much as Anne Bradstreet three centuries earlier felt the necessity to cajole the men of her day by saying: "Men can do best, and women know it well. / Preheminence [sic] in all and each is yours."

Millay's poem defies too neat an allegorical reading and remains lighthearted, but it once again suggests the way her attempt to transcend inhibiting structures of power returns her in spite of herself to confrontation with disabling forces: "And I clutched the stalk and jabbered, / With my eyes shut blind,—" Climbing, it turns out, is not a transcendental activity. The farther up one goes, the closer one gets to what Millay called in an early letter "the assembled [male] deities" who confer value on poetry by careful control of the (library?) "shelf."

Where, one might ask, is a stabilizing female presence in Millay's early work to operate as an alternative to the hegemony of male power? Millay's life was full of women. In fact, her father was merely a shadowy figure in it after the early day on which he and her mother separated. In contrast, Millay's mother emerges as a strong continuing presence, a wonderfully energetic and unconventional woman who raised three talented and strong-minded daughters. Millay adored her mother and, in addition, had many close women friends, Elinor Wylie among them.

Nevertheless, in her poetry women usually provide comfort only outside the "normal" social and cultural realm, suggesting that what is female cannot become a force potent enough to transform the Law. Millay did write a number of memorable elegies to women—Dorothy Coleman, Elinor Wylie, her mother—but these tend to undermine the value of a life lived *in* the world. In the Wylie sequence (V), she admits that her love for a woman (Wylie) makes her complicitous with anti-life forces: "Someone within these walls has been in love with Death longer than I care to say; / It was not you! . . . but he gets in that way" (CP, 373).

In "The Return" and "Ode to Silence"—a fascinating poem in its own right— female figures are sought out as an escape from the tensions of the social world; the speaker wants a "frigid" bosom where "unquestioned, uncaressed" she can find respite from both language and social relations. In each case it is a woman who provides this service. Yet we sense in both poems that this will be only a brief interlude, after which the speaker will presumably return to the world, leaving the sister/mother behind.

Even the mother in "The Ballad of the Harp-Weaver," who has the magical capacity to weave clothes for her son on "a harp with a woman's head," must die in the effort, reminding us once again of the connection between creativity and bodily harm in Millay, and further confirming our sense that other women are given mainly instrumental functions in her early work. Though as Nature women can be effective, in the realm of Culture their effectiveness is limited, Millay seems to say.

Perhaps this is one reason why the persona in "Sonnets from an Ungrafted Tree" finds herself for much of the poetic sequence unable to deal with Culture at all, her "quiet ear" preferring the soothing sounds of Nature. Yet these sonnets, coming at the end of Millay's early period, actually move that persona beyond the essentially limited position we have seen Millay's women occupy before, and at the end new vistas of possibility begin to open up.

Such possibilities may have something to do with the mood Millay was in during the time of composition. Since her relationship with Arthur Davison Ficke had collapsed, she was no doubt examining the costs of romantic love for women like herself. In January 1922 she wrote to Ficke: "I hold a very nervous pen lately. Does your hand get that way sometimes, so that you want to dig in the earth with it, or whittle it, or thrust it into a broad fat back,—anything but write with it?" (*L*, 143). In "Sonnets from an Ungrafted Tree" it is possible to see her using her art to develop a perspective on the aggressive impulses she was feeling.

However, this sonnet sequence is interesting for more than biographical reasons.[28] It explores not only the neurotic behavior of an individual woman but also a set of problems confronting all of us who discover sexual desire to be fraught with dangers. Though the protagonist of "Sonnets from an Ungrafted Tree" is plagued by agoraphobia, a hypersensitivity to noises, and hallucinations, at the end of the poem she is the one who possesses the gaze whereas her husband's eyes have been permanently closed in death. She is the one able to look at the world in a new way and that new way is liberating.

The plot of the sonnet sequence involves a woman who has been separated from her husband returning to him because he is ill and needs a nurse. The whole poem is filled with images of decay and disillusionment—with marriage, with men, but equally with the hopeful young woman who haunts the wife's memory, her gullible early self who thought to find in what Blake called "the lineaments of satisfied desire" an expansion of opportunities gratifying the young woman's narcissism and need for mystery.

The sonnet sequence is notable in Millay for its rendering of character, its imagism (since almost everything is "told" in pictures of the body and the domestic and natural worlds), and for its restraint. We are never informed, for instance, of the reasons the woman left her husband or precisely why she returned "loving him not at all." In some ways her madness is reminiscent of the wife's in Charlotte Perkins Gilman's "The Yellow Wallpaper" since she doesn't herself make the connections to the position of women under patriarchy that the reader is invited to make.

As readers, we are the ones who see her engaging in the tasks assigned to women: setting the house to rights, making the tea and the fire, giving "of her body's strength" to the man as though he were a child whose hands needed steadying about the cup. Furthermore, Millay invites us to see this woman's impulses as both mediated by culture and masochistic in the sense Mary Ryan uses that term, where gratification comes from an activity which is stressful and self-defeating. Like a magazine housewife, this woman learns to:

> Polish the stove till you could see your face,
> And after nightfall rear an aching back
> In a changed kitchen, bright as a new pin,
> An advertisement, far too fine to cook a supper in.
>   (CP, 612)

The use of "you" and "your" instead of "she" and "her" seems to make this activity a ritual of capitalism, "an advertisement" of the role assigned to women who must make their kitchen "bright as a new pin" despite the fact that it then becomes unusable.

The last line of the couplet, with its extra syllables, suggests a metaphor for the disillusionment the woman feels with her life in general. In pursuing the pattern of romantic love given by patriarchy, she discovers, not that her husband is a brute, but that he becomes an accomplice in continuing, rather than a partner in terminating, her frustration.

Like the speaker in "Renascence" this woman feels hemmed in by her circumstances. Her husband's mute, thick body operates as an image of that frustration.

> Familiar, at such moments, like a friend,
> Whistled far off the long, mysterious train,
> And she could see in her mind's vision plain
> The magic World, where cities stood on end . . .
> Remote from where she lay—and yet—between,
> Save for something asleep beside her, only the window screen.
>   (CP, 617)

That "something asleep beside her" which is her husband's body is hardly a strenuous antagonist. "She gave her husband of her body's strength / Thinking of men, what helpless things they were" (CP, 617). Yet his need for her is enough to bring her back within the circle of his desire. Sexual desire seems as much as anything the source of the woman's original fascination with this man who was "not over-kind nor over-quick in study / Nor skilled in sports nor beautiful" (CP, 614).

But the woman now seems to feel that her body has in some way betrayed her. By flashing a mirror in her eyes at school, he appeared to give her her body in a new way. He appealed to her narcissism. But like the male gaze which promises subjectivity to the woman only to betray that promise in the end, desire for the other's body that is actually desire for her own selfhood confuses the woman as to her real goal. The young woman cannot know herself by looking into this mirror. But she believes her needs addressed by the desire he seems to arouse in her: "And if the man were not her spirit's mate, / Why was her body sluggish with desire?" (CP, 615). The younger woman cannot answer such a question.

Only when her husband is dead, and "From his desirous body the great heat /

Was gone at last" (CP, 622), can she begin to find her own way. At the end the poet says:

> She was as one who enters, sly, and proud,
> To where her husband speaks before a crowd,
> And sees a man she never saw before—
> The man who eats his victuals at her side,
> Small, and absurd, and hers: for once, not hers, unclassified.
>
> (CP, 622)

In this way she becomes "an ungrafted tree," set free from her younger self who has been inscribed within the structure of another's life. The poem suggests that even during their separation the woman was not wholly free, so that when she returns to "the wan dream that was her waking day," she is merely "borne along the ground / Without her own volition" (CP, 618). Who, then, is the "strange sleeper on a malignant bed"? Is it her husband or herself, grafted onto his need for her?

This poetic sequence seems to me an important declaration of independence for Millay. No longer does she insist on regarding life fatalistically; in the end the woman has begun to wake into a new world where the possibility of freedom is marked simply by the word "unclassified." Not only is the husband's body no longer what it was, but by implication her body and thus her life are now unclassified, also. Like the wife in Kate Chopin's "Story of an Hour," this woman is able to become a subject only after her husband's death allows her to see herself separate from his needs and desires.

BODY LANGUAGE IN MIDDLE AND LATE MILLAY

From some points of view, middle Millay—which includes *The Buck in the Snow, Fatal Interview, Wine from These Grapes,* and *Huntsman, What Quarry?*—is Millay's strongest period of achievement. Jean Gould says that "the years from 1930 to 1936 represent the peak of Millay's career professionally and financially, as well as creatively." *Fatal Interview* (1931) marked the height of Millay's popularity.[29] Several of the sonnets from that book are still widely known and often anthologized.

However, Millay seems even more tormented by the problems of the flesh in this period than she was earlier. Whereas before she expressed a certain bravado about the pleasures of the senses, here she is "rolled in the trough of thick desire" (CP, 359). In "Menses" she is tortured by the psychological problems attendant upon menstruation. Though "Menses" should be recognized as a brave and original poem, perhaps the first to deal openly with P.M.S.,[30] it is also a confession of helplessness, climaxing with a cry of anguish: "Just Heaven consign and damn / To tedious Hell this body with its muddy feet in my mind!" (CP, 347).

Physical disabilities are more keenly felt in this period than they have been previously: "For the body at best / Is a bundle of aches," the poet says in "Moriturus"

(CP, 200). Even death is no longer so much a temptation to be toyed with as a frightening prospect which shadows the life of the poet and her friends. The elegies for Elinor Wylie and Millay's mother appear in this period, as well as one of Millay's most beautiful lyrics, "To the Wife of a Sick Friend."

Identifying with the hunted in her buck and rabbit poems, Millay conveys a sense of physical vulnerability more urgent than the fantasies she nourished earlier precisely because she presents these as not fantasies but realities. The threat of war certainly overshadows these poems, as where she advises the rabbit:

> "You are bigger than a house, I tell you, . . .
>   you are a beacon for air-planes!
> O indiscreet!
> And the hawk and all my friends are out to kill!
> Get under cover!" But the rabbit never stirred; she never will.
>   (CP, 326)

In the interesting detail that even her friends are "out to kill," one senses that Millay was beginning to feel danger closing in on her even from intimate relations.

In another much more humorous hunting poem, "Huntsman, What Quarry?" the lady offers herself to the hunter so that the fox may go free, but he, though tempted, finds the fox sexier:

> Her hand was on his knee;
> But like a flame from cover
> The red fox broke—
> And "Hoick! Hoick!" cried he.
>   (CP, 334)

Having chosen the title of this poem as the title for her collection, Millay implies that this predatory relation governs more than the simple roles of man and beast in the fox hunt.

In *Conversation at Midnight* and "Intention to Escape from Him," economic relations, in particular patriarchal and capitalist economics, invade all other realms of life: domesticity, art, friendship, politics, and religion. Millay shows her affinity with 1930s-style leftism where she insists on a view of humanity as "a special thing and no commodity, a thing improper to be sold" (CP, 384).

Of course, Millay's reliance on the sales of her books and her reading tours meant that her rejection of commercialism was neither so wholehearted nor so uncontaminated as it sometimes appears in the poems. Millay was certainly gratified when *Wine From These Grapes* sold 40,000 copies within a short time of its publication. Furthermore, Millay was more of a populist than a socialist, as one can see from *Conversation at Midnight*, a book-length work published in 1937. Yet Millay's insights into the compromises exacted from women living under these particular economic and social conditions are not negligible. For instance, when the commercially successful and misogynistic short story writer in *Conversation* says:

"I can't make love to a woman I really respect," Millay foreshadows much later critiques.[31]

Are women still on the market in Millay's middle period poems, still determined by the male gaze, their bodies not entirely their own? Millay denies this in *Fatal Interview* where the speaker addresses this issue directly:

> Heart, have no pity on this house of bone:
> Shake it with dancing, break it down with joy.
> No man holds mortgage on it; it is your own;
> To give, to sell at auction, to destroy.
>
> (CP, 658)

Yet in the three alternatives she provides, the gift of the body to another, prostitution or slavery, and suicide, one hears her eloquent silence on the subject of independent pleasure in the senses. As for selling the body at auction, who but Millay among the nightingale poets would even mention this as a choice. As rabbit, as doe, and as saleable commodity, Millay's females do indeed seem to be, as Berger says, born, within a limited and confined space, into the keeping (or killing) of men.

Since *Fatal Interview* is probably Millay's most highly respected book of poems, it deserves consideration at some length. It also illustrates the extreme tension between Millay's frustration and her complicity with patriarchal practice, though perhaps "complicity" is the wrong word, since it suggests the voluntary acceptance of a participatory relation.

In *Fatal Interview* the speaker admits from the beginning her comparatively powerless position, asking, "What thing is this that [though merely mortal] . . . / Has power upon me?" (CP, 630). In the second sonnet she calls her love "This beast that rends me in the sight of all" (CP, 631). These fifty-two sonnets explore a relationship between an older woman and a younger man, reminding us of H. D.'s late poems about Lionel Durant. However, where H. D. was able to transform her pain into a poignant vision of integrity and transcendence in the face of death, Millay's sonnets move toward madness and despair. Though both poets record the story of an aging woman plunged by her desirous body into a tormented relationship, H. D.'s is more cerebral than visceral, while Millay's reflects that her body is a marked-down commodity unable to tear itself loose from the larger system of values that govern her culture.

The sonnets of *Fatal Interview* were inspired by Millay's adulterous love affair, which neither she nor her husband made any attempt to hide, with a younger man. The identity of the younger man, whom we now know to have been George Dillon, was kept secret. She was thirty-six, he was twenty-one. Though the speaker pretends to be not a mortal woman but a goddess who cannot die, she is a fully incarnated entity only fitfully endowed with transcendental options. Once again the male gaze is important ("Your look which is today my east and west") and once again her body has become a text; waking while she sleeps, it records the scar of this encounter written upon it by the sword of sexual desire. As early as Sonnet III, the speaker acknowledges that she must use deception and coyness to hold her lover, though she despises resorting to "a philtre any doll can brew." She is no mythical exception, "Since that which Helen did and ended Troy / Is more than I can do" (CP, 635).

Women are her only allies in this tormented state. But they *are* allies as they have not often been before. In Sonnet XXXVI the speaker pays tribute to the strong island women of Maine. In "Night is my sister," the most beautiful lines of this beautiful and witty poem describe a moment of female camaraderie memorable for its poignance:

> Small chance, however, in a storm so black,
> A man will leave his friendly fire and snug
> For a drowned woman's sake, and bring her back
> To drip and scatter shells upon the rug.
> No one but Night, with tears on her dark face,
> Watches beside me in this windy place.
>
> (CP, 636)

Yet, like the speaker's scorn for the "doll" who brews a philtre, mortal women represent to her a history of inadequate versions of love. She longs to be an exception, offering "Love in the open hand, no thing but that" (CP, 640). Though she is ready to admit that "Women have loved before as I love now" (in Sonnet XXVI), she pretends to think herself the sole contemporary advocate of "unregenerate passions." "I think however that of all alive / I only in such utter ancient way / Do suffer love" (CP, 655), she says.

"Love" as sufferance rather than choice leaves the speaker defenseless. Therefore, her occasional defiance, as in "I know my mind and I have made my choice; / Not from your temper does my doom depend" (Sonnet XLV), does not ring true. Her mind is not a refuge from the pain of the lover's dismissal of her body; the body corporal is still Millay's first adjutant, and still her primary antagonist.

As in other poems from Millay's middle period, the imagery of war permeates this sequence. But the female self here seems less muscular, less agile than it has seemed in other poems. Consider, for instance, Sonnet XXIV:

> Whereas at morning in a jeweled crown
> I bit my fingers and was hard to please,
> Having shook disaster till the fruit fell down
> I feel tonight more happy and at ease:
> Feet running in the corridors, men quick-
> Buckling their sword-belts bumping down the stair,
> Challenge, and rattling bridge-chain, and the click
> Of hooves on pavement—this will clear the air.
> Private this chamber as it has not been
> In many a month of muffled hours; almost,
> Lulled by the uproar, I could lie serene
> And sleep, until all's won, until all's lost,

And the door's opened and the issue shown,
And I walk forth Hell's mistress . . . or my own.

(CP, 653)

This poem demonstrates both the strength and the weakness of the sonnets in *Fatal Interview*. I have always liked it because it does express so perfectly a woman's view; the delight some of us can take in getting things stirred up as long as we don't have to witness the carnage, as long as the aggression is displayed at a distance; our luxuriant indulgence of ourselves in solitude (perhaps the only place in the midst of such conflict where such a woman can let down her hair and experience genuine *jouissance*); our willingness to adapt ourselves to the outcome, whatever it may be. But in the imagined dialectic between active, aggressive men and a passive, waiting queen, we find ourselves returned to Millay's gender conflicts.

Her handling of the sonnet form here is certainly impressive.[32] But it needs saying that her sensual evocation of the physicality of war, so tautly rendered in the second quatrain, alternates with the languor and resistlessness of the lines in the first and third quatrains, which are about the woman herself. She is most active at the beginning; after that she would rather leave others to decide her fate.

The poem climaxes with the double stresses of "door's opened" and "issue shown" in a line which actually reads like tetrameter rather than pentameter, suggesting a condensation of feeling, a coming to grips. But who is opening the door and showing the issue? Presumably, in the terms of the knightly metaphor, men are in control at these moments. If we are to interpret this as mental combat, the male side of the speaker's psyche is the most forceful here. When Millay wrote "I am possessed of a masterful and often cruel imagination" (*L*, 22), perhaps she meant to imply that her experience as a poet involved indulgence of aggressive fantasies, but in fact her poetry is only rarely cruel and it usually preserves a sexual dichotomy allocating to men and women fairly conventional attributes.

Like the distraught speakers in poems by Amy Lowell, Elinor Wylie, H. D., and Louise Bogan, Millay's woman/goddess in *Fatal Interview* dissolves into madness. Despite her proclamations, it is clear that she has not been able to preserve a female self independent of the male. Part of the madness of the ending is evident in the fact that she has projected the violence of her own anger onto her lover.

After all the poems claiming her right to her own desire, even her willingness to manipulate a hesitant lover into bed, she now imagines a scene of rape in which she indentifies with an unwilling victim. The rape itself may be a metaphor, of course, for her sense of being imposed upon by masculine values denying integrity and power to her love. Yet, there is something peculiar about ending the sonnet sequence with this reversal of Keats, beginning "Oh, sleep forever in the Latmian cave, / Mortal Endymion, darling of the Moon." Endymion becomes the villain, the moon his victim:

Whom earthen you, by deathless lips adored,
Wild-eyed and stammering to the grasses thrust,
And deep into her crystal body poured
The hot and sorrowful sweetness of the dust:

> Whereof she wanders mad, being all unfit
> For mortal love, that might not die of it.
> (CP, 681)

Here this poem seems tortured by bad faith, and perhaps this form of bad faith is what we understand to be her madness. From a reading of the entire sonnet sequence, we know she knows she is both innocent and guilty, her guilt exposed in Sonnets II and XV; she is both aggressive (in Sonnet XXXIV) and passive; she is both consumer and consumed. But in this last poem, she tries to blot out half of each of these pairs of oppositions, making the female object wholly innocent, wholly passive, consumed by her madness. The Elizabethan pun on the word "die," used throughout the sequence, suggests a link between desire and suicidal longings. The woman, caught in the meshes of a relationship, where she is indeed unable to realize her will, longs to kill off the powerless self. The desire for consummation becomes itself consuming in the end.

Though *Mine the Harvest*, Millay's last published book, contains some beautiful lyrics, such as "Ragged Island" and "The Parsi Woman," it continues to present a vulnerable persona whose body is sometimes violently assaulted, sometimes already dead. Furthermore, *Mine the Harvest* is the collection most occupied with "the mind" as though, in defiance of T. S. Eliot, whose influence she felt had been ruinous to her own career, she were now herself attempting to compete with more abstract intellectual poets.[33] In fact, "Journal," a long, amorphous, stream-of-consciousness poem, raises a number of issues about the mind, mentioning Descartes and Bergson along the way, only to come up short against Death and the dissolution of the body.

> When I see my netted veins
> Blue and busy, while the grains
> In the little glass of ME
> Tumble to eternity,—
> When I feel my body's heat
> Surge beneath the icy sheet,
> (CP, 523)

then, the poet says, she imagines herself in the room with Death, Death who "Caught his image fleetingly / In the glass that mirrors me." Mirrors no longer serve the function of catering to the speaker's narcissism or returning her to the Imaginary as they do in "Sonnets from an Ungrafted Tree" and "Renascence." In fact, what one feels in late Millay is that the poet is unable to find potency in the female body. Unfortunately, for a poet who made her reputation out of her ability to feed a hungry public with her own flesh as text, this spells disaster.

Female bodies in the late poems are epitomized by their helpless or sorrowful gestures. Women are allies but the alliance is one of pain. Feminist critics have recovered "An Ancient Gesture," for instance, in which the speaker wipes her eyes on her apron, thinking as she does so that Penelope also wept with fatigue and loneliness. The poem ends bitterly.

> Ulysses did this too.
> But only as a gesture,—a gesture which implied
> To the assembled throng that he was much too moved to speak.
> He learned it from Penelope . . .
> Penelope who really cried.
>
> (CP, 501)

The female alliance renders the quintessential experience of womanhood as suffering, much as nineteenth-century nightingale poets suggested a hundred years earlier.

Similarly, the Parsi woman watches the sky, which is "thick and cloudy with the bold strong wings / Of the vulture, that shall tear your breast and thigh" (CP, 506), since in Parsi culture corpses are left in "the tall Tower of Silence" to be devoured by predatory birds. The poet thinks to herself that she has done what the Parsi woman is here doing, admiring the beauty of an array of forces to which in the end she will fall prey. The irony is that her response to beauty, like the Parsi woman's, actually makes her complicitous with death instead of helping her to fight against it.

One new and interesting theme in this last collection concerns infancy and the birth trauma. In two poems Millay speaks of the baby's desire to remain within the womb and the anger and frustration consequent upon "the crimson betrayal of his birth into a yellow glare." "Intense and terrible, I think, must be the loneliness / Of infants" (CP, 548–49) is an original poem that casts a shadow unusual for its time on the "dainty abode of Baby." The poet seems to admire the sheer willfulness of infants.

> If you wish to hear anger yell glorious
> From air-filled lungs through a throat unthrottled
> By what the neighbours will say;

try taking an infant's favorite security toy away. Does Millay envy the infant because it need not make compromises and smother its anger? Perhaps. In any case, this poem, though uneven, is refreshing in its lack of sentimentality. Baby's life is shadowed too with the memory of betrayal: "The pictures painted on the inner eyelids of infants just before they sleep, / Are not in pastel."

In spite of moments of freshness, however, problems of many sorts weaken this final collection, which is tedentious, prosy, and self-pitying in parts. One feels the lack of careful editing, of pruning, grafting, fertilizing, and plowing under, as Millay called the process of revision. Yet significantly, this is the only place where Millay actually recognizes, if only indirectly, a woman poet's struggle. In "Black hair you'd say she had," she speaks of the "desperate notes" of the female songbird ("with unmelodious throat and wing"). She counsels the bird to sit on her eggs, "bring /

Beauty to birth, that it may sing / And leave you." But for the bird herself, her voice being inferior to her drunken mate's (a reference to Dylan Thomas?), she counsels submission. If the male songbird is good at all, "Why, shut your lids and hear him sing, / And when he wants you, take him back" (CP, 497–98).

Perhaps, at this stage of her life Millay was ready to acknowledge defeat not only for herself but for female ambition in general, as Amy Lowell did twenty-five years earlier in "Ronde du Diable": "Therefore, Sisters, it's my belief / We've none of us very much chance at a leaf."

A generally disregarded but fascinating poem, "Men Working" (CP, 532–34), implies a similarly pessimistic perspective. The poem purports to be about workmen putting in power lines but, considered metaphorically, its implications are much broader and more disturbing. It begins with a seemingly innocent reflection:

> Charming, the movement of girls about a May-pole in May.
> Weaving the coloured ribbons in and out,
> Charming; youth is charming, youth is fair.

It then continues by turning these thoughts into an invidious distinction:

> But beautiful the movement of men striking pikes
> Into the end of the black pole, and slowly
> Raising it out of the damp grass and up into the air.
> The clean strike of the pike into the pole: beautiful.

Here we find again what one has come to respect in Millay's treatment of the body, her genuine delight in muscular movement, which she is the best of all nightingale poets in rendering. We also recognize her late style with its preference for long and rather flat lines with irregular rhyme schemes. These elements in the end, however, both remind us of Millay's earlier successes and suggest criticism of them.

The middle section of the poem includes dialogue between the men and the boss as they work together democratically, the boss never simply imposing his will but taking his cue from the good sense and skill of his men. Why does it stir the poet so deeply to watch this scene, real as it was to Millay when electricity was installed in her rural retreat at Steepletop? She is watching something that calls into question the whole thrust of her early and middle poetry, a set of actions she idealizes as male, working class, clean, unemotional, and adept. Yet, it is not, I think, a work written in bad faith. It is instead a poem we might justifiably read as tragic, for in her seemingly quite genuine admiration for these men and what they are able to achieve lies the complete annihilation of her own project.

> One by one the pikes are moved about the pole, more beautiful
> Than coloured ribbons weaving.
>
> The clean strike of the pike into the pole; each man
> Depending on the skill
> And the balance, both of body and of mind,

Of each of the others: in the back of each man's mind
The respect for the pole: it is forty feet high, and weighs
Two thousand pounds.

In the choice between female decorative bodily gestures, girls dancing around the maypole in the ancient ritual of worshipping the phallus, and men establishing their power over something they construct as female, she chooses to admire the masculine over the feminine project. Furthermore, she admires it because it represents the balance of body and mind, something Millay herself was never able to achieve. As a group project, it also reminds us that nowhere in Millay do women help one another to balance body and mind in the interests of transforming civilization; they do so only in the interests of personal healing.

Though in the back of their minds, these men respect the weight and stature of the pole,

In the front of each man's mind: "She's going to go
Exactly where we want her to go: this pole
Is going to go into that seven-foot hole we dug
For her
To stand in."

Surely the repetition of the men's thoughts—"she's going to go," "to go," "to go"—draws our attention to the contamination of these instrumental reflections by a rhetoric of male dominance. As these long lines abruptly diminish into two and three words, we are troubled by the complacency with which the men control the implicit power of the feminine by positioning it in a seven-foot hole "for her / To stand in." Even the understatement of the last two lines does not provide much reassurance. "This was in the deepening dusk of a July night. / They were putting in the poles: bringing the electric light."

In this "electric light" the illumination that Millay had at the end of her life, that women stay put and do not threaten male power because even in their mythic materiality (here two thousand pounds!) they operate *merely* as matter, as undifferentiated bodies, whose meaning is determined by men, stabilized in an economic "repetition of the same"? I find this poem fascinating, and far more revealing to consider in a feminist context than "An Ancient Gesture," where Ulysses is too easily denigrated as an emotional plagiarist and Penelope too one-dimensionally presented as a victim.

Having explored Millay's work at some length, we are left, it seems to me, with a question. Does every woman poet worth her salt need to be subversive? Today, we can find subversion everywhere, even in the works of the most unlikely writers. Millay, however, is a rare case within the nightingale tradition: a woman who was actually a likely candidate for a subversive, who supported women's rights, who spoke out emphatically when she was discriminated against on the basis of sex. At New York University, for instance, where she was given an honorary degree in

1937, she discovered that the male recipients were being honored at the Waldorf-Astoria, whereas she would be honored "at a dinner given for a small group of ladies" by the wife of the Chancellor. She wrote decrying this procedure and she insisted: "I register this objection not for myself personally, but for all women" (*L*, 291). No other nightingale poet of her generation would have done such a thing, not even Amy Lowell, who was outspoken in other ways.

As a poet, Millay was flamboyant, exuberant, sinewy, rebellious, wry. But only in places. In truth, Millay was not really subversive. She never worked out a large conception of women's place in American culture, women's oppression under patriarchy, or even the dynamics of male-female relations. H. D. was much more analytical about these issues, but even Louise Bogan was more consistent in her evaluation of the relative merits of the sexes. Therefore, we are likely to be disappointed in Millay if we want from consciously feminist poetry more than the beginnings of feminist consciousness, if we want subtlety and range of application capable of revising our categories.

What one does find in Millay again and again is evidence of the difficulty women have in thinking outside those pernicious limits. Unlike some of the less "feminist" but more acute poets, Millay fought against the new ways of thinking about the psyche that were introduced with psychoanalysis. Only in her last book does she begin to acknowledge the existence of the unconscious and suggest the possibility that a deeper analysis of the psyche might be valuable.

If we are fair, however, it seems to me that we must understand Millay as a poet formed by her culture, choosing from that cultural matrix those elements that particularly fit her self-understood needs and interests. She was daring in some ways, but she was also, in others, a casualty of the sexual revolution of the 1910s and 1920s. Encouraged to see herself as a particular kind of consumer of sensual pleasure, she placed herself and her work within a matrix of market relations only briefly and superficially rewarding.

What she did not see at first was the vulnerability of that position and once she saw it, it was too late. Though Millay exploited the roles of both consumer and commodity, her poetry—like her body—failed to charm after a certain point. Then she was consigned, like an aging fashion model, to the ash heap of literary history. Hugh Kenner, for instance, dismisses her as a writer of "unread, unreadable books," calling her "what's her name, the candle woman, Miss Millay, Edna St. Vincent."[34]

In fact, Edna Millay was not before and is not now the author of "unread, unreadable books." For some readers, not exclusively female, her work continues to have semiotic power. For our purposes we can see in it both an index of cultural strains and a defiant rejection of those who insist that woman *as* body/text cannot write *of* body/text, that is, of our own cultural positioning. Now that we understand this better, her poetry deserves more profound, and more profoundly feminist, readings than it has received.

WOMEN AND THE
RETREAT TO THE MIND
Louise Bogan and the Stoic Persona

"Henceforth, from the mind," wrote Louise Bogan in the early 1930s, "For your whole joy, must spring / Such joy as you may find / In any earthly thing."[1] The difference from Millay's typical embodiment of desire is striking. For Bogan, as for Elinor Wylie and H. D., a retreat to the mind, not some carnal corruption, was often the temptation figured in the siren's song. And for this Bogan has been praised. Her Pulitzer prize–winning biographer, Elizabeth Frank, for instance, speaks admiringly of Bogan's "stoic indifference and stoic endurance."[2]

In fact, though Frank compares her disadvantageously to Bogan, Edna St. Vincent Millay also had her moments of stoicism, as in poems like "Ragged Island," where she sounds like Bogan herself:

> There, there where those black spruces crowd
> To the edge of the precipitous cliff,
> Above your boat, under the eastern wall of the island;
> And no wave breaks; as if
> All had been done, and long ago, that needed
> Doing; and the cold tide, unimpeded
> By shoal or shelving ledge, moves up and down,
> Instead of in and out;
> And there is no driftwood there, because there is no beach;
> Clean cliff going down as deep as clear water can reach;
>
> No driftwood, such as abounds on the roaring shingle,
> To be hefted home, for fires in the kitchen stove;
> Barrels, banged ashore about the boiling outer harbour;
> Lobster-buoys, on the eel-grass of the sheltered cove:
>
> There, thought unbraids itself, and the mind becomes single.
>
> There you row with tranquil oars, and the ocean
> Shows no scar from the cutting of your keel;
> Care becomes senseless there; pride and promotion
> Remote; you only look; you scarcely feel.
>
> Even adventure, with its vital uses,
> Is aimless ardour now; and thrift is waste.

Oh, to be there, under the silent spruces,
Where the wide, quiet evening darkens without haste
Over a sea with death acquainted, yet forever chaste.
(CP, 443–44)

Though Louise Bogan's oeuvre is the smallest of all the poets treated here and her persona, the stoic, in some ways the most severe, the issue we will consider in this chapter—woman's retreat to the mind—is one that has considerable resonance within the tradition as a whole. When Edna Millay writes of Ragged Island, "There, thought unbraids itself, and the mind becomes single," when she rejects her earlier amorous persona in the lines "Even adventure, with its vital uses, / Is aimless ardour now;" she is imagining a sharpening of mental powers and a concomitant reduction of emotionality—"You only look; you scarcely feel"—which has a strong appeal to women poets within the nightingale tradition.

In *Helen in Egypt* H. D. presents it as the island world of Leuke, governed by Artemis as Moon-goddess. In "Sagesse" of *Hermetic Definition*, the Leuke-spirit is apostrophized as "Lady of chaste hands and the quiet mind" (HD, 82), reminiscent of the sister-spirit toasted with a "chilly thin green wine, / . . . trod by pensive feet / From perfect clusters ripened without haste / Out of the urgent heat" in Millay's "Ode to Silence" (CP, 117). Yet, the mentalistic female, unlike the muse figure in most male poems, still manages to be simultaneously intellectual and earthy in these women's works, both *Brillante Mère Féconde* and *Sombre Mère Stérile* in H. D.'s "Sagesse," both earth mother and nun.

Not every woman poet who imagines a retreat to the mind personifies the presiding spirit of that retreat as female, of course. In Bogan's "Henceforth, from the Mind" only the image of the shell, also a feature of H. D.'s Leuke poems, suggests that this mind is gendered.

Henceforward, from the shell,
Wherein you heard, and wondered
At oceans like a bell
So far from ocean sundered—
A smothered sound that sleeps
Long lost within lost deeps,

Will chime you change and hours,
The shadow of increase,
Will sound you flowers
Born under troubled peace—
Henceforth, henceforth
Will echo sea and earth.
(BE, 64)

Surely a sign of the female, the shell is a complex choice for both women's idealization of an interior mental realm. It also summons up Wordsworth's use of the shell in *The Prelude* prefigured in Book One as "the mind's / Internal echo of the imperfect sound," later recurring in the Arab dream when the Poet hears a "loud prophetic blast of harmony" by listening to the shell the Arab offers.[3] In Wordsworth the shell is a second ear (Dorothy?) which, as for H. D., helps him hear "a music yet unheard" in the mind's imagination.

Another association with the shell may be found in Paul Valéry, a favorite of Louise Bogan's, where he says: "A *crystal*, a *flower*, or a *shell* stands out from the usual disorder that characterizes most perceptible things. They are privileged forms that are more intelligible for the eye, even though more mysterious for the mind, than all the others we see indistinctly."[4] Thus, the shell suggests resistance to chaos and the mysterious ordering at the heart of life that H. D. found in the chambered nautilus and that Bogan alludes to in "Old Countryside," where the beleaguered spirit stands "braced against the wall to make it strong, / A shell against your cheek" (*BE*, 52).

In addition, both women's linkage of the shell with the mind evokes the dream of tranquility that accompanies the idea of "withdrawing into a shell." Gaston Bachelard comments perceptively on this set of associations in his chapter on shells in *The Poetics of Space*. Bachelard insists that "by living this image, one knows that one has accepted solitude," and he further comments that, though the dream of living in a shell is absurd, "it is a dream that, in life's moments of great sadness, is shared by everybody, both weak and strong, in revolt against the injustices of men and of fate."[5]

These associations with the shell (solitude and self-protection) are very much a part of its iconography in the poetry of Bogan and H. D. Preoccupied with symbolic structures and well-versed in Freud, both of them would also have been aware of the essentially *female* configuration of shell images, their repetition of the interiority of the female body.

Furthermore, for them the feminine is also the realm of vulnerability, in need of defense, of the armor we call a "shell." Here Bogan's retreat to the mind can be linked to Teasdale's crystal gazer who watches the world from a safely defended position, and to Elinor Wylie's lens of crystal in "Self-Portrait." There Wylie gives her mind the power to "disentangle fox-fires" and "calm queer stars to clarity," though in Wylie's case such calm was never entirely secure. The shell and the crystal are, after all, fragile constructions.

Against the background of the fact that all of the women in the nightingale tradition have at times hungered to retreat from the social scene, that most have had strongly reclusive tendencies, that many have suffered terrible repercussions from overburdened and highly strung sensibilities, and that Lowell, Teasdale, Wylie, H. D., and Millay were all treated at some point in their lives for nervous breakdowns, it comes as no surprise to find that Louise Bogan was hospitalized three times for depression and after her mid-thirties found—to a greater or lesser extent—her main consolation in the life of the mind.

Nevertheless, Bogan remains a special case, and for this reason, it is she who most readily furnishes us with the opportunity to investigate the nature and significance of the stoic persona. In her life and in her work, we can see her tendency from the very earliest period to meet every crisis with a tightening of her belt, a stiff upper lip, a desire to persevere in her duty and, above all, to endure. The framework of her stoicism was both psychic and social.

What's more, it was aesthetic, amounting to a commitment to form so stringent that Gloria Bowles has named it "an aesthetic of limitation."[6] Bogan believed that to live well and to write well requires grace, the grace *not* to say and *not* to do, so that what is said and done comes out compactly, memorably, in form. She celebrated the old prophetic voice: "I kept silent, even from good words . . . the fire kindled, and at the last I spoke with my tongue."[7] Thus, she belongs to the austere branch of the nightingale tradition.

In the rest of this chapter, it will be important to see both what is special to Louise Bogan's poetic temperament and what is generic, what links her to the other nightingale poets and to her culture. The stoic persona she chose was certainly influenced by her New England upbringing; it was also one of the masks available to intelligent, ambitious, vulnerable but proud young women living in New York in the 1920s. If we can see in distilled form through reading Louise Bogan a tendency other nightingale women—to a greater or lesser extent—also share, we will see the whole tradition more clearly. With the tradition as background more in focus, we can also see Louise Bogan more clearly, more generously, with a fuller and deeper respect.

LOUISE BOGAN AND THE LONG REALITY

The first letter Ruth Limmer reprints in *What the Woman Lived: Selected Letters of Louise Bogan 1920–1970* is written to William Carlos Williams and concerns John Coffey, Bogan's friend then incarcerated in Matteawan. In it she says: "Write to John. Tell him, as well as you can in a letter that will be read by various people before it reaches him, that because of the thing he knows[,] endurance can become the long reality. Tell him that there are sources undiscovered and not yet spilled out."[8]

This letter is enigmatic and yet, in the context of Bogan's life as a whole, it is both paradigmatic and prescient. For Bogan herself, endurance would become "the long reality." Her own traumatic experiences would cause her to search for and ultimately to find sources of strength suited to her needs. These resources would come to seem not emotional so much as intellectual; occasionally reached through the will, they were also stronger and more persistent than the will. Such resources gave the poet's life grace and form and yet, after a certain period, they stifled her poetry.

If the stoic in Bogan saved her from hysterical lapses like Millay's and Wylie's, and from a suicide like Teasdale's, the stoic was also a severe custodian whom Bogan herself never entirely trusted. "The Alchemist," written in 1922, sets up the dilemma with which Bogan was to struggle all her life.

> I burned my life, that I might find
> A passion wholly of the mind,
> Thought divorced from eye and bone,

Ecstasy come to breath alone.
I broke my life, to seek relief
From the flawed light of love and grief.

With mounting beat the utter fire
Charred existence and desire,
It died low, ceased its sudden thresh.
I had found unmysterious flesh—
Not the mind's avid substance—still
Passionate beyond the will.

(*BE*, 15)

Of this poem Diane Wood Middlebrook has written: "In 'The Alchemist' the contradiction between woman and artist is an implication latent within the explicit subject of the poem: the desire to attain self-transcendence through brutal self-control."[9] Middlebrook is right when she interprets the realm of the mind as a space inflected as masculine in Bogan's culture. She is also shrewd in her comprehension that Bogan sought to escape her female body in order to "ascend to that high plane occupied by the greatest spirits."[10]

But the triumphant liberation of the female carnal spirit that Middlebrook finds at the end of "The Alchemist" was only intermittently possible to the poet herself. Louise Bogan would at times feel the necessity to let go, to go under, to give up her severe discipline and her stoic attitude, perhaps to fall in love, to have an affair. In these instances we can say that she found "unmysterious flesh— / Not the mind's avid substance—still / Passionate beyond the will." But these moments would pass and once again she would return to the mood that possessed her more and more in what she called "the iron years" of her later life. During this thirty-year period, her most characteristic statement was "It is fine to have a layer of Stoicism, in all this" (*WWL*, 300).

It was mostly fine, according to Bogan, to have a layer of stoicism, no matter what the problem, after the age of thirty-five. Though Bogan made fun of her own tendencies in a poem first titled "Lines Written After Detecting in Myself a Yearning Toward the Large, Wise, Calm, Richly Resigned, Benignant Act Put on by a Great Many People After Having Passed the Age of Thirty Five" (*WWL*, 82), she frequently advocated that others adopt this spirit and did so herself when she could. Bogan's Law, as she called it in a letter to Rolfe Humphries in 1938, meant restraining one's impulses as much as possible for "action usually comes from meanness and frustration" (*WWL*, 180).

What exactly were the problems that Louise Bogan struggled with so painfully and continued to write about all her life? What was her "long reality"? Three of the most painful problems concerned her relationships with her mother, her second husband (Raymond Holden), and herself.

Her early life was spent in Massachusetts, New Hampshire, and Maine, where she was born (five years after Edna St. Vincent Millay) in 1897. Her father was a mill superintendent and the family moved around a lot. But this in itself was not the cause of those tremendously difficult early memories, which would continue

to dog Bogan's mental footsteps all her life and which were still capable of precipitating a mental crisis in 1965.

It was more than the family's rootlessness, its working-class contours, its Irish
Catholic marginality, that haunted Bogan. Though these stresses took their toll,
others more personal were more deeply wounding. Some of Bogan's most famous
poems hint at traumatic incidents that somehow also become the imagined scenes
of writing. Thus, "Medusa," from Bogan's first book, mythologizes the experience
of psychic injury:

> When the bare eyes were before me
> And the hissing hair,
> Held up at a window, seen through a door.
> The stiff bald eyes, the serpents on the forehead
> Formed in the air.
>
> (BE, 4)

Since this scene becomes frozen in the mind, and since it retains not only terror
but beauty, as we shall see, the poet seems to be inviting us to note the connection
between the traumatized individual and the artist who would preserve in *form* the
content of psychic crisis.

"Medusa" is early, but one of Bogan's last poems, "Psychiatrist's Song," returns
to the paralyzing moment of visual insight.

> Those people, and that house, and that evening, seen
> Newly above the dividing window sash—
> The young will broken
> And all time to endure.
>
> (BE, 134)

Whatever these traumatic early incidents were, they mostly involved her
mother. May Bogan was discontented with her husband and prone to clandestine
extramarital affairs. Sometimes violent and hysterical, she was also unintentionally
cruel to Louise, as when she abandoned her husband and children for extended
periods of time. It was not easy to grow up under such conditions and Bogan's
visual memories of the New England towns she lived in are strangely infected by
what must have been her emotional torment.

In her journal she talks about "the incredibly ugly mill towns of my childhood,
barely dissociated from the empty, haphazardly cultivated, half wild, half deserted
countryside around them."[11] She writes of the "pale, lonely light" and of the men
and women who, in her mind's eye, all seem disfigured by ugly scars. Probably the
most significant memory, however, is the following:

But one (and final) scene of violence comes through. It is in lamplight, with
strong shadows, and an open trunk is the center of it. The curved lid of the trunk
is thrown back, and my mother is bending over the trunk, and packing things
into it. She is crying and she screams. My father, somewhere in the shadows,

groans as though he has been hurt. It is a scene of the utmost terror. And then my mother sweeps me into her arms, and carries me out of the room. (*JAR*, 26)

Even Bogan herself seems not to know precisely what the details of her mother and father's problems were. They involved her mother's longing for a different and more exciting life, her mother's beauty and tendency to seek out other men, her passionate presence that exacted total devotion from those around her. And yet, after returning from one of her typical escapades, she would be humble, contrite, vulnerable. Bogan herself described her mother as a "terrible, unhappy, lost, spoiled, bad-tempered child" and a "tender, contrite woman with, somewhere in her blood, the rake's recklessness, the baffled artist's despair" (*LB*, 11).

Louise Bogan's mother did not provide a very strong or reliable image of womanhood for her daughter to emulate. And yet the poet was never tempted to renounce her gender like Amy Lowell or to seek a female lover to repair the damage done to her young psyche. She did become what she would later describe as "the semblance of a girl, in which some desires and illusions had been early assassinated: shot dead" (*JAR*, 27).

She also began to shape a persona who could depend upon her own strengths. As she later remembered it: "With my mother, my earliest instinct was to protect— to take care of, to endure. This, Dr. Wall once told me, is the instinct of a little boy . . . Well, there it is. I *did* manage to become a woman" (*JAR*, 172).

But she also sought out a refuge, a sanctuary we might call it, where she would not be so emotionally vulnerable. In this world she might adopt some of the privileges of "a little boy" without seeming in any way to make herself conspicuous. This sanctuary was her own eager and developing mind. In her journal she describes: "The life of the mind, growing up inside the outer life, like a widely branched vine [like an ungrafted tree?] . . . The individual *free* being, forced to begin small, like a sturdy root, but humble, which does not make much of a target for the wind" (*JAR*, 23).

Quietly, she began to study Latin, Greek, French, the English poets, especially Swinburne and the Rossettis, and the early issues of *Poetry: A Magazine of Verse*. She wrote imitations and was designated Class Poet at the Girls' Latin School in Boston. As Frank puts it: "Her apprenticeship was steady, and by the age of eighteen she had accumulated [in Bogan's words] 'a thick pile of manuscript, in a drawer of the dining room—and had learned every essential of my trade' " (*LB*, 26).

Nevertheless, she was also keen to nourish the needs of the body, especially its sexual passions. After one year at Boston University, Bogan dropped out, married a soldier named Curt Alexander, and became pregnant. It was not a fortuitous marriage since she had little in common with Alexander outside of sex, and perhaps she married only to escape from her family situation. The marriage lasted less than three years but it did produce Mathilde (Maidie) Alexander in October 1917.

In 1956 Louise would write to Robert Phelps: "I myself came into responsibility at the birth of my daughter, when I was twenty; and I have not been able to get away from it entirely, although the death of my father, five years ago, at the great age of ninety, eased it somewhat. Responsibility forms and teaches . . ." (*WWL*,

305–6). On the other hand, Bogan was still eager for life. When she and Alexander separated, she deposited her young daughter with her parents and went directly to New York.

In fact, Bogan, like Elinor Wylie in the aftermath of leaving Horace, like Edna St. Vincent Millay set free from Vassar, was grateful to get to the city and to get a job. New York was a good place to be in 1920 for a talented young woman who wrote poetry. In the city Bogan made many friends who would stand her in good stead: Edmund Wilson, Rolfe Humphries, Edna Millay, Ruth Benedict, Margaret Mead, and Marianne Moore. She even parlayed her connections into a Guggenheim traveling fellowship to Vienna. Her first book, *Body of This Death*, was published in 1923 by Robert M. McBride and Company.

It was also about this time, after a series of unproductive affairs, that she met Raymond Holden, the one person, other than her mother, whose effect on her was so strong that, despite years of separation, she was unable entirely to set it aside. By the time she met Raymond, she had already lived through a number of distressing episodes: her brother and only sibling was killed in France in 1918; her first marriage had fallen apart and her husband had died (of natural causes) in 1920; her mother had given up her earlier erratic behavior after the death of her son, but had become instead a critical, ultra-religious lower middle-class matron who was hardly a calming, supportive influence on her daughter's life. Louise had already explored some depths by the time she met Raymond, including terrible bouts of fear and guilt during which she sought the help of a psychiatrist. Still, she married Raymond Holden in 1925 with the highest hopes. She was a courageous woman and deeply in love.

The unraveling of Bogan's marriage to Raymond Holden is dramatically brought to life in Frank's biography and I will not discuss it at length here. Suffice it to say that in Holden's defense one could argue that Bogan was obsessively jealous and prone to giving Holden bizarre tests, such as inviting a friend to spend the weekend and then mysteriously disappearing for several days to see what would happen. On Bogan's side, it seems clear that Holden was peculiarly unreliable and evasive, a man who enjoyed the romantic sugar rush of being tormented by passion without being able to sustain the genuine human sympathy and loyal support which might have helped his distressed wife gain control of herself.

When Bogan went to Europe on a Guggenheim, Holden's letters were full of defiance and self-justification in response to the poet's suggestions that he would soon find a replacement for her. Nevertheless, Bogan's paranoia turned out in the end to have had some roots in reality: Holden *did* have an affair, did have his mistress move into the apartment he was supposed to be sharing with his wife, and, after his divorce from Bogan, would marry (and divorce) this intermediary before finally (with his fourth wife) forming a lasting relationship.

In 1933 Louise Bogan and Raymond Holden were separated. In 1936 she described her own misery in her life with Holden to Rolfe Humphries: "I fought one fight—a crusade designed to make the man I loved tell the truth—for about five years, over and over again" (*WWL*, 124–25). However, by 1954 she was looking back on this period of her life in somewhat different terms when she wrote to May Sarton:

But what has never been explained thoroughly, by me to you, is the really dreadful emotional state I was trapped in for many years—a state which Raymond struggled manfully against, I will say, for a long time. In those days, my devotion came out all counter-clockwise, as it were. I was a *demon* of jealousy, for example; and a sort of *demon* of fidelity, too: "morbid fidelity," Dr. Wall came to call it. A slave-maker, really, while remaining a sort of slave. Dreadful! (*WWL*, 282)

Many of these dysfunctional mechanisms were connected to Bogan's earlier relationship with her mother and the terrible sense of betrayal and morbid jealousy she felt over her mother's extramarital liaisons and periodic abandonments.

Bogan eventually made these connections herself but not before several mental breakdowns for which she was hospitalized, one in 1931 and another in 1933. During one of her most difficult periods, she wrote the autobiographical piece published as "Journey Around My Room" in the *New Yorker* (1933), in which she connects her present living arrangements with her early experiences in the mill towns of New England. Frank comments: "The 'journey' recounted here is a descent into psychic depths, past memory and past fear, into the most primitive sources of serenity and acceptance of fate, of time, of the isolation and loneliness of individual destiny" (*LB*, 216–17). In other words, Louise Bogan's way out of her private hell was to become a woman capable of stoic detachment.

However, this mask would slip a number of times in the next thirty-five years. On a trip to Ireland in 1937 she was overcome with paranoid terrors, made utterly helpless on the boat-train to Southampton, and forced to rely on an Irish-American electrician who took care of her like a baby. Another slippage of the mask was the fact that, despite her earlier belief that there can be no new love for a woman of thirty-seven, she carried on an eight-year very private but thoroughly satisfying relationship with this same man, writing jubilantly to Theodore Roethke (a previous lover turned friend): "O, why didn't I know about the trades, years ago? I wasted a lot of time on the professions" (*LB*, 286). Bogan's electrician seems to have served some of the same functions—passion combined with independence—that the forbidden lover served for Sara Teasdale, Elinor Wylie, H. D., and others.

Yet many close to Bogan believe that, though the poet never saw Raymond Holden after 1937, she continued to love him all her life. Even after the divorce, she never changed the name Holden on her apartment doorbell.

Through her final years Louise Bogan became a woman obsessed with the memories she had accumulated in her childhood and in her young life with Raymond. Thus, the "Medusa" poem written in the early 1920s may be read in part as a terrifying prolepsis:

> This is a dead scene forever now.
> Nothing will ever stir.
> The end will never brighten it more than this,
> Nor the rain blur.
>
> The water will always fall, and will not fall,
> And the tipped bell make no sound.

The grass will always be growing for hay
Deep on the ground.

And I shall stand here like a shadow
Under the great balanced day,
My eyes on the yellow dust, that was lifting in the wind,
And does not drift away.

                                                    (BE, 4)

This is a scene whose beauty and terror has pollinated her imagination with its "yellow dust" that does not drift away. The shadow to which she refers in line eighteen suggests both the sense of her own insubstantiality in the face of this trauma and the embodiment of her desire to echo it, to become the shadow of suffering. In her poem "To My Brother" she insists that "all things endure," and "all things remain," because the mind refuses to let them go.

Though burned down to stone
Though lost from the eye,
I can tell you, and not lie,—
Save of peace alone.
                        (BE, 77)

Peace Louise Bogan was never to know in any thorough and uninterrupted form. Though her life was rich in many ways, with conversation, friendship, music, reading, writing of various kinds, travel, teaching, admiration from others, and length of years, her internal weather was often stormy. For certain periods she seems to have been driven by resentment and jealousy of others' successes. Often she was lonely, depressed.

The last decade of her life was particularly hard when it should have been a time for basking in the recognition beginning to come to her through awards, prizes, and honorary positions. The position of Poet-in-Residence she was offered in 1964 at Brandeis University brought her back to places she remembered as a child and set off another series of traumatic disturbances. In 1965 she was hospitalized again and this time received a brief series of shock treatments. After that she was dependent on Librium, cried frequently, drank too much, and retreated almost completely within herself, just as Sara Teasdale had done at the end of her life. Louise Bogan died of a coronary occlusion, *not* a suicide, but a woman for whom death, though resisted, became one way of perfecting the stoic persona.

THE CHOICE OF THE STOIC PERSONA

Why did Louise Bogan assume the mask of the stoic instead of Lowell's androgyne, Teasdale's passionate virgin, Wylie's woman warrior, H. D.'s Greek sylph, or Millay's bodily spirit? There are indications that she toyed with all of these, even associating the voice of the lyric poet with "the maenad cry" in an early Grecian moment. In "Ad Castitatem" she praised the "beautiful futility" of chastity in terms very reminiscent of Sara Teasdale. Like Amy Lowell she loved hanging around with the boys, drinking whiskey and smoking cigarettes well into the night, and she took up Lowell's androgynous role as a poet-critic. As for Elinor Wylie, Wylie and Bogan were temperamentally similar in many ways; of all the nightingale women, they were the best haters. "Step forth, then, malice, wisdom's guide, / And enmity, that may save us all" (*BE*, 70), wrote Louise Bogan.

But Millay was probably the woman to whom Bogan most often compared herself; not because they were similar in temperament but because Millay dominated so completely the female side of the poetry scene. Both women were born in Maine. Both were literary ingenues notorious for their high living in the New York of the early 1920s. In 1923 Bogan actually published a poem called "Pyrotechnics" in clear imitation of Millay's "First Fig":

> Mix prudence with my ashes;
> Write caution on my urn;
> While life foams and flashes
> Burn, bridges, burn![12]

Yet Louise Bogan was temperamentally unsuited to Millay's mask and soon dropped it. Reflecting on this time in her life in a *Partisan Review* interview, she responds to the interviewer's description of her as both "a fool and a careerist" by saying: "Yes. In minor ways. I had the desire of surpassing the self through the self. But the pattern of self-abnegation was also strong" (*JAR*, 58). What she calls her sentiments, her "sensitive, delicate, generous side" might have made her a foolish imitation of Millay but her stern, disciplined, tougher side intervened.

For whatever reason, Bogan came to stigmatize Millay as representative of everything she wanted to avoid in private and public life, especially intemperance and volubility. Bogan's reflections on Millay in 1939 suggest the way she saw herself as having chosen a different path, thus avoiding Millay's worst excesses. Wondering what a woman poet should write about as she grows older, Bogan reflects that it may be of primary importance "to withdraw more and more, as time goes on, [the woman poet's] own personality from her productions."[13] If Millay could not do this, she would never develop into a fully mature poet. She would never achieve a woman's wisdom.

The kind of woman's wisdom Bogan particularly admired was encapsulated in Louise Imogen Guiney's poem "A Talisman." Elizabeth Frank tells us that this poem, copied into Bogan's notebook in 1915, was one she continued to admire all her life. It begins:

> Take Temperance to thy breast,
> While yet is the hour of choosing,
> As arbitress exquisite
> Of all that shall thee betide.
> (*Happy Ending*, 87)

Temperance was Bogan's fortress and her guard. In "After the Persian" she claims: "I am the dweller on the temperate threshold" (*BE*, 115). As she wrote in her journal in 1933: "The calm and unperturbed front is the one weapon against everything" (*LB*, 181). But what began as a defense became in time an orientation to life. In 1939 she answered the question, do you suffer, by saying: "No: that has been expensively excised." When asked what her wishes were, she responded: "To live without apology. . . . To live my life, at last delivered from ambition, from envy, from hatred, from frightened love, to live it until the end *without the need for philosophy*" (her emphasis; *JAR*, 58). Such goals differentiated Bogan from many ambitious women of her era and made her more deeply akin to the later Sara Teasdale than to Amy Lowell, Elinor Wylie, H. D., or Edna Millay.

But was Louise Bogan unaffected by her times in her choice of the stoic persona? She wanted others to think so. To Morton Zabel she wrote: "I never was a member of a 'lost generation.' . . . I had no relations whatever with the world around me; I lived in a dream, . . . What I did and what I felt was, I assure you, *sui generis*" (*LB*, 285).

Yet the stoic persona was no simple product of an inborn temperament nourished by a New England upbringing, any more than it was a purely literary affectation adopted from Louise Imogen Guiney. The choice of the stoic persona was also culturally determined, and an acknowledgment of this allows us to see Bogan as connected to a special set of women of her era who were equally bent on avoiding the pitfalls of the past.

One such woman was Leonie Adams, whose difficult modernist poetry Bogan admired. According to Gloria Bowles, "Adams agreed with Bogan that modernist women poets had to avoid overabundant expressions of feeling; for women, form is the clue; the compression of the modern lyric helps women keep feeling in check."[14] By adhering to an "aesthetic of limitation," both women hoped especially to avoid falling into the traps of sentimentality and shoddy craftsmanship they associated with second-rate women poets of the past.

Yet the stoic persona, as I hope to show, was more than a literary mask. It was also a social maneuver typical of Bogan, Adams, and other "modern women." Mary Austin, writing in 1926, talks about the necessity for women to overcome the fear of being disliked that has so often limited our choices:

> As for not being under the necessity of being liked, which began as a defense, it has become part of my life philosophy. I see now that too many of the impositions of society upon women have come of their fear of not being liked. Under disguising names of womanliness, of tact, of religion even, this humiliating necessity, this compulsive fear goes through all our social use like mould, corrupting the bread of life.[15]

Therefore, according to Austin, women must develop a self-relying stoicism in the face of criticism.

The twenties and thirties were full of women determined *not* to give way to emotion. Lillian Hellman called her generation's modus operandi "the cool currency of the time." In *An Unfinished Woman* (a book Bogan described as "kooky but nice"), Hellman reflects upon the lack of emotionality in her first sexual experience:

"But my generation did not often deal with the idea of love—we were ashamed of the word, and scornful of the misuse that had been made of it—and I suppose that the cool currency of the time carried me past the pain of finding nastiness in what I had hoped would be a moving adventure."[16] For Hellman such detachment made the disappointments in life easier to bear.

In Katherine Anne Porter's "Flowering Judas"—which Bogan reviewed admiringly for the *New Yorker* in 1930—Laura is another young woman who has made up her mind not to let herself get carried away. In the story her willful resistance to all emotional risk is both explored and criticized by Porter. Of Laura, Porter writes: "She . . . persuades herself that her negation of all external events as they occur is a sign that she is gradually perfecting herself in the stoicism she strives to cultivate."[17]

Indeed, literary history of the 1920s and 1930s is full of women who made it their policy to cultivate stoicism. Though far from cool herself, Dorothy Parker's mordant wit is consistent with the stoic persona. Mary McCarthy, whom Bogan knew well, is another figure from this era known for her reserve and tough-mindedness.

Though Louise Bogan's case is not precisely similar to that of any of these literary women, their presence in the world Bogan inhabited suggests that the stoic was a mask available for appropriation, a mask in the sense that Erving Goffman uses the term, not in opposition to a "real self" but as the crystallization of performed character.[18]

It is important to pay attention to the positive value of the stoic persona, the fact that it helped women like Louise Bogan feel a greater degree of control over themselves and their lives. However, one must also take account of one of its sources in negation; Bogan wished to achieve a degree of detachment so as *not* to become a member of what she and Leonie Adams called the "Oh-God-the-pain-girls" school of women writers.

Like a number of women already mentioned in the nightingale tradition, Bogan had ambitions to compete with the men of her generation and only sporadically saw herself as part of a female alliance. As Elizabeth Frank says: "Crankily sympathetic with women, she was nevertheless aware, through her own mistakes and her acute observations of others, of the ways in which women seem to perpetuate their own patterns of defeat and failure, and with these she was impatient" (*LB*, 65). Her impatience sometimes verged on cattiness, as when she turned down Malcolm Cowley's offer to do a women's anthology, writing to John Hall Wheelock: "the thought of corresponding with a lot of female songbirds made me acutely ill" (*WWL*, 86).

In fact, Louise Bogan is the only woman under discussion here who actually knew a considerable amount about the nightingale tradition. In "Poetesses in the Parlor," published in the *New Yorker* in 1936, she provides a rare twentieth-century view of early nineteenth-century women poets. Though she describes them as gloomy and conventional, she finds later nineteenth-century women seething with feeling and eager to celebrate "the unfettered joys of the here-and-now."[19]

In *Achievement in American Poetry*, Bogan's historical overview published in

1951, her assessment of the contributions of nineteenth-century women is even more enthusiastic, as it is less tainted by condescension. This supports Gloria Bowles's thesis that Bogan (like Amy Lowell) became more sympathetic to the plight of women as she grew older. In the later work she writes:

> Freshness and sincerity of emotion, and economical directness of method were, it can be seen early apparent in formal poetry written by women well before the turn of the century. Women's subsequent rejection of moral passivity, economic dependence, and intellectual listlessness in favor of active interests and an involvement with the world around them—a rejection which, at crucial moments in the English suffragist movement, became exteriorized in actual physical combat—changed the direction and tone of their writing.[20]

Thus, Louise Bogan found elements to praise in women poets and was able to see the effects of political and cultural change upon the poetry women composed. Her brief anthology of American poems appended to *Achievement* contains works by Louise Imogen Guiney, Lizette Woodworth Reese, Emily Dickinson, Gertrude Stein, Sara Teasdale, Edna St. Vincent Millay, Elinor Wylie, H. D., Leonie Adams, Marianne Moore, and Elizabeth Bishop as well as some by Stephen Crane, Trumbull Stickney, Ezra Pound, Robert Frost, Edgar Lee Masters, Edwin Arlington Robinson, Carl Sandburg, T. S. Eliot, William Carlos Williams, Wallace Stevens, Vachel Lindsay, John Crowe Ransom, Allen Tate, Hart Crane, Karl Shapiro, Robert Lowell, Peter Viereck, and Richard Wilbur.

In spite of the evenhandedness of *Achievement*, however, Bogan was evidently prone to jealousy of other women writers and preferred to read and review male rather than female poets. After declaring that she wanted to smash Babette Deutsch's face for an unfavorable review of *Body of This Death*, Bogan declared sarcastically: "How women poets love one another!" (*LB*, 370). When she objected to the work of women writers, it was frequently because the work was childish, girlish, adolescent, theatrical, or illogical, according to Elizabeth Frank (*WB*, 368). So the stoic persona was also helpful because she felt it allowed her to put distance between herself and traditions of female writing she abhorred or tendencies toward female emotionality she feared.

However, as Bowles has observed, this placed Louise Bogan in a double bind because she also admired women writers for their ability to capture subtlety and intensity of feeling. Reviewing the current poetry scene in 1947, Bogan saw:

> The fear of some regression into typical romantic attitudes is, at present, operating from feminine talent; and this is not a wholly healthy impulse, for it negates too strongly a living and valuable side of woman's character. In women, more than in men, the intensity of their emotions is the key to the treasures of their spirit. (*PA*, 428)

This warning might have been a red flag Bogan was setting up for herself as she assessed the problems implicit in her own achievement of a calm and wise detachment.

If "a woman writes poetry with her ovaries" (*LB*, 328), as Bogan once claimed, later life will pose a particularly difficult problem for the poet who happens to be a woman. After the age of thirty-five Bogan felt the necessity to remake herself into a much less vulnerable creature. Yet the stoic, it turned out, had limited creative resources. Bogan felt the limitation, as we can see from her review of Dylan Thomas's wife Caitlin's *Leftover Life to Kill* from 1957, where she makes the following revealing comments, comments that resonate ominously against Bogan's own typical preferences:

> In maturity, it is necessary, mankind has discovered, to suppress outbursts of strong emotion—joy, rage, grief—that may, in their irrationality, disturb the general peace. . . . Yet it is true, and always has been, that innocence of heart and violence of feeling are necessary in any kind of superior achievement; the arts cannot exist without them. (*PA*, 388)

In what follows I will explore the way Louise Bogan's poetry struggles to achieve perspective on violence of feeling through a retreat to the mind. I will also consider the relevance of Bogan's gender to the way she coped with psychic crisis and artistic sterility and to the particular importance of "mind" to her work. Finally, I will attempt to place Louise Bogan's achievement in the context of the nightingale tradition, suggesting both the strengths and the weaknesses of a persona constructed in some ways to elude the problems of that tradition's influence.

THE MIND AND THE WOMAN POET

Louise Bogan was not a prolific poet. The bulk of her work was published in her first three volumes: *Body of This Death* (1923), *Dark Summer* (1929), and *The Sleeping Fury* (1937). After that she revised her opus and added a few poems here and there in *Poems and New Poems* (1941), *Collected Poems 1923–1953*, and *The Blue Estuaries* (1969), but basically her style and her literary persona were fully formed and almost fully expressed by 1940. She is a poet whose voice belongs definitively to the 1920s and 1930s.

During her lifetime Bogan received a good deal of praise. In 1923 her portrait appeared in *Vanity Fair* together with those of Elinor Wylie, Amy Lowell, Genevieve Taggard, Aline Kilmer, Edna St. Vincent Millay, Sara Teasdale, and Lizette Woodworth Reese under the heading: "Distinguished American Women Poets Who Have Made Lyric Verse Written by Women in America More Interesting Than That of the Men" (*LB*, 54). At twenty-six she was a comparatively young woman but her arrival on the scene coincided with the full flowering of the modern nightingale tradition.

During the next twenty years she would receive the support and admiration of

Harriet Monroe, John Hall Wheelock, Morton Dauwen Zabel, Theodore Roethke, Allen Tate, Robert Frost, Ivor Winters, Kenneth Rexroth, Malcolm Cowley, Hayden Carruth, Maxine Kumin, and Edmund Wilson, among others. Marianne Moore audited Bogan's class at the YMHA in 1956; she admired Bogan's "laboratory detachment." One of Bogan's most enthusiastic supporters was W. H. Auden, who in 1941 thought her among the very few important American poets, classing her with T. S. Eliot and Marianne Moore. In his memorial Auden summed up what he saw as her achievement by saying: "What, aside from their technical excellence, is most impressive about her poems is the unflinching courage with which she faced her problems, her determination never to surrender to self-pity" (LB, 416–17). In death she achieved her apotheosis as a stoic.

Yet she has had a deeper influence on contemporary women poets than the stoic persona might give us reason to expect. Her lyric mode made a strong impression on Maxine Kumin, Martha Collins, Alicia Ostriker, May Sarton, and, surprisingly, Robin Morgan.[21] Furthermore, Bogan is now more frequently represented than she used to be in anthologies of American literature, where she appears alongside Wylie, Millay, and H. D.[22]

For many of us, Louise Bogan's poetry has a talismanic quality; the hard polished lines, written with such patience, have become precious. Though Bogan probably found more readers for her intelligent *New Yorker* reviews than she did for her poetry, her intellectual character is observable in both media. All in all, one must conclude that the joys available "henceforth from the mind" were by no means negligible, but what exactly were these joys?

Bogan places a tribute to the power of the mind at the end of her first book, *Body of This Death*:

> My mouth, perhaps, may learn one thing too well,
> My body hear no echo save its own,
> Yet will the desperate mind, maddened and proud,
> Seek out the storm, escape the bitter spell
> That we obey, strain to the wind, be thrown
> Straight to its freedom in the thunderous cloud.
>
> (BE, 26)

Though flawed, this sonnet is still worth pausing over for the clues it provides to Bogan's 1920s' vision of mental experience.

One should notice, for instance, that the personal is associated not with the mind but with the body: *my* mouth, *my* body become "we." Over and against these is "*the* mind," a courageous impersonal spirit which, unlike the former, will claim its freedom. However, this mind is not stoic. In its "maddened and proud" recoil from entrapment, it recalls Edna St. Vincent Millay's Bluebeard sonnet and Elinor Wylie's "Demon Lovers," where the proud woman eludes her lovers while seeming to serve them physically. Wylie notes ironically: "Like quicksilver, her absent mind / Evades them both, and is not missed" (CP, 74).

There are hints of stoicism in Bogan's first book, hints that the body is vulnerable and emotional life treacherous. Generally, however, the poet seems eager to insist upon her own intensity. Though in "Knowledge" her persona hopes to "Lie here and learn / How, over their ground, / Trees make a long shadow / And a light sound" (BE, 9), and in "My Voice Not Being Proud," she looks forward to a time when she'll be "separate, eased and cured" (BE, 13), her most characteristic advice is not retrenchment but full address. The alchemist's flesh is "still / Passionate beyond the will." In "Memory" images from the past must not be harbored in secret but instead laid out in the open like stones "That any spade may strike" (BE, 18). In "Sub Contra" the speaker insists:

> Let there sound from music's root
> One note rage can understand,
> A fine noise of riven things.
> Build there some thick chord of wonder;
> Then, for every passion's sake,
> Beat upon it till it break.
>
> (BE, 5)

How different this is from the enormous appeal accorded silence in the later books. The mind in *Body of This Death* is an ephemeral refuge precisely because it is seen here as an "avid substance" (BE, 15), less personal but no less appetitive than the body. There is no implication in St. Paul's question—"Who shall deliver me from the body of this death?"—that the mind unaided by God offers any effective counterforce to desire, dissolution, and death. Bogan's title is, in fact, a tribute to the power of carnal love though it preserves through Paul a dark sense of suspicion about the reliability of desire.

> The woman who has grown old
> And knows desire must die,
> Yet turns to love again,
> Hears the crows' cry.
>
> (BE, 17)

In contrast, *Dark Summer* wears the colors of a different spirit. Here the main theme may be stated as the necessity to adjust to a reality that flies in the face of emotional needs. Though Bogan would take up madness as a theme elsewhere (in "Evening in the Sanitarium," for instance), *Dark Summer* is Bogan's maddest book and contains some of her most obscure poems, like "Division," "Feuer-Nacht," and "The Mark." It is hard at first to make sense of the visual imagery of light and shadow, fire and storm, which seems to be intended to carry so much psychological weight but which the poet refuses to gloss or even to assist the reader with understanding.[23]

It is now clear that Bogan wrote these poems in the midst of her marital problems with Raymond Holden. *Dark Summer* also contained a long poem about a young wife's obsession with betrayal, called "The Flume," later excised by Bogan from the final collection she authorized in *Blue Estuaries*.

From some points of view *Dark Summer* is a transitional book. It lays all the groundwork for the retreat to the mind without fully advocating that retreat. A clue to its hesitation in this regard may be found in "I Saw Eternity," which seems to me not a poem *about* insanity, like "Evening in the Sanitarium," but a poem *of* insanity.

> O beautiful Forever!
> O grandiose Everlasting!
> Now, now, now,
> I break you into pieces,
> I feed you to the ground.
>
> O brilliant, O languishing
> Cycle of weeping light!
> The mice and birds will eat you,
> And you will spoil their stomachs
> As you have spoiled my mind.
>
> Here, mice, rats,
> Porcupines and toads,
> Moles, shrews, squirrels,
> Weasels, turtles, lizards,—
> Here's bright Everlasting!
> Here's a crumb of Forever!
> Here's a crumb of Forever!
>
> 						(BE, 50)

Bogan herself was very proud of this poem and one can see why. But it is also a very disturbing lyric.

In Henry Vaughan's poem "The World," which begins "I saw eternity the other night," and which—as an admirer of the metaphysical poets—Bogan surely knew, the vision of eternity is "Like a great ring of pure and endless light, / All calm as it was bright." Against the serenity of the spiritual world, Vaughan juxtaposes the "madness" of the lover, the miser, the politician. In Bogan's poem, however, there is no perfection in eternity. Instead it is as though the speaker has seen the vision of the universe's absurdity soon to become a staple of Existentialist literature. Her "cycle of weeping light" is more akin to Wylie's "sudden excess of light" in "O Virtuous Light," where "A private madness has prevailed / Over the pure and valiant mind" (CP, 199). "I Saw Eternity" is more deeply akin to the nihilistic vision Bogan described to Ruth Limmer in 1965 than it is to Vaughan's poem. In the letter to Limmer, Bogan says: "One evening with a gibbous moon hanging over the city (such *visions* we have!) like a piece of red cantaloupe, and automobiles showing red danger signals, . . . I thought I had reached the edge of eternity, and *wept* and *wept*" (WWL, 363). This is the mood of "I Saw Eternity" and the reason why the mind in this book provides no reliable refuge. Though the First Voice in

"Summer Wish" tantalizes with the offer of "The mind for refuge, the grain of reason, the will" (*BE*, 57), to the First Voice's optimism the Second Voice responds with a powerful countervision: "See now / Open above the field, stilled in wing-stiffened flight, / The stretched hawk fly" (59). This "refuge" is open to depredations from above and below.

When I say that the groundwork for a retreat into the mind is laid in *Dark Summer*, I mean that over and over again the poems suggest that the world of the senses, of *time*, will ultimately betray our trust. Thus, one might ask, what can one do except retreat into an interior world not dependent for its satisfactions on the body, on love, on others. A representative and beautiful sonnet from this period is "Simple Autumnal":

> The measured blood beats out the year's delay.
> The tearless eyes and heart, forbidden grief,
> Watch the burned, restless, but abiding leaf,
> The brighter branches arming the bright day.
>
> The cone, the curving fruit should fall away,
> The vine stem crumble, ripe grain know its sheaf.
> Bonded to time, fires should have done, be brief,
> But, serfs to sleep, they glitter and they stay.
>
> Because not last nor first, grief in its prime
> Wakes in the day, and hears of life's intent.
> Sorrow would break the seal stamped over time
> And set the baskets where the bough is bent.
>
> Full season's come, yet filled trees keep the sky
> And never scent the ground where they must lie.
>
> (*BE*, 40)

This poem is about the *need* to break down. In Bogan's images of the autumn leaves which refuse to fall, she picks up the fire imagery also used in "Feuer-Nacht," where the flame *has* achieved its harvest: "Sworn to lick at a little, / It has burned all" (36). Here, however, the torment is that the "tearless eyes and heart" are "forbidden grief." Suffering lingers. Still, it is "life's intent" that we learn to bear our suffering.

The stoic, therefore, enters as one participant in a conversation underlying a number of poems in this volume: "Winter Swan," "Late," "Didactic Piece," "Summer Wish," and "Come, Break With Time." Whereas "Memory" in Bogan's first book advocated an openness toward pain, setting out the "rich stuff" for others to handle, "If We Take All Gold" in *Dark Summer* advocates storing "sorrow's gold" in the "shelved earth's crevice": "If it be hid away / Lost under dark heaped ground, / Then shall we have peace" (*BE*, 30). This acceptance of repression is one of the maneuvers necessary to the stoic.

Yet there is bitterness in the need for such maneuvers, as "Come, Break With Time" conveys.

> Come, break with time,
> You who were lorded
> By a clock's chime
> So ill afforded.
> If time is allayed
> Be not afraid.
>
> *I shall break, if I will.*
> Break, since you must.
> Time has its fill,
> Sated with dust.
> Long the clock's hand
> Burned like a brand.
>
> Take the rocks' speed
> And earth's heavy measure.
> Let buried seed
> Drain out time's pleasure,
> Take time's decrees.
> Come, cruel ease.
>
>   (51)

In Louise Bogan's struggle with time in this book, she reenacts H. D.'s early temporal crisis, which H. D. then tried to resolve through the poppy dream. However, for Bogan there is no poppy dream possible. What she has instead is her intellect. Significantly, Bogan would soon apply for a Guggenheim travel fellowship in order to distract herself from pain. In her letter to Morton Zabel, whom she was asking for a letter of recommendation, she urged: "Bear, bear on the mind, on the capacity of the brain, on the long scholar's head, on the know-without-having-learned intuition, on the bred-in-the-bone aptitude, . . . on the made-a-life-for-herself-through-choice-in-spite-of-evil-chance stamina" (*LB*, 155).

Like the stamina of this letter, "Come, Break With Time" is a poem which advocates not escape but acceptance and endurance. It suggests a much tougher attitude toward experience than Wordsworth's "A slumber did my spirit seal," which Bogan plays upon in her last stanza. Yet the last line betrays the fact that even the first speaker does not really believe the stoic attitude superior to the world of guilt and sorrow inhabited by its alter ego. Though it advocates detachment, this is a bitter poem not unlike "Exhortation" and "Kept" in *The Sleeping Fury*.

Eight years intervened between the publication of *Dark Summer* and *The Sleeping Fury*. These were years of great pain for the poet but they were also productive years during which she learned German and read Heine with Edmund Wilson. She was building up her intellectual world as her emotional and personal life crumbled. In her journal she recorded:

> Edmund spoke of Emerson's lack of real intellectual power. The essays are flashes, held together by no structure of "fundamental brainwork." And the thought struck me that I should take notes happily all my life, not even troubling to put them

into form. I am a woman, and "fundamental brainwork," the building up of logical structures, the abstractions, the condensations, the comparisons, the rea-sonings, *are not expected of me*. But it is only when I am making at least an imitation of such a structure that I am really happy. It is only when the notes fall into form, when the sentences make *at least the sound of styles*, that my interest really holds. (her emphasis; LB, 201)

It is worth noticing that Bogan vacillates here between identifying with Emerson's resistance to "fundamental brainwork"—a phenomenon she also constructs as fem-inine—and insisting on her own capacity and need for tensile structures, for the abstractions, condensations, and reasonings she associates with men. Thus, she imagines herself at first taking notes "happily all my life," only to remember that as a woman such dilettantism is precisely what is expected of her. Women are not expected to produce logical structures, abstractions, condensations. Yet suddenly Bogan recognizes that "it is only when I am making at least an imitation of such a structure that I am really happy." Thus, in order to be "really happy," she must undertake that fundamental brainwork previously delegated to men.

Before we criticize Bogan for making the activities of the intellect masculine, we should remember that Bogan's life as a female intellectual was a product of the cultural changes belonging to the early twentieth century. Only the privileged few (and they were very few) could pursue an intellectual course so unswervingly in earlier eras, only women like Madame de Staël and Margaret Fuller. In the first half of the twentieth century, such women became commonplace: Mary Austin, Anna Julia Cooper, Clelia Mosher, Elizabeth Hardwick, Mary McCarthy, Margaret Mead, Hannah Arendt, to name but a few. In the twentieth century, the female intellectual became a recognizable feature of a progressive urban environment.

In Louise Bogan's case, her intellectual development was fostered to a great degree by her friendship with Edmund Wilson, who deserves considerable credit for the respect he showed intellectual women, not only Bogan but Millay, Wylie, and Mary McCarthy, among others. Though there were frictions at times, Bogan's friendship with Wilson lasted through four decades. In his letters to her, Wilson gives the impression that he regards Bogan as fully equal to consider the intellectual matters he takes most seriously. At one point in their correspondence, he looks forward to getting back from his trip to Russia in order to talk it all over with her, whom he calls, perhaps a bit imperiously, "my best audience." Their conversations covered a variety of topics including architecture, painting, music, film, Marxism, history, the nature of the artist, America, Ireland, Russia, Upstate New York, New England, poverty, sex, original sin, magic, and bees.

Wilson was sensitive but also sensible in his responses to Bogan's neurotic breakdowns, urging her to get on with her work, to use her intellectual and artistic talents to regain control of herself. "The only thing we can really make is our work," Wilson advised. "And deliberate work of the mind, imagination, and hand, done, as Nietzsche said, 'notwithstanding,' in the long run remakes the world."[24] Bogan was not slow to see the value of this advice, and during the 1930s and 1940s she read voraciously and worked hard. Wilson continued to respect her mind.

When he took over as book reviewer from Clifton Fadiman at the *New Yorker* in 1943, he wrote to Harold Ross:

> Louise Bogan, of course, does all the poetry, and is one of the best people writing on the subject. I believe that in her case there have been one or two conflicts of interest between Fadiman and her. That will not happen with me, because she is an old friend of mine, and I should be glad to have her write not only about poetry but about books of criticism of poetry and biographies of poets, if she wants to.[25]

The Sleeping Fury, which is dedicated to Edmund Wilson, is Bogan's most impressive book. Less tormented than *Dark Summer*, it exposes her growing sense that the universe is not absurd after all but orderly and meaningful: "Motion beneath us, fixity above," (*BE*, 84) she says in "Putting to Sea." It is also a volume in which her several conceptions of mind—as psyche, as intellect, as intuition, as vision—come together.

One might well begin by considering the portrayal of the mind as psyche. For Bogan, like many moderns, psychology seemed to have replaced religion by offering a human mode (in "Putting to Sea" she calls it significantly The Way) of pursuing mystery and essence. However, like Freud's psychic economy with its superego, ego, and id reminding one of the Father, Son, and Holy Ghost, Bogan's language of the psyche is mystical. She never fully exorcised her early Catholic upbringing.

Bogan calls the peace she seeks "serenity" but her idea of it has real affinities to mystical traditions of desirelessness, as she herself knows. In one letter she writes: "Jung states that such serenity is always a miracle, and I think the saints said that, too. Though there were certain ways, and a certain road that may bring it about, when it comes, it is always a miracle. I am so glad that the therapists of my maturity and the saints of my childhood agree on one score" (*LB*, 238).

Stoicism and serenity are different, of course—one emphasizing resistance and the other acceptance. But for Bogan both served the function of quieting her torments and detaching her from the world in which love brought only violence of feeling and carnal struggle.

"The Sleeping Fury" itself is a triumphant poem which demonstrates the positive side of Bogan's retreat to the mind. In this poem the speaker is able to face her emotional guilt (imaged here as Megaera, the Fury bent on punishing sexual crimes), because she has retreated from the fray. She is alone, contemplating a symbol, a piece of art. Elizabeth Frank tells us that the sleeping fury is the Erinni Addormentata that Bogan saw in the Museo delle Terme in Rome. But the experience described in the poem is not part of historical time. It is a moment of pleroma occurring in the mind where she contemplates the image.

The speaker in "The Sleeping Fury" remembers the terrible emotional struggles of her past, but these are now in abeyance.

> Your hair fallen on your cheek, no longer in the semblance of serpents,
> Lifted in the gale; your mouth, that shrieked so, silent.

> You, my scourge, my sister, lie asleep, like a child,
> Who, after rage, for an hour quiet, sleeps out its tears.

How has this change come about? According to this poem, two qualities are necessary to quiet the fury: courage and insight, efforts of heart, on the one hand, and mind on the other.

> You who know what we love, but drive us to know it;
> You with your whips and shrieks, bearer of truth and of solitude;
> You who give, unlike men, to expiation your mercy.
>
> Dropping the scourge when at last the scourged advances to meet it,
> You, when the hunted turns, no longer remain the hunter
> But stand silent and wait, at last returning his gaze.

It is interesting that the process of achieving this mental attitude transforms the hunted from a female spirit, sister and double of the fury, to a male one: "at last returning *his* gaze."

The realm of the mind would always be ambiguously gendered for Bogan. The intellect she tended to make masculine, though for the purely abstract world of intellectual categories she had little patience, speaking contemptuously, for instance, of Kenneth Burke as "one of those providential characters put into the world to show how the human mind should not be used" (*WWL*, 99). Other capacities of mind, however, intuitive and visionary capacities, she often rendered female. She appreciated Dorothy Richardson's belief that woman "should claim her birthright as a being whose knowledge of, and intuition concerning, reality are profound" (*JAR*, 146).

Her own preference was for the compassionate, visionary, detached, and ironic minds of Rilke and Yeats at their most serene. Achieving this distance from emotional life, however, meant renouncing many of the joys of womanhood for Bogan. The fury is "bearer of truth" but also "of solitude."

"The Sleeping Fury" is a poem about learning to face, and then to distance oneself from, the sources of mental torment that provide the subject matter for art. Its conclusion is a benediction but also a farewell.

> Beautiful now as a child whose hair, wet with rage and tears
> Clings to its face. And now I may look upon you,
> Having once met your eyes. You lie in sleep and forget me.
> Alone and strong in my peace, I look upon you in yours.
>
> (78–79)

One cannot help feeling the sense of loss implicit in "You lie in sleep and forget me." But though the speaker is alone, she also feels herself to be *strong* in her peace, stoic and serene.

After *The Sleeping Fury* (1937) Bogan never again wrote enough to publish a whole book of new verse. Yet she did write some very beautiful and powerful poems in the last years, including "To Be Sung on the Water," "After the Persian," and "Song for the Last Act." Representative of Bogan's lighter style, "Several Voices Out of a Cloud" is memorable for its poet-critic polemics saluting the true artist and denouncing tame imitators.

> Come, drunks and drug-takers; come, perverts unnerved!
> Receive the laurel, given, though late, on merit; to whom and wherever deserved.
>
> Parochial punks, trimmers, nice people, joiners true-blue
> Get the hell out of the way of the laurel. It is deathless
>   And it isn't for you.
>
>   (BE, 93)

As a poem about the costs and benefits of Bogan's stoicism, her retreat to the mind, "The Musician" (published first in *Poems and New Poems*, 1941) provides as good an example as any.

> Where have these hands been,
> By what delayed,
> That so long stayed
> Apart from the thin
>
> Strings which they now grace
> With their lonely skill?
> Music and their cool will
> At last interlace.
>
> Now with great ease, and slow,
> The thumb, the finger, the strong
> Delicate hand plucks the long
> String it was born to know.
>
> And under the palm the string
> Sings as it wished to sing.
>   (BE, 106)

This poem delights in the triumph of art over life; and yet, and yet. . . . To the question "where have these hands been?" we must assume the answer is out in the world of feeling, in the world of love and loss anatomized in "Spirit's Song":

> But you, fierce delicate tender touch,
> Betrayed and hurt me overmuch,
>
> For whom I lagged with what a crew
> O far too long and poisoned through!
>   (BE, 86)

Now these hands have found a different world where "Music and their cool will / At last interlace."

The third stanza always evokes for me the sound of deep stringed instruments which, as in Vaughan Williams's "Fantasia On a Theme from Thomas Tallis," at last express something we have been waiting to hear, a music which suddenly surges up from the heart after a stretch of anti-rhythm in the earlier sections. But this music is both beautiful and heartbreaking. One wants to ask of this delicate hand, so in tune with the string "it was born to know," is there no adaptation beyond one to a "lonely skill"? No resolution but through retrenchment?

Though the last two stanzas seem more than a little erotic, the eroticism is almost onanistic. It suggests that the best that can be accomplished for this musician is sublimation. Here the retreat to the mind, to the world of artistic sublimation, provides an alternative reality we may justly call both rich and thin, reminding one of Sara Teasdale's "Effigy of a Nun": "Is she amused at dreams she has found?" Like Teasdale, Bogan seems to answer, yes and no.

Looked at as a whole, how does Louise Bogan's work suggest the danger and the value of a retreat to the mind for American women poets in the nightingale tradition? Like H. D.'s early imagist poems, which were also produced under pressure, the Bogan lyric at its best is both brilliant and subtle. More than one critic has seen the relevance of the third section of "After the Persian" to Bogan's own aesthetic product:

> All has been translated into treasure:
> Weightless as amber,
> Translucent as the currant on the branch,
> Dark as the rose's thorn.
>
> (BE, 116)

The strengths of this kind of poetry are refinement, resonance, and durability. It sings. It lasts.

That Louise Bogan was also capable of a high level of intellectual badinage is evident not only in her letters but also in a number of poems like "Hypocrite Swift" and "Animal, Vegetable, and Mineral." Her stoic sensibility often nourished itself on a pungent irony that skewers its victims.

There is no doubt, however, that Louise Bogan (like Elinor Wylie) understood herself to be a minor poet, whose exclusions, though necessary for psychic balance and resilience, narrowed the range of her potential. Ultimately Bogan's need to keep herself under tight rein stifled her creative spirit. H. D. and Elinor Wylie, who kept writing up to the last, seem to have had more fertile ways of dealing with psychic chaos.

In assessing the hazards for women poets of a retreat into the mind, and thus a refusal of emotional risk or political engagement, it is important to keep before one the example of Emily Dickinson. Though Dickinson shares some biographical similarities with Bogan and Teasdale in their tendencies toward isolation, Dickinson—whose retreat was more complete and long-lasting—was able to produce a much larger and more wide-ranging collection of poems. A retreat to the mind does not always stifle creativity.

Yet this brings me to my last point about Bogan's limitations. When comparing Louise Bogan to writers like Emily Dickinson, Amy Lowell, H. D., and Marianne Moore, we also need to remember that Bogan wrote criticism in order to support herself financially, that this writing demanded an entirely different kind of orientation to language, that it was often exhausting and sometimes debilitating. If Bogan had been financially independent like Dickinson, Lowell, H. D., and Moore, she might have produced far more poems in far fewer years. She might have.

All we can say with certainty is that Louise Bogan succeeded in creating some superb lyrics. She never prostituted her talent and what she has left us has a granitic edge. If her opus is small, it is also durable. Using Millay's words, we might describe Louise Bogan's poetry in the language of a New England landscape. Clean cliff going down as deep as clear water can reach.

THE SOUND OF NIGHTINGALES

Looking back, we can see that the twentieth-century nightingale poets were deeply imbued with the ambivalent spirit of their nineteenth-century sisters. Their poems often pay tribute, consciously or unconsciously, to the traditions of women's poetry they inherited willy-nilly from that obscured and neglected past.

In spite of similarities, however, there is one tone in their collective voice which characterizes them as modern, and thus of Dorothy Parker's generation rather than Lydia Sigourney's: that tone is irony. For the most part, these women were sharp-witted and sharp-tongued, ready to laugh at themselves as well as others. As Elinor Wylie wrote, "None has quite escaped my smile."

How is their wry candor exemplified in their poems? Sometimes it comes through quite plainly in the sardonic poems each of these women writes: Lowell's "Ronde du Diable," Teasdale's "In the End," Wylie's first "Subversive Sonnet," H. D.'s "A Dead Priestess Speaks," Millay's "Black Hair You'd Say She Had," Bogan's "At a Party," for instance. Each of these poems speaks unsentimentally both about the poet's "self" and about the frustrations of having to cope with problematic "others."

But also characteristic of these women, and deeply embedded in the nightingale tradition, is a certain kind of poem which defies the "oh-God-the-pain-girls" school of poetry they all trained for but in the end disdained. It is a poem of forbearance and fortitude. In Sara Teasdale we hear its cadences in "In a Darkening Garden":

> Gather together, against the coming of night,
>   All that we played with here,
> Toys and fruits, the quill from the sea-bird's flight,
>   The small flute, hollow and clear;
> The apple that was not eaten, the grapes untasted—
>   Let them be put away.
> They served for us, I would not have them wasted,
>   They lasted out our day.
>
> (CP, 209)

Louise Bogan surely remembered the Teasdale poem when she wrote "After the Persian" (V):

Goodbye, goodbye!
There was so much to love, I could not love it all;
I could not love it enough.

Some things I overlooked, and some I could not find.
Let the crystal clasp them
When you drink your wine, in autumn.

(BE, 117)

Though William Butler Yeats was supremely important to many of these women, this is not quite Yeats's Irish airman balancing life against death.[1] Both Teasdale's and Bogan's poems suggest an urge to tidy up which is missing from Yeats's. But like Yeats in his last poems, these women feel a need both to salute the blessings of life and to withdraw the ego from them. H. D.'s long poem "Winter Love," Wylie's "Farewell, Sweet Dust," Lowell's "The Anniversary," and Millay's "Ragged Island" provide other examples.

Looking back on the nightingale tradition, on its bragging, spiteful, mournful, lofty moods, its masks outrageous and austere, I am struck less by the deviousness of its strategies than by the courage of its commitments. If these poets were not always consistent on issues of gender, in their poems they "actively structured," as Cora Kaplan says, "the meaning of sexual difference."[2] This meant that they identified areas of concern to women as a group and often worked through several positions regarding those issues during their lifetimes. Their poems structured the way their many women readers came to see their own experiences, and now, in our turn, they may help us to think more clearly about the way cultural constructions of femininity affected certain kinds of women between 1910 and 1940.

Amy Lowell's struggle to find a voice both "powerful and womanly" alienated her until late in her life from the subjects which in What's O'Clock and Ballads for Sale she handles so well, the traditional female subjects of love and longing. Her choice of an androgynous persona seemed a solution to Lowell, as it did to other women in the early years of the twentieth century. Yet this choice was made at a cost which we are now better able to count.

Sara Teasdale's work provides us with the first extended example of a woman in search of autonomy, turning against her own early idealization of love in order to chart a lonely and ultimately self-destructive course. Teasdale's struggle looks forward to Sylvia Plath's, though comparing the two poets, one is struck by both similarities and differences in the cultural patterns in play. For example, Plath felt the need to split up her passionate and virginal personae, while it was important to Teasdale to keep them together.

Elinor Wylie's work makes those similarities and differences even more apparent. Her marriage of rage to abjection, also reminiscent of Plath, is enacted in conventions she adapted from both Romantic and Renaissance sources, distancing her poems from Plath's and from our own time. Nevertheless, the woman warrior persona she adopted still justifies renewed attention in the late twentieth century, as feminist scholars search for historical examples of resistance and subversion.

The heroine of the modern nightingale tradition is, from most perspectives,

H. D. Like Amy Lowell, however, H. D. only belongs here if we treat the boundaries of the tradition flexibly. Her very early poems attempt to find a way around the gender minefield without giving voice to the nightingale's sense of frustration. Furthermore, her epic poems are too long to fit the nightingale mode and postdate the decline of the tradition's dominance, which I roughly identify as coinciding with the end of the Second World War, and the publication of works like Elizabeth Bishop's *North & South* (1946). Finally, one can begin to feel that H. D. is too much of a modernist to be a nightingale.

However, the poems written between 1915 and 1935 make a much better fit. Furthermore, a close examination of the development of H. D.'s Greek persona reveals her engagement with many of the issues of female positionality in patriarchal culture that preoccupy these women poets. Within her modernism, H. D. did rework the material of her emotional life in her poems and her cold, crystal, shell, sanctuary images are often strikingly consistent with those of other nightingales.

In addition, her poetry demonstrates, perhaps more clearly than the others', the impact of a strong father-presence on a developing woman poet. Mapping H. D.'s relationship to various incarnations of Father Time provides support for Cora Kaplan's contention that "strong-minded daughters of dominating men will inevitably find them a site of 'all those patriarchal ideas' with which our culture is saturated, will often cut their political teeth in opposing their sanctions however mild, will, almost certainly imagine a gentler, more loving father."[3]

Literature helps us to see the complications of such relationships because it encodes both social and psychological reality while at the same time exploring worlds of material and imaginative possibility. H. D.'s half-century of literary production provides evidence of the difficulties as well as the opportunities present "when," as Barbara Clarke Mossberg has framed it, "a writer is a daughter."[4]

A fatherless daughter, or a woman poet who grows up in a household entirely made up of strong women, will not necessarily avoid the dangers of patriarchal influence on identity formation, as the work of Edna St. Vincent Millay illustrates. The culture does the work of patriarchal ideology with perhaps more devastating invisibility. In consumer culture both the female poet and her poems become commodities. That liberation requires more than fearless sensuality is an unhappy fact Millay's body language helps us to comprehend in greater detail.

Yet the strategy employed repeatedly by the nightingale poets, the retreat to the mind, is also problematic, since there are no really effective sanctuaries. The lofty voice of Louise Bogan's stoic persona carries with it its own echoes of isolation and loneliness. Ultimately the stoic's range is limited, her weapons directed as much at herself as at others.

Avoiding the dangers of too complete a retreat to the mind, William Butler Yeats balanced his poems of lofty imperturbability with bawdy complaints. Why couldn't Louise Bogan do likewise? Was it only the times in which she lived that circumscribed her talent? Or was there something peculiarly inadequate about her? How did her gender influence her response to her emotional and literary crises?

Perhaps these questions will never be fully answered. However, only through a critical practice that takes seriously the intersection of culture with psyche, of history and gender with creativity, can we start to fill in the gaps in this picture. For those interested in how conceptions of gender have affected the type and degree of productivity of women poets, there is still much work to be done.

Can we actually say that the battles fought and suffered by American women poets in the modern period have now been won? Have we surpassed the need to imagine ourselves as Other to the dominant discourse? Do we genuinely live in a postfeminist era, (as most of my students seem to believe), in which the anger, the pain, and the self-assertions of even my postwar generation seem a bit passé? I sincerely doubt it.

Yet it is true that women are writing poems today in strong, unapologetic voices, many of which convey a belief in the empowered self few women could have mustered before 1940. The very critical edge of these women suggests a capacity to address their audiences from the vantage point of power, of a reasonably adequate sense of selfhood. One's poetic persona is always a mask but women today can assume a wider variety of masks, not simply models outrageous or austere.

And where in this brave new world do we hear the sound of nightingales? Have those tones of melancholy stringency disappeared entirely from our poetry? Without attempting anything like a complete survey of contemporary poets, I will in what remains of this chapter tease out a few examples of nightingale echoes. These echoes simply make us aware that, though nothing like an intact tradition is still in force, some women poets remember the nightingales and some poems in the old vein are being written today.

One recently published volume which immediately invites discussion in this context is Carolyn Kizer's *Mermaids in the Basement: Poems for Women* (1984).[5] This volume brings together poems from earlier books (of special interest are those from *Knock Upon Silence* [1965]) with later work done in the seventies and eighties. The book is divided into sections called Mothers and Daughters; Female Friends; Pro Femina; Chinese Love; Myth: Visions and Revisions; A Month in Summer; and Where I've Been All My Life. The convergence of these topics with nightingale themes is obvious.

Furthermore, *Mermaids in the Basement* contains recognizable echoes of the nightingale poets. "Afterthoughts of Donna Elvira," for instance, is written in four-line stanzas, using a varying trimeter form with an emphasis on rhyme unusual if not entirely absent from contemporary poetry. Its formal aspects as well as its diction suggest the work of Louise Bogan.

The poem begins:

> You, after all, were good.
> Now it is late, you are kind.
> Never too late, to my mind.
> The mind catches up with the blood.

In this poem Donna Elvira emerges as a wise woman figure somewhat akin to Bogan's late persona as it manifested itself in her relations with May Sarton. Elvira is a woman unwilling to enter into an intense one-on-one involvement but she is nevertheless kind in a detached sort of way. The poem begins its last stanza: "Now that I see, I see / What you have known within" (100). Could Kizer have been unaware of the echo of Bogan's "Song for the Last Act," the last line of which is "Now that I have your heart by heart, I see"?

Kizer's "Myth: Visions and Revisions" immediately calls to mind H. D.'s revisionist work with myth. "A Month in Summer," which anatomizes in thirty-day-journal form the progress and ending of a love affair, reminds one of Edna St. Vincent Millay's similar experiment in *Fatal Interview* and her use of the journal motif in *Mine the Harvest*. Kizer has always worked with the haiku form. Here the haiku about love and loss offer the possibility of interesting comparisons with Amy Lowell's "Twenty-Four Hokku on a Modern Theme." I also find fascinating the Wylie-esque rage and abjection in "Bitch" and "Threatening Letter."

Kizer was quick to admit her relation to and disgust with the nightingale poets as early as "Pro Femina," published in 1965. The poem is too long to quote entire but it refers in passing to Elinor Wylie, Sara Teasdale, Edna Millay, and Amy Lowell. Here is the first stanza of section three:

> I will speak about women of letters, for I'm in the racket.
> Our biggest successes to date? Old maids to a woman.
> And our saddest conspicuous failures? The married spinsters
> On loan to the husbands they treated like surrogate fathers.
> Think of that crew of self-pitiers, not-very-distant,
> Who carried the torch for themselves and got first-degree burns.
> Or the sad sonneteers, toast-and-teasdales we loved at thirteen;
> Middle-aged virgins seducing the puerile anthologists
> Through lust of the mind; barbiturate-drenched Camilles
> With continuous periods, murmuring softly on sofas
> When poetry wasn't a craft but a sickly effluvium,
> The air thick with incense, musk, and emotional blackmail.
>
> (MB, 43)

This poem, besides being witty, is an excellent index of the hostility to nightingale poets that dominated American literary culture in the post–World War II period. The irony, of course, is that in summoning up these disquieting muses in order to exorcise them and distinguish herself from the past, Carolyn Kizer is doing exactly what Amy Lowell did, in the 1920s, in "The Sisters": misreading and misjudging, in part to establish credibility and in part to move forward.

A more sympathetic approach to our relationship with our literary foremothers is suggested by Lisel Mueller in *The Need to Hold Still* (1980).[6] Even Mueller's title evokes the nightingale tradition's emphasis on repression. Her wonderful poem "Why We Tell Stories" is not precisely about relations between women poets but it helps us see the poet's attitude toward inheritance.

> Because the story of our life
> becomes our life

Because each of us tells
the same story
but tells it differently

and none of us tells it
the same way twice
Because grandmothers looking like spiders
want to enchant the children
and grandfathers need to convince us
what happened happened because of them

and though we listen only
haphazardly, with one ear,
we will begin our story
with the word *and*

(*NHS*, 62–63)

Lisel Mueller is not afraid to memorialize Elinor Wylie in her poem on the many different kinds of snow, called "Not Only the Eskimos." In fact, in the closing stanzas, Mueller mentions first "the snow Elinor Wylie walked in / in velvet shoes," as though to continue the list she has been making, a list which includes snow as rendered in literature. However, instead of merely leaving Wylie there in her velvet shoes, she dilates this image into "the snow before her footprints / and the snow after" (24–25), as though to suggest that Wylie's literary footprints changed what came after as shoes on snow alter the winter landscape indelibly.

Her mood is frequently reminiscent of the nightingale poets. "Among daughters, I am the recluse," the speaker says in "Night Song" (33). Yet probably the poem most typical of the nightingale tradition is not either of these but "The Escape"— a work which consciously invokes Elinor Wylie's poem "Escape." This is a poem about a woman in pain who imagines a release for herself in which she is magically transported out of her present circumstances. Mueller's poem begins: "Pain lines the inside of her skin." The woman has given up speech, a "shift of denial" which itself might be designed to signal the flight of the nightingale. Wylie's protagonist in "Escape" imagines herself shrinking to fairy size "with a whisper no one understands" (*CP*, 24). Mueller has her woman perform a similar operation.

How silent it is,
the labor of getting smaller
until so little is left of her
that she can escape through a pinhole.

As Frances Osgood's heroine escaped patriarchal imprisonment through a keyhole in "Fancy" and Emily Dickinson evaded capture by mental gymnastics in "They shut me up in prose," Mueller's anorexic, like so many nightingale figures, is "dreaming a dream of flight":

a disappearance so perfect
that we suspect nothing:
she imagines us at her bedside,
accepting her muteness, her turned-away face
as usual, while she speeds
outward through unimagined space,
already a star without memory.

(57)

In this fantasy of a perfect apotheosis, we may recognize a classic female separation between mind and body in which the body remains in a realm of frustration and imperfection while the mind zooms off "straight to its freedom in the thunderous cloud," as Louise Bogan would have it (*BE*, 26).

Another poem in this genre is Alicia Ostriker's "A Young Woman, A Tree," in which a young girl experiences that old hunger:

Passing that fiery tree—if only she could

Be making love,
Be making poetry,
Be exploding, be speeding through the universe

Like a photon, like a shower
Of yellow blazes—[7]

Instead, "what she's doing is plodding / To the bus stop, to go to school." She feels herself facing only frustrating alternatives in which she "senses her infinite smallness / But can't seize it." Like many a nightingale poet, she is left to recognize "the folly of desire, / The folly of withdrawal."

It may be significant that Kizer, Mueller, and Ostriker were all born before 1945, Kizer quite a bit before. Women poets of the younger generation often write about women who seem to feel more confidence in their right to occupy physical space and thus less frequently imagine transubstantiation. Still, an ongoing theme of this work is the objectification of the female in what remains androcentric culture.

Louise Gluck's "Aphrodite" presents this view:

A woman exposed as rock
has this advantage:
she controls the harbor.
Ultimately, men appear,
weary of the open.
So terminates, they feel,
a story. In the beginning,
longing. At the end, joy.
In the middle, tedium.

In time, the young wife
naturally hardens. Drifting
from her side, in imagination,
the man returns not to a drudge
but to the goddess he projects.

On a hill, the armless figure
welcomes the delinquent boat,
her thighs cemented shut, barring
the fault in the rock.[8]

Though Gluck ends her poem with Aphrodite "barring / the fault in the rock" and
thus forbidding entrance, this denouement is hardly triumphant. In the middle
stanza of the poem, we hear the story of tedium from the man's point of view but
we have already been invited to keep in mind that there is a counternarrative.
The "woman exposed as rock" to whom the man returns offers him an ambiguous
welcome, "her thighs cemented shut." What we do not hear, however, is a counternarrative in which that fault in the rock is repaired. Why not liberate Aphrodite
from being "exposed as rock"? This possibility remains beyond the poem's ambitions.

Though different from Gluck's clipped New England accent, Jana Harris's bluesy
twang in "Glitter Box" also addresses the female body rendered spectacular in the
male gaze and examines the limits of one female position:

What do these men really want
I said.
What they really want
is some hassle-free woman.
What they're looking for,
I said,
is no depressions,
light to medium moods
and not too often.
What they really want
in a woman
is a glitter box,
Carmen Miranda fruits
in a gypsy skirt.
But underneath,
under the dress,
the frilly red French bikini
panties and bra,
underneath
it had better be mama,
I said.
It had better be mama
and not any flaming parrot.[9]

Harris explains that women cater to these male fantasies, "as the only way / of getting by."

Cleopatra Mathis's "Rearranging My Body" sounds at first reading like a challenge to this fatalism.

> I have a woman's feel for time,
> hands that know when to be innocent.
> When you watch me, I am graceful
> like any southern girl
> who learned to yield, easily
> borrowed the rhythms of walking.
> Black women washed my skin
> and showed me when to leave well enough alone.
>
> Now this changes: my mouth widens.
> I am wild with hair. I strip
> off this cotton dress, tear apart
> my legs that will learn their own time.
> I reach inside,
> my stomach becomes a new fist,
> I rearrange the obedient fingers of my ribs.
>
> You'll see my body,
> the new hard curves
> of a woman bent over in a soybean field.
> You'll smell the overcooked greens,
> the brown sweat. Even now, see my wrist,
> the underside thin and pale
> as a fish's belly, the veins
> strong as catgut.
> I am no longer familiar. It is all right
> if you never want me again.[10]

At first this poem seems to be about self-transformation and liberation. One of its ironies, of course, is that the lighter-skinned woman (Mathis is part Greek and part Cherokee) is taught "to leave well enough alone" by her darker sisters. If in the end her independence involves taking on the persona of a black fieldworker, another victim who has learned to be tough, this may spell change, but as liberation it seems self-consciously limited.

Nevertheless, I find this poem particularly interesting because it suggests a certain canniness about its own contradictions. This woman hasn't really made herself independent of her lover, and surely this is Mathis's point. She keeps parading herself before his gaze: "when you watch me," "you'll see." Furthermore, her wrist remains a representation of vulnerability: "the underside thin and pale" despite the veins "strong as catgut." So it's not *really* okay "if you never want me again"; this is a poem less about reclaiming the body than about learning to wear a mask.

If it is true that women poets are still writing about their hunger and their pain, still seeing them as part of a battle between male and female, are there signs of hope? In the work of some women, perhaps especially women of color, it seems there are.

Rita Dove, for instance, is a poet of great imaginative range who writes not only poems that refigure the nightingale tradition but others that are wide open to new possibilities. One critic has written of her: "While restraint is one of the strengths of Dove's poems, her work can sometimes seem austere."[11] On the other hand, in "Parsley," she imagines herself in the mind of Rafael Trujillo, ordering the execution of 20,000 blacks because he dislikes their pronunciation of the Spanish word for parsley. This is not a poetic project a nightingale poet would have undertaken.

Dove is herself "African-American," though in *Thomas and Beulah* (1986) she imagines her grandmother's response to that designation as unenthusiastic: "What did she know about Africa?"[12] The signs of hope one can feel in Dove's work have less to do with political change than with the power of the imagination to reorient the world. In Dove's most recent book, *Grace Notes* (1989), she gives the mother-daughter relation a positive spin that bodes well for the future. One poem of hope has a title immediately winning to a contemporary parent: "After Reading *Mickey in the Night Kitchen* for the Third Time Before Going to Bed." Here mother and daughter delight in their shared anatomical features: "the same glazed / tunnel, layered sequences."[13] The female body, innocently explored, is not paralyzed here in the male gaze.

Furthermore, "Genetic Expedition" gives women the imaginative power to redeem their own objectification in patriarchal culture.

> Each evening I see my breasts
> slacker, black-tipped
> like the heavy plugs on hot water bottles;
> each day resembling more the spiked fruits
> dangling from natives in the *National Geographic*
> my father forbade us to read.
>
> Each morning I drip coffee onto my blouse
> and tear into one slice of German bread,
> thin layer of margarine, radishes, the years
> spreading across my dark behind, even more
> sumptuous after childbirth, the part of me
> I swore to relish
>
> always. My child has
> her father's hips, his hair
> like the miller's daughter, combed gold.
> Though her lips are mine, housewives
> stare when we cross the parking lot
> because of that ghostly profusion.
>
> *You cant be cute*, she says. *You're big.*
> She's lost her toddler's belly,

that seaworthy prow. She regards me
with serious eyes, power-lit,
atomic gaze
I'm sucked into, sheer through to

the gray brain of sky.[14]

Why does this poem seem to me hopeful? The mother here regards her own body somewhat ambivalently. Though she has sworn to relish her sumptuous behind, she is dieting. At the beginning she sees her breasts in the camera's gaze, as spiked fruits dangling from "natives" in *National Geographic*.

Here we must remember Elizabeth Bishop's poem "In the Waiting Room," where the little girl comes to see her own identity as linked to "those awful hanging breasts" in *National Geographic*. The cry of pain she utters involuntarily is a recognition that she is "one of *them*," a human female.[15] In what way is Rita Dove's vision more hopeful?

"Genetic Expedition," like "In the Waiting Room," ends with a reorientation. The child in Bishop's poem clings desperately to the facts of historical and material reality. The mother in Dove's poem, confronting her daughter's "power-lit" gaze, is transported "sheer through to / the gray brain of sky," to a realm somehow dynamic. This realm seems to me positioned in the poem as an alternative to the stories of imperialism, of the miller's daughter, of the sailor's figurehead—those narratives of the female body the mother has, in spite of herself, internalized. Is "the gray brain of sky," which she merges with through her daughter's gaze, capable of rewriting the cultural code so that the female body becomes associated with power and possibility?

Perhaps one of the most significant aspects of post-nightingale poems is that frequently the end of the story remains open, undecidable. Often these are women's stories, like Louise Gluck's "Aphrodite" and Rita Dove's "Genetic Expedition," written in defiance of the predictable beginning, middle, and end handed down to us from the past.

In Sharon Olds's "Photograph of the Girl," for instance, a Russian peasant confronts the seemingly ruthless narrative of the 1921 famine, but the poem ends ambiguously:

the caption says
she is going to starve to death that winter
with millions of others. Deep in her body
the ovaries let out her first eggs,
golden as drops of grain.[16]

Late-twentieth-century women poets leave open possibilities for rewriting the stories given to us in the dominant discourse. Perhaps, in defiance of the patriarchal narratives of the past, we can bring to birth new possibilities, "golden as drops of grain."

But what about the stories of weakness, of failure, of madness, of the mistaken hopes and dashed illusions that are *part* of our inheritance from the women poets of our past? Should we say, like Toni Morrison's narrator at the end of *Beloved*: "This is not a story to pass on"?[17]

Like Morrison herself, I believe we cannot follow this advice without risking losing part of our own history, a history precious to those who would both understand what American culture has been and what it can conceivably become. If the present offers *some* hopeful images to cherish in spite of time and history, the sound of nightingales still haunts our cultural moment and our literary dreams.

Notes

INTRODUCTION

1. H. D., *Bid Me to Live (A Madrigal)* (New York: Dial Press, 1960), 7.

2. Giles Gunn, *The Culture of Criticism and the Criticism of Culture* (New York: Oxford UP, 1987), 71.

3. Alan Trachtenberg, "Comments on Evan Watkins' 'Cultural Criticism and the Literary Intellectual,' " *Works and Days* 3 (Spring 1985), 37; quoted in Gunn, 171.

4. Cheryl Walker, *The Nightingale's Burden: Women Poets and American Culture before 1900* (Bloomington: Indiana UP, 1982).

5. Cora Kaplan, *Sea Changes: Culture and Feminism* (London: Verso, 1986), 3.

6. Sacvan Bercovitch, "New England's Errand Reappraised," *New Directions in American Intellectual History*, ed. John Higham and Paul Conkin (Baltimore: Johns Hopkins UP, 1979), 87.

7. Although Tocqueville thought American girls freer than their European counterparts, he felt that women after they reached maturity were allowed much more independence in Europe, where wives led lives often virtually independent of their husbands. The quotation from James comes from *The Portrait of a Lady*, (1881; rpt. New York: Modern Library-Random House, 1966), 49.

8. Elaine Sproat, ed., " 'Woman and the Creative Will': A Lecture by Lola Ridge, 1919," *Michigan Occasional Papers in Women's Studies*, No. 18, Spring 1981. The quotation is from Sproat's introduction, 2. The following quotation is from p. 17.

9. Harold E. Stearns, "The Intellectual Life," in *The Culture of the Twenties*, ed. Loren Baritz (Indianapolis: Bobbs-Merrill, 1970), 339, 341, 343. Henry James makes similar arguments in *The American Scene*. Furthermore, this attitude is still with us, as one can see from Ann Douglas's *The Feminization of American Culture*, which also emphasizes the way women control cultural discourses and the loss of rigor which ensues.

10. Sara Josepha Hale, *Ladies' Magazine* 2 (1829), 142.

11. Ridge, 10.

12. The quotations from Ransom are taken *passim* from John Crowe Ransom, "The Poet as Woman," *Southern Review* 2 (1937), 783–806. In light of this article, I was particularly delighted recently to find Dave Smith's poem, "Figure from an Elder Lady," which begins:

> Don't women, Mr. Ransom, as much as geese
> Deserve a voice? Must we be tasked
> with silence, be always the antecedents
> of your pedantic? What is the purpose?

This poem is from *Cumberland Station* (Urbana: U of Illinois P, 1976).

13. Florence Howe, "Introduction," *No More Masks! An Anthology of Poems by Women*, ed. Florence Howe and Ellen Bass (New York: Doubleday-Anchor, 1973), 6–7.

14. T. J. Jackson Lears, "The Concept of Cultural Hegemony: Problems and Possibilities," *American Historical Review* 90 (1985), 567–93.

15. Works which portray Emily Dickinson as centrally concerned with gender include Wendy Martin, *An American Triptych* (Chapel Hill: U of North Carolina P, 1984); Barbara Antonina Clarke Mossberg, *Emily Dickinson: When a Writer Is a Daughter* (Bloomington: Indiana UP, 1982); and Paula Bennett, *My Life a Loaded Gun: Female Creativity and Feminist Poetics* (Boston: Beacon, 1986). By listing these works here, I do not intend a sweeping dismissal of them since I have learned from all of them, especially from Mossberg.

16. I have written elsewhere about my views on the status of the author in recent feminist criticism and will not rehearse those arguments here. See Walker, "Feminist Theory and the Author," *Critical Inquiry* 16 (Spring 1990), 551–71.

17. William Drake, *Sara Teasdale, Woman & Poet* (San Francisco: Harper and Row, 1979), 73.

18. Drake, 116.

19. Patrick Moore, "Symbol, Mask, and Metre in the Poetry of Louise Bogan," in *Gender and Literary Voice*, ed. Janet Todd (New York: Holmes and Meier, 1980), 79.

20. Alicia Ostriker, "The Nerves of a Midwife: Contemporary American Women's Poetry," *Parnassus: Poetry in Review* 6 (1977), 75.

21. Sandra Gilbert, "Costumes of the Mind: Transvestism as Metaphor in Modern Literature," *Critical Inquiry* 7 (1980), 391–417.

22. Judith Kegan Gardiner, "The (US)es of (I)dentity: A Response to Abel on '(E)merging Identities,' " *Signs: Journal of Women in Culture and Society* 6 (1981), 442; emphasis mine.

23. See Virginia M. Kouidis, *Mina Loy: American Modernist Poet* (Baton Rouge: Louisiana State P, 1980).

24. Gloria T. Hull, "Afro-American Women Poets: A Bio-Critical Survey," in *Shakespeare's Sisters*, ed. Sandra M. Gilbert and Susan Gubar (Bloomington: Indiana UP, 1981), 165–66.

25. Hull, *Color, Sex, and Poetry: Three Women Writers of the Harlem Renaissance* (Bloomington: Indiana UP, 1987), 20, 24, 22.

26. Erlene Stetson, *Black Sister: Poetry by Black American Women, 1746–1980* (Bloomington: Indiana UP, 1981), esp. 63, 65, and 72. See also Maureen Honey, ed., *Shadowed Dreams: Women's Poetry of the Harlem Renaissance* (New Brunswick: Rutgers UP, 1989).

27. Sandra Gilbert and Susan Gubar, *No Man's Land: The Place of the Woman Writer in the Twentieth Century—Volume Two: Sexchanges* (New Haven: Yale UP, 1989).

28. Stetson, 58–59.

29. William Heyen, ed., *American Poets in 1976* (Indianapolis: Bobbs-Merrill, 1976) includes twenty-four male poets and four females: Joyce Carol Oates, Linda Pastan, Adrienne Rich, and Anne Sexton. Stephen Berg and Robert Mezey's *The New Naked Poetry: Recent American Poetry in Open Forms* (Indianapolis: Bobbs-Merrill, 1976) presents twenty-three men plus three women: Denise Levertov, Adrienne Rich, and Muriel Rukeyser.

30. Alicia Suskin Ostriker, *Stealing the Language: The Emergence of Women's Poetry in America* (Boston: Beacon, 1986).

2. WOMEN AND FEMININE LITERARY TRADITIONS

1. *The Complete Poetical Works of Amy Lowell* (Boston: Houghton Mifflin, 1955); all the poems in this chapter are quoted from this work. Subsequent references will be given in the text, the page number following the quotation.

2. Robert Lowell, *Life Studies* (New York: Farrar Straus, 1967), 38. Gilbert and Gubar read *Life Studies* as suggesting Lowell's participation in his family's denigration of Amy. Though this cannot be ruled out entirely, and Robert does seem to express some amusement at Amy's expense, the whole thrust of the essay in *Life Studies* is to suggest the alienation Robert himself feels from a family so thoroughly devoted to respectability.

3. Alicia Ostriker, *Writing Like a Woman* (Ann Arbor: U of Michigan P, 1983), 132.

4. I use these terms throughout this chapter not to suggest essential qualities of males and females but as a shorthand to designate qualities assigned to men and women by Lowell's culture. I personally believe that there *are* inborn differences between men and women but since such differences always result in a range of physical and mental types, and since we know so little as yet about sociobiology, it seems unwise to speculate further. Clearly, the

"androgyne" was not a physical type but an unstable form of cultural combination which actually reinstated the force of essentialist distinctions even as it marked the need of some women to find a way around them.

5. See Elizabeth Shelpley Sergeant, *Fire under the Andes* (Port Washington, N.Y.: Kennikat Press, 1966), 3–32, esp. 23.

6. Harold Bloom, *The Anxiety of Influence* (New York: Oxford UP, 1973) and *A Map of Misreading* (New York: Oxford, 1975). Bloom's theory posits an oedipal struggle between a strong precursor poet and a modern who must misread "his" predecessor in order to clear a space for his own poetic projects. Latecomer poets are portrayed as suffering from anxiety due to their filial sense of inadequacy and hostility toward the strong parent poet.

7. Bennett, *My Life a Loaded Gun: Female Creativity and Feminist Poetics* (Boston: Beacon, 1986), 10.

8. Ostriker, *Stealing the Language*, 192. The interpolated quotation here comes from Joanne Feit Diehl (see below).

9. See *The Nightingale's Burden*, 26–27; Sandra Gilbert and Susan Gubar, *The Madwoman in the Attic* (New Haven: Yale UP, 1979), 51; Joanne Feit Diehl, "Come Slowly—Eden: An Exploration of Women Poets and Their Muse," *Signs: Journal of Women in Culture and Society* 3 (1978), 572–87. Feit Diehl is mainly concerned with women poets' relation to a masculine tradition but also sees the need to revise Bloom.

10. Sandra Gilbert and Susan Gubar, *No Man's Land: The Position of the Woman Writer in the Twentieth Century—Volume One: The War of the Words* (New Haven: Yale UP, 1988), 195.

11. Jean Gould, *Amy: The World of Amy Lowell and the Imagist Movement* (New York: Dodd Mead, 1975), 15; hereafter cited in the text as Gould, page reference following.

12. S. Foster Damon, *Amy Lowell: A Chronicle* (Boston: Houghton Mifflin, 1935), 65; hereafter cited in the text as Damon, page reference following.

13. Louis Untermeyer, "Introduction" to *The Complete Poetical Works of Amy Lowell*, xxvi.

14. Glenn Ruihley, *The Thorn of the Rose: Amy Lowell Reconsidered* (Hamden, Conn.: Archon Books, 1975).

15. Hugh Kenner, *The Pound Era* (Berkeley: U of California P, 1971), 291.

16. Margaret Widdemer, "The Legend of Amy Lowell," *Texas Quarterly* 2 (1963), 200.

17. T. J. Jackson Lears, *No Place of Grace: Antimodernism and the Transformation of American Culture, 1880–1920* (New York: Pantheon, 1981), 124–25.

18. Susan Gubar, "Blessings in Disguise: Cross-Dressing as Re-Dressing for Female Modernists," *Massachusetts Review* 22 (1981), 481.

19. Gubar, "Blessings," 485.

20. See "To Two Unknown Ladies" for an example of Lowell's derogatory treatment of frustrated women. Her attitude is not unlike the political unconscious which haunts Adrienne Rich's early poem "Aunt Jennifer's Tigers." In both poems a frustrated woman uses an art to convey what she refuses to admit openly. Lowell is by turns angry and sympathetic with the plight of these women whose "patient, stupid zeal" is the mark of the amateur. Since Lowell makes them two halves of one whole—"a frail half and a virile"—one suspects she is, like Rich, projecting her own concerns on the figures she describes with such ambivalence (562–65).

21. Carroll Smith-Rosenberg, *Disorderly Conduct: Visions of Gender in Victorian America* (New York: Oxford UP, 1985), 265.

22. Amy Lowell, *Poetry and Poets* (Boston: Houghton Mifflin, 1930), 116.

23. According to several biographers, Lowell became involved with a young Bostonian in 1897 who supposedly proposed marriage but then broke off the engagement. Very little is known about this affair and the story seems to have come principally from S. Foster Damon. It is likely that the deaths of both her mother and her father during this period plus her serious depression over her weight also influenced her seven years' despair.

24. *Poetry and Poets,* 111.

25. Louise Imogen Guiney, "Borderlands," in *Happy Ending* (Boston: Houghton Mifflin, 1909).

26. Horace Gregory, *Amy Lowell: A Portrait of the Poet in Her Time* (New York: Thomas Nelson, 1958), 207.

27. "Bronze Horses" is one of Lowell's historical spots-of-time poems in *Can Grande's Castle,* one of her least successful books. It is written in polyphonic prose and focuses on Roman decadence. The lady in the bath is pampered and bored, derided by Lowell. "Legionaries ravish Egypt for her entertainment." Yet the vision of the woman bathing is strangely seductive.

> Aqua Claudia, Aqua Virgo, Aqua Marcia, drawn from the hills to lie against a woman's body. Her breasts round hollows for themselves in the sky-green water, her fingers sift the pale water and drop it from her as a lark drops notes backwards into the sky. The lady lies against the lipping water, supine and indolent, a pomegranate, a passion-flower, a silver-flamed lily, lapped, slapped, lulled, by the ripples which stir under her faintly moving hands. (178)

In this poem the clear suggestions of auto-eroticism are complicated by the mixture of waters given women's names. Claudia, Virgo, and Marcia, through the correspondence of water and woman, "lie against a woman's body," lapping, slapping, and lulling her with pleasure.

28. *Poetry and Poets;* all three quotations are on p. 121.

29. See Clement Wood, *Amy Lowell* (New York: Harold Vinal, 1926). This study of Lowell reflects the response to the poet's lesbianism by some of her contemporaries and is full of homophobia.

30. Winfield Townley Scott, "Amy Lowell after Ten Years," *New England Quarterly* 8 (1935), 326.

31. Adrienne Rich, *Your Native Land, Your Life* (New York: Norton, 1986), 3–27.

3. WOMEN AND SELFHOOD

1. All the quotations from Teasdale's poetry, except where otherwise noted, are from *The Collected Poems of Sara Teasdale* (New York: Macmillan, 1966). I have used this edition instead of the more recent, expanded *Mirror of the Heart: Poems of Sara Teasdale,* ed. William Drake (New York: Macmillan, 1984), because it is more widely available and was for a long time in paperback.

2. See Carol Gilligan, *In a Different Voice: Psychological Theory and Women's Development* (Cambridge: Harvard UP, 1982). Gilligan's argument, with its emphasis on a female ethic of affiliation, is much more relevant to Teasdale's first three books than it is to the later ones.

3. William Drake, *Sara Teasdale: Woman and Poet* (San Francisco: Harper and Row, 1979), 151. All future quotations from this work will appear in the text as *WP,* page reference following. Also see Drake's other works, the introduction to *Mirror of the Heart* and his fascinating recent study of women poets and social issues, *The First Wave: Women Poets in America 1915–1945* (New York: Macmillan, 1987).

4. Toril Moi, *Sexual/Textual Politics* (London: Methuen, 1985), 67–68.

5. For a useful discussion of romantic thralldom, see Rachel Blau DuPlessis, *Writing beyond the Ending* (Bloomington: Indiana UP, 1985), 66–83.

6. In *Feminism and Poetry,* Jan Montefiore examines Christina Rossetti's "Self-Definition by Renunciation." Her assessment of Rossetti, similar to mine of Teasdale, concludes that Rossetti's defining characteristic is the creation of a voice of inhibited longing (see 125–34). For a discussion of Rossetti's influence on Teasdale, see note 12 below.

7. Freud's articulation of penis envy appears particularly in the essay "Femininity," in

The Standard Edition of the Complete Psychological Works of Sigmund Freud, James Strachey, ed., Vol. 22. For Lacan on lack, see Jacques Lacan, *The Four Fundamental Concepts of Psycho-Analysis*, ed. Jacques-Alain Miller, trans. Alan Sheridan (New York: Norton, 1981), esp. "The Subject and the Other: Alienation," 203–15.

8. For a discussion about the way sorrow became literary capital for women, see *The Nightingale's Burden*, esp. 88–93.

9. See Mossberg, "Hunger in the House," in *Emily Dickinson: When a Writer Is a Daughter*, 135–46.

10. Maria Brooks, *Zóphiël; or, The Bride of Seven* (Boston: Carter and Hendee, 1933), 230–31.

11. *The Answering Voice*, Sara Teasdale, ed. (Boston: Houghton Mifflin, 1917); revised, with fifty recent poems added (New York: Macmillan, 1928), ix–xii.

12. WP 287. Teasdale's relationship with Christina Rossetti is discussed by Drake in *Sara Teasdale: Woman and Poet*, esp. 282–88, and *The First Wave*, esp. 13–14.

13. Margaret Haley Carpenter, *Sara Teasdale, A Biography* (New York: Schulte, 1960), 311.

14. In 1926 my mother, who published under the name "Marilyn," received a letter from William Briggs of Harper & Bros. The letter indicates as much as anything that Harper's, who also published Edna St. Vincent Millay, was on the lookout for more female talent. Briggs wrote: "One who has the skill of expression, and the power of feeling, in the degree that you have, is well equipped to write poetry of more than passing interest. It occurred to me that probably you had enough verse in hand to make a collection. . . . I can assure you now of our genuine interest in the possibility of publishing it, and we shall give you a prompt decision." My mother at the age of twenty was both shy and cynical; she considered the offer both an intrusion on her privacy and an attempt to get her to give them money; she never responded. As an indication of how thoroughly young women poets like my mother were influenced by Teasdale, here is part of a poem my mother wrote called "Gift." It begins: "I would give you a song all fragrant of heather" and ends:

> Yes, I would give you a song but lest I falter
> In my fine words and fail my final vow,
> I have laid silence for you as an altar
> And silence I do believe is better now.

Such poems were surely written by young women all over the United States in the twenties. Silence and renunciation were still profoundly attractive to these early twentieth-century women.

15. Paula S. Fass, *The Damned and the Beautiful: American Youth in the 1920s* (New York: Oxford UP, 1977), 6. All future references to Fass's work will appear in the text with the page number following the quotation.

16. Dorothy Dunbar Bromley, "Feminist New-Style," *Harper's* 155 (1927), 552–60, esp. 555.

17. Quoted in Elaine Showalter, ed., *These Modern Women: Autobiographical Essays from the Twenties* (Old Westbury, N.Y.: Feminist Press, 1978), 67; hereafter cited in the text with page reference following quotation.

18. For a discussion of these and other studies affecting this period, see Mary P. Ryan, *Womanhood in America from Colonial Times to the Present*, 2d ed. (New York: Franklin Watts, 1979).

19. Frank D. Watson, "What Some College Men Want to Know about Marriage and the Family," *Social Forces* 11 (1932), 240; Clifford Kirkpatrick, "Student Attitudes toward Marriage and Sex," *Journal of Educational Sociology* 9 (1936), 550.

20. For discussions of women on the poetry scene, see H. L. Davis, "Enter the Woman," *Poetry* 30 (Sept. 1927), 338–46, esp. 338; Llewellyn Jones, "The Younger Woman Poets," *The English Journal* 13 (May 1924), 301–310; Mark Van Doren, "Women as Poets," *Nation*

114 (April 26, 1922), 498–99; Virginia Moore, "Women Poets," *Bookman* 71 (July 1930), 388–93; Harriet Monroe, "Voices of Women," in *Poets and Their Art* (New York: Macmillan, 1926), 141–54, esp. 141.

21. Elizabeth Breuer, "The Flapper's Wild Oats," *Bookman* 57 (March 1923), 1–6, 57; esp. 5.

22. Jean Starr Untermeyer, "Response to Breuer," *Bookman* 57 (June 1923), 480–81.

23. For a prominent proponent of these ideas, see Luce Irigaray, "And the One Doesn't Stir Without the Other," trans. Helene Vivienne Wenzel, *Signs: Journal of Women in Culture and Society* 7 (Autumn 1981), 60–67; and *This Sex Which Is Not One*, trans. Catherine Porter with Carolyn Burke (Ithaca: Cornell UP, 1985), esp. "When Our Lips Speak Together," 205–18.

24. Carpenter, 33.

25. Ruth Perry and Maurine Sagoff, "Sara Teasdale's Friendships," *New Letters* 46 (Fall 1979), 101–7, esp. 101. See also Drake, *First Wave*, 52–63 and 241–49.

26. Marya Zaturenska, "The Strange Victory of Sara Teasdale," introduction to *The Collected Poems*, xxx.

27. For a discussion of "The Tiger," by Wilcox, see *The Nightingale's Burden*, 126–27.

28. Drake, *Mirror of the Heart*, xxxiv.

29. Monroe, *Poets and Their Art*, 74.

30. Kaplan, *Sea Changes*, 225.

31. Though this may be using the term *virgin* somewhat loosely, applying to a person a meaning usually reserved for flora (as in virgin timber), we should remember that the conception of detachment Teasdale chooses is inextricable from antihumanistic spiritual traditions connected to the Virgin Mary. In this sense we can say that the idea of the virgin as a being unaltered by human activity is relevant to Teasdale toward the end of her life.

32. Sylvia Plath, *The Collected Poems*, ed. Ted Hughes (New York: Harper and Row, 1981), 172–73.

33. Gloria Erlich, *Family Themes and Hawthorne's Fiction: The Tenacious Web* (New Brunswick: Rutgers UP, 1984), 6.

34. Louise Bogan, *Achievement in American Poetry* (Chicago: Henry Regnery, 1951), 75–76.

35. Carolyn Kizer, *Knock Upon Silence* (Seattle: U of Washington P, 1968), 47.

36. See Lowell, *A Critical Fable*, in *Complete Poems*, 420.

4. WOMEN AND AGGRESSION

1. *Last Poems of Elinor Wylie* (New York: Knopf, 1943), 46; hereafter cited in the text as *LP*, page following. Though several feminist critics have recently attacked the tendency to read all women's writing as about rage, their useful warnings should not preclude the possibility of discussing rage as an issue of particular importance to a poet like Wylie.

2. Comment made in conversation with Alicia Ostriker. For other works which address the issue of violent anger in women writers, see Gilbert and Gubar's *No Man's Land* and Bennett's *My Life a Loaded Gun*.

3. *Collected Poems of Elinor Wylie* (New York: Knopf, 1932), 75; henceforth referenced in the text as *CP*, page number following.

4. For a discussion of power fantasies in women poets, see *The Nightingale's Burden*, esp. 38–43.

5. Ostriker, *Stealing the Language*, 126.

6. Much of my argument about the abject is indebted to Julia Kristeva's *Powers of Horror: An Essay on Abjection* (New York: Columbia, 1982). This quotation can be found on p. 2.

7. Stanley Olson, *Elinor Wylie: A Life Apart* (New York: Dial Press/James Wade, 1979), 329; henceforth given in the text as Olson, page reference following.

8. Carl Van Doren, *Three Worlds* (New York: Harper, 1936), 219. This is an essential source on Wylie's life.

9. These masochistic rituals of Wylie's have eerie parallels in the biographies of nineteenth-century women. The poet Elizabeth Oakes-Smith also burned her fingers and applied a mustard plaster to her leg until she fainted from the pain. Lucy Larcom's sister bathed in ice water in winter and slept on a hard chest to test her courage and stamina.

10. Quoted in Edmund Wilson, *The Shores of Light* (New York: Farrar Straus, 1952), 393.

11. The Macdowell Colony, which still operates in Peterborough, N.H., provides accommodations and studios to creative artists during the four months of summer. Attendance at the colony is by invitation only.

12. Louis Untermeyer, *From Another World* (New York: Harcourt Brace, 1939), 241.

13. Eunice Tietjens, "Armor of the Spirit," *Poetry* 24 (February 1924), 96–99.

14. Van Doren, *Three Worlds*, 238. For a discussion of the pervasiveness of the forbidden lover motif among nineteenth-century American women poets, see *The Nightingale's Burden*, esp. 91 and 149. Sara Teasdale also became obsessed with a forbidden lover, John Hall Wheelock, for whom she carried a torch all her adult life.

15. Louise Imogen Guiney, *Happy Ending*, 3–4.

16. Lears, *No Place of Grace*, 248.

17. Quoted in Gilbert and Gubar, *No Man's Land*, I, 63 and 78.

18. Anaïs Nin, *Ladders to Fire* (Chicago: Swallow Press, 1959), 47; for a discussion of this quotation and other examples of the woman warrior, see Susan Gubar, "Blessings in Disguise," 477–508.

19. *Scouting for Girls: Official Handbook of the Girl Scouts* (New York: Girl Scouts Inc., 1920), 19.

20. Quoted in Gilbert and Gubar, *No Man's Land*, I, 78. This quotation is actually taken from Martha Vicinus's *Independent Women: Work and Community for Single Women, 1850–1920* (Chicago: U of Chicago P, 1985).

21. Judith Farr's *The Life and Art of Elinor Wylie* (Baton Rouge: Louisiana State UP, 1983) is the most recent book about Wylie. Though it glosses over the disruptive violence in Wylie's work, this book makes a good case for the influence of Aestheticism on Wylie as well as noting Wylie's resistance to certain aspects of Aestheticism.

22. William Drake, *The First Wave*, 90.

23. *The Collected Prose of Elinor Wylie* (New York: Knopf, 1933), 879.

24. Dayton Kohler, "Elinor Wylie: Heroic Mask," *South Atlantic Quarterly* 36 (April 1937), 218–19.

25. *Collected Prose*, 873 and 874.

26. R. P. Blackmur called this novel "a fable for frigidity," but the most peculiar aspect of the poet's relationship to it is that once the work was published Wylie expressed surprise and disappointment at the weakness of her hero. She confessed to Carl Van Doren: "I am heartily disgusted with the . . . gutless Virginio now that I have him between dull commonplace blue cloth covers." See Van Doren, "Elinor Wylie," *Harper's*, September 1939, 362.

27. For another use of Artemis by Wylie as a woman warrior resistant to anger, see "A Birthday Cake for Lionel" in *Collected Prose*, esp. 817.

28. See *The Nightingale's Burden*, 28–29, for discussion of Frances Osgood's similarly peculiar poem "Woman." Other nineteenth-century poems which exhibit unstable perspectives of this sort include Lucy Larcom's "Fern-Life" and Helen Hunt Jackson's "Acquainted with Grief."

29. For a discussion of nineteenth-century clitoridectomy, see Peter Gay, *Education of the Senses* (New York: Oxford, 1984), 303–4.

30. Virginia Woolf, *A Room of One's Own* (New York: Harcourt Brace, 1929), 108. Also see Jane Marcus, *Art and Anger* (Columbus: Ohio State UP, 1988), 122–54.

31. "Anti-Feminist Song, For my Sister," *New Yorker*, February 16, 1929, 22.

32. Hélène Cixous and Catherine Clément, *The Newly-Born Woman*, trans. Betsy Wing (Minneapolis: U of Minnesota P, 1986), 33. "Imaginary" and "mirror stage" are terms in Jacques Lacan's post-structural analysis and will be discussed further in chapter 6.

33. See Adrienne Rich, "Vesuvius at Home: The Power of Emily Dickinson," in *On Lies, Secrets, and Silence* (New York: Norton, 1979), 157–84; also see Rich's use of volcano imagery in "Twenty-One Love Poems," in *The Fact of a Doorframe: Poems Selected and New 1950–1984* (NY: Norton, 1984), 236–46.

34. Julia Kristeva, *Powers of Horror*, 1; hereafter page references given in the text following quotation.

35. Readers who have noted the masochism in Elinor Wylie include Stanley Olson, Judith Farr, and Josephine O'Brien Schaefer in "Elinor Wylie," *American Writers*, Supp. 1 (New York: Scribner's, 1979), 707–30.

36. Simone de Beauvoir, *The Second Sex* (New York: Random House, 1974), 447.

37. Though the woman warrior persona is much more typical of literary women in the first half of this century, an interesting contemporary usage may be found in the work of Audre Lorde who, as a young woman, was a great reader of Elinor Wylie. Lorde discusses the woman warrior motif in *Zami: A New Spelling of My Name* (Freedom, Calif.: Crossing Press, 1982), esp. 82–83; in *The Cancer Journals* (San Francisco: Spinsters/Aunt Lute, 1980), and in poems like "For Each of You," "Cables to Rage," and "A Poem for Women in Rage" in *Chosen Poems—Old and New* (New York: Norton, 1982). It is not hard to see why Wylie's combination of rage and abjection would speak to an African-American lesbian feminist poet like Lorde.

5. WOMEN AND TIME

1. This phrase comes from Walter Pater's conclusion to *The Renaissance* (1873) where he urges the sensitive individual "to burn always with this hard gem-like flame." Such ideas had a strong influence on both H. D. and Elinor Wylie. H. D.'s modernism, however, would require her to come to terms with the historical realities of war and the disintegration of the social fabric on a scale Elinor Wylie could hardly imagine.

2. For a comparison between H. D. and Elinor Wylie, see Thomas Burnett Swann, *The Classical World of H. D.* (Lincoln: U of Nebraska P, 1962), 191.

3. David Perkins, *A History of Modern Poetry, from the 1890s to the High Modernist Mode* (Cambridge: Harvard UP, 1976), 340.

4. Ricardo J. Quinones, *Mapping Literary Modernism: Time and Development* (Princeton: Princeton UP, 1985), 73.

5. *HERmione* (New York: New Directions, 1981), 10; hereafter cited in the text as *H*, page reference following.

6. Barbara Guest, *Herself Defined: The Poet H. D. and Her World* (Garden City, N.Y.: Doubleday, 1984), xii; hereafter cited in the text as Guest, page reference following.

7. *Bid Me to Live (A Madrigal)* (New York: Dial Press, 1960), 123; hereafter cited in the text as *BML*, page following.

8. *The Gift* (New York: New Directions, 1969), 7; hereafter cited in the text as *G*, page reference following.

9. On April 1, 1978, Mary Barnard, the distinguished translator of Sappho's lyrics, told a faculty seminar at the Radcliffe Institute for Independent Study (now the Bunting Institute) that Pound had advised her in the early days to undertake a study of sapphics. According to Barnard, Pound said that the only way to avoid writing "girls' stuff," that is, sentimental poetry, was to study Greek sapphics and get them down so that she could do them "dead drunk or asleep." Here too Greek was seen as a means of entry into the previously forbidden temple of art.

10. Bryher [Winifred Ellerman], *The Heart to Artemis: A Memoir* (London: Collins, 1963).

11. For a good discussion of H. D.'s reading, see Swann, *The Classical World of H. D.* For other works about H. D.'s connection to Greek culture, see Guest, *Herself Defined*, and Rachel Blau DuPlessis, *H. D.: The Career of That Struggle* (Bloomington: Indiana UP, 1986), esp. "Sheer Young Classicism circa 1917."

12. Ostriker, *Writing Like a Woman*, 13.

13. *Collected Poems: 1912–1944*, ed. Louis L. Martz (New York: New Directions, 1983), 29–32; hereafter all poems contained in this text will be cited as *CP* with the page numbers of the complete poem following the quotation given in the chapter.

14. Pound's poem as well as his pronouncements on imagism are included and discussed in a useful little book by William Pratt called *The Imagist Poem* (New York: Dutton, 1963).

15. Julia Kristeva, "Women's Time," *The Kristeva Reader*, ed. Toril Moi (New York: Columbia, 1986), 191; hereafter cited in the text. All references to Kristeva in this chapter are to this text, pp. 188–213.

16. *Tribute to Freud* (Boston: Godine, 1974), 13. Hereafter cited in the text as *TF*, page reference following.

17. DuPlessis, *H. D.: The Career of That Struggle*, 116.

18. Susan Stanford Friedman, *Psyche Reborn: The Emergence of H. D.* (Bloomington: Indiana UP, 1981), 108.

19. Joseph N. Riddel, "H. D. and the Poetics of 'Spiritual Realism,' " *Contemporary Literature* 10 (1969), 447–73, esp. 457.

20. *Palimpsest* (Carbondale: Southern Illinois UP, 1968), 158.

21. "Notes on Recent Writing" is located in the Beinecke Library at Yale University, where most of H. D.'s papers are held. Quotation reprinted here by permission.

22. Louis L. Martz, "Introduction," in *Collected Poems: 1912–1944*, xxv.

23. Albert Gelpi, "Hilda in Egypt," *Southern Review* 18 (1982), 233–50.

24. Horace Gregory, "Introduction," in *Helen in Egypt* (New York: New Directions, 1961), x.

25. So much criticism of H. D. has come out in the past twenty years that it is impossible to list here all the material that relates to *Helen in Egypt*. However, excellent readings of the poem as a feminist epic may be found in Friedman's *Psyche Reborn*, DuPlessis's *Writing Beyond the Ending*, Gelpi's "Hilda in Egypt," and Lucy Freibert's "From Semblance to Selfhood: The Evolution of Woman in H. D.'s Neo-Epic *Helen in Egypt*," *Arizona Quarterly* 36 (1980), 165–75. For an excellent annotated bibliography of the criticism up to 1986, see *H. D. Woman and Poet*, ed. Michael King (Orono, Me.: National Poetry Foundation, 1986).

26. H. D., *Helen in Egypt*, 2. Hereafter cited in the text as *HE*, page reference following. *Helen in Egypt* was written in two stages, first as an epic poem and then with the addition of the prose headnotes to each section. "Helen"—the Greek persona—thus shares the poem with the writer of the prose glosses, who does not always agree with Helen. The prose persona confirms the reader's sense of uneasiness with some of Helen's statements, telling us when to doubt Helen, allowing us a sense of fragmentation, incompletion, even failure. The notes suggest that H. D. was aware that the hieratic voice of Helen might by its very power seem to elude time, though Helen herself is forced to rejoin it. The prose voice, outside of the "time" of the poem's narrative plot, represents our time, a modern consciousness. By juxtaposing the notes to the poems, H. D. offers us a complicated layering of temporal consciousnesses.

27. Frank Kermode, *The Sense of an Ending* (New York: Oxford UP, 1967), 72.

28. Gelpi, "Hilda in Egypt," esp. 245–47.

29. One other buried allusion may be designed to undercut the absolutism of Theseus's "Myth, the one reality dwells here." H. D. was deeply versed in Hawthorne's work while she was growing up and continued to speak respectfully of him. In "My Kinsman, Major Molineux," Hawthorne's Robin is almost tempted to give up his quest by the false words of a pretty young woman in a red petticoat who says: "Major Molineux dwells here." Perhaps H. D. saw Freud's interpretations as similarly tempting but in the end similarly endangering to the success of the quest.

30. Friedman made this statement in a paper on "Women as Epic Poets" given at the 1984 Modern Language Association convention in New York.

31. H. D., *Hermetic Definition* (New York: New Directions, 1972), 19; hereafter cited in the text as *HD*, page reference following.

6. WOMEN ON THE MARKET

1. *The Letters of Edna St. Vincent Millay*, ed. Allan Ross Macdougall (New York: Harper and Row, 1952), 71; hereafter cited in the text as *L*, page reference following.

2. *Collected Poems* (New York: Harper and Row, 1956), 688; hereafter poems from this edition will be cited in the text as *CP*, page reference following.

3. These remarks are from Floyd Dell, one of Millay's early lovers, cited in Allen Churchill, *The Improper Bohemians* (New York: Dutton, 1959), 264; and John Hyde Preston, "Edna St. Vincent Millay," *Virginia Quarterly Review* 3 (1927), 343.

4. The negative views of Millay quoted here are from Louise Bogan, *A Poet's Alphabet: Reflections on Literary Art and Vocation*, ed. Robert Phelps and Ruth Limmer (New York: McGraw-Hill, 1970), 299; Bette Richart, "Poet of Our Youth," *Commonweal*, May 10, 1957, 150; Maureen Howard, "City of Words," *Women, the Arts, and the 1920s in Paris and New York*, ed. Kenneth W. Wheeler and Virginia Lee Lusier (New Brunswick, N.J.: Transaction Books, 1982), 45.

5. See Jane Stanbrough, "Edna St. Vincent Millay and the Language of Vulnerability," in *Shakespeare's Sisters*, ed. Gilbert and Gubar, 183–99; Walter S. Minot, "Millay's 'Ungrafted Tree': The Problem of the Artist as Woman," *New England Quarterly* 48 (1975), 260–69; and Elizabeth Perlmutter Frank, "A Doll's Heart: The Girl in the Poetry of Edna St. Vincent Millay and Louise Bogan," *Critical Essays on Louise Bogan*, ed. Martha Collins (Boston: G. K. Hall, 1984), 130–31. Nancy Milford has been working on the biography of Millay for many years. Her reviews have appeared in the *New York Times*, always tantalizing.

6. Churchill, 246.

7. Cited in Churchill, 263. Edna Millay started a novel to be called *Hardigut*, which comically depicted a group of people whose eating habits were always dealt with in an embarrassed and secretive manner, obviously a transformation of sexuality into alimentary terms. Though very private about her own love affairs, Millay clearly felt that sex itself should not be treated with embarrassment.

8. Elizabeth Atkins, *Edna St. Vincent Millay and Her Times* (Chicago: U of Chicago P, 1936), 70.

9. In the headnote to this poem, Macdougall says: "Miss Millay and her two friends, John Peale Bishop and Edmund Wilson, had amused themselves one evening writing poetic self-portraits." One longs to compare Bishop's and Wilson's to Millay's; would they have described themselves in such terms?

10. For an interesting essay concerning Stein's relationship with her body, see Catherine Stimpson, "The Somagrams of Gertrude Stein," in Susan R. Suleiman, ed., *The Female Body in Western Culture: Contemporary Perspectives* (Cambridge: Harvard UP, 1986).

11. Stanbrough says: "The language pattern of vulnerability suggests strongly that Millay saw herself as a misfit and a failure and that she believed that some external forces in her life impeded her development and inflicted permanent injury," 191. Stanbrough compiles a startling list of poems in which the speaker is violently assaulted.

12. See "Women on the Market," in Luce Irigaray, *This Sex Which Is Not One*, trans. Catherine Porter with Carolyn Burke (Ithaca: Cornell UP, 1985), 170–91.

13. John Berger, *Ways of Seeing* (New York: Penguin, 1972), 46.

14. For some time biographers of Millay, particularly Nancy Milford and Jean Gould, have been throwing out hints about Millay's connection to lesbianism. In her biography, *The Poet and Her Book* (New York: Dodd Mead, 1969), Gould indicated that Millay was willing to describe herself as both homosexual and heterosexual but Gould was careful to

indicate that people connected to the poet, possibly her sister Norma, had kept the full story from being told.

15. Berger, 47.

16. Joan Dash, *A Life of One's Own* (New York: Harper and Row, 1973), 215.

17. Dash, 152.

18. Susan Gubar, " 'The Blank Page' and the Issues of Female Creativity," *Critical Inquiry* 8 (1981), 248.

19. T. J. Jackson Lears, "From Salvation to Self-Realization: Advertising and the Therapeutic Roots of Consumer Culture, 1880–1930," in *The Culture of Consumption*, ed. Richard Wrightman Fox and T. J. Jackson Lears (New York: Pantheon, 1983), 8.

20. Mary Ryan, *Womanhood in America*, 2d ed. (New York: Franklin Watts, 1979), both quotations 179.

21. Rachel Bowlby, *Just Looking: Consumer Culture in Dreiser, Gissing, and Zola* (New York: Methuen, 1985), 32.

22. In 1950, after her husband's death from cancer, Millay wrote a frustrated letter to a friend who was collecting money for cancer research. "The American Cancer Society doesn't know how to advertise itself. This is a pity. Infantile Paralysis is all over the radio and all over everything else with its tricky slogans . . . and Heart Disease has gone and spoiled St. Valentine's Day with its National Heart Week. . . . But all that the American Cancer Society ever does is simply to announce, in a dignified way, that it exists, and is not averse to contributions" (*L*, 367).

23. "Renascence" has inspired a number of readings which seem to me to miss crucial aspects of the poem. James Gray, in his monograph on the poet in *American Writers* (ed. Leonard Unger [New York: Scribner's, 1979]), says: " 'The soul can split the sky in two, / And let the face of God shine through.' This confrontation with the divine can be dared and endured because man is one with the divine" (125). It seems to me crucial that the speaker is *not* one with the divine. Edmund Wilson thought the poem described sexual love. This, of course, ignores almost all of its specific elements. Wilson also had a hunch that the images of claustrophobia were important but he does not analyze them beyond saying that "this poem gives the central theme of Edna Millay's whole work: she is alone; she is afraid that the world will crush her; she must summon the strength to assert herself, to draw herself up to her full stature, to embrace the world with love: and the storm—which stands evidently for sexual love—comes to effect a liberation" (*The Shores of Light* [New York: Farrar, Straus, 1952], 758–59. After this chapter was complete, I discovered Suzanne Clark's fascinating essay on this poem; Clark reads "Renascence" in ways startlingly similar to mine, using Lacan and Kristeva. Clark, however, sees Millay struggling to repress the maternal and agrees with Frank that Millay's persona remains "the girl." See Clark, "Jouissance and the Sentimental Daughter: Edna St. Vincent Millay," *North Dakota Quarterly* 54 (Spring 1986), 85–108. I was also interested to discover that the black feminist lesbian poet Audre Lorde memorized all eight pages of this poem in the 1940s according to *Zami: A New Spelling of My Name* (Freedom, Calif.: Crossing Press, 1982). To her at that time "the words were so beautiful they made me happy to hear, but it was the sadness and the pain and the renewal that gave me hope" (83–84).

24. Sigmund Freud, *On Creativity and the Unconscious* (New York: Harper and Row, 1958), 153.

25. Michelet is quoted in Clément and Cixous, *The Newly-Born Woman*, 4; hereafter cited in the text as *NW*, page following.

26. *NW*, 33. For Catherine Clément, to touch the integrity of the masculine body image, which is what the sorceress and Millay's speaker do, is to participate in a demonic festival of liberation possible to the female only outside of cultural sanity. "It is the moment at which the woman crosses a dangerous line, the cultural demarcation beyond which she will find herself excluded" (*NW*, 33).

27. Jan Miel, "Jacques Lacan and the Structure of the Unconscious," *Structuralism*, ed. Jacques Ehrmann (Garden City, N.Y.: Doubleday-Anchor, 1970), 99.

28. Walter S. Minot's article, "Millay's 'Ungrafted Tree': The Problem of the Artist as Woman," referenced above, is sympathetic to the plight of the woman poet but tends to reduce the sonnet sequence to an autobiographical struggle between Millay and her father. In a typical passage, he writes: "The lack of fatherly affection and the general dominance and aggressiveness of her mother produced in Millay an uncertainty about sexual roles and a distrust of men that may have crippled her as a person, and could be the cause of her failure to achieve the poetic greatness that many predicted for her" (265). I do not see Millay's biological father as an important presence in her work and Millay's mother seems to me a strong and positive model, very unlike the speaker in these sonnets. If the sequence suggests distrust of men, this is amply justified by her critique of both "masculinity" and "femininity" in their socially constructed forms, and not an aberration with its source in Millay's personal biography.

29. Gould, *American Women Poets*, 253–54.

30. In fact, my first knowledge of this poem came when Adrienne Rich quoted these lines from memory to me in 1972. Rich has admitted several times that Millay was an important early influence.

31. *Conversation at Midnight* (New York: Harper, 1937), 51. Though trounced by the critics (Louise Bogan thought it dreadful), *Conversation* is a fascinating period piece. The dinner guests, who are all men, discuss women on pp. 45–51 with the short story writer, the ad man, and the capitalist making derogatory remarks eventually broken up here and elsewhere by Ricardo's reformist interventions. However, even Ricardo (the host character supposedly a combination of Millay and Eugen) does not enjoy the conversation of women at Merton's, the stockbroker's, house. In the course of this polylog, there are insightful discussions of language change, the impact of labor-saving devices on women's lives, and the relative strengths and weaknesses of various political ideologies.

32. For an excellent article on Millay's use of sonnet form, see Debra Fried, "Andromeda Unbound: Gender and Genre in Millay's Sonnets," *Twentieth Century Literature: A Scholarly and Critical Journal* 32 (Spring 1986), 1–22.

33. According to Joan Dash, during the late forties Millay poured her pent-up feelings about the high priest of poetry and criticism, T. S. Eliot, into a collection of poems, never published, that satirized him unmercifully. See Dash, 213.

34. See Hugh Kenner, *A Homemade World: The American Modernist Writers* (New York: William Morrow, 1975), 14.

7. WOMEN AND THE RETREAT TO THE MIND

1. All quotations from Bogan's poems in this chapter come from *The Blue Estuaries* (New York: Ecco Press, 1977), 64; henceforth referenced in the text as *BE*, page number following.

2. Elizabeth Frank, *Louise Bogan: A Portrait* (New York: Knopf, 1985), 244; henceforth referenced in the text as *LB*, page number following.

3. William Wordsworth, *The Prelude* (New York: Holt Rinehart, 1954), 205 and 272.

4. Paul Valéry's essay "Les Coquillages" is quoted in Gaston Bachelard, *The Poetics of Space* (Boston: Beacon, 1969), 105–6.

5. Bachelard, 123.

6. Gloria Bowles, *Louise Bogan's Aesthetic of Limitation* (Bloomington: Indiana UP, 1987).

7. "The Springs of Poetry," *New Republic*, 5 December 1923, 8.

8. *What the Woman Lived: Selected Letters of Louise Bogan 1920–1970*, ed. Ruth Limmer (New York: Harcourt Brace, 1973), 3; hereafter referenced in the text as *WWL*, page number following.

9. Diane Wood Middlebrook, "The Problem of the Woman Artist: Louise Bogan, 'The Alchemist,' " in *Critical Essays on Louise Bogan*, ed. Martha Collins (Boston: G. K. Hall, 1984), 174–80, esp. 175.

10. Middlebrook, 179.

11. *Journey Around My Room: The Autobiography of Louise Bogan*, ed. Ruth Limmer (New York: Viking, 1980), 23; hereafter referenced in the text as *JAR*, page number following.

12. See Elizabeth Frank, "A Doll's Heart: The Girl in the Poetry of Edna St. Vincent Millay and Louise Bogan" in Collins, ed., *Critical Essays*, 128–49, esp. 136.

13. *A Poet's Alphabet: Reflections of the Literary Art and Vocation*, ed. Robert Phelps and Ruth Limmer (New York: McGraw-Hill, 1970), 299; hereafter referenced in the text as *PA*, page number following.

14. Bowles, 41; Gloria Bowles and Elizabeth Frank both do an excellent job of connecting Louise Bogan's work to that of other women poets in the nightingale tradition.

15. *These Modern Women*, 85.

16. Lillian Hellman, *An Unfinished Woman* (Boston: Little, Brown, 1969), 27.

17. Katherine Anne Porter, *The Collected Stories of Katherine Anne Porter* (New York: Harcourt Brace, 1979), 90–102.

18. Erving Goffman, *The Presentation of Self in Everyday Life* (Garden City, N.Y.: Doubleday-Anchor, 1959). See especially pages 56–57, where Goffman quotes George Santayana at length to the effect that to become a self means assuming a mask that defines our "sovereign temper." In this guise "we compose and play our chosen character," which is "more truly ourself than is the flux of our involuntary dreams." As our soul crystallizes into an idea of ourself, "our animal habits are transmuted by conscience into loyalties and duties, and we become 'persons' or masks." Goffman suggests that the two terms are interchangeable.

19. "Poetesses in the Parlour," *New Yorker*, 5 December 1936, 42, 45, 46, 48, 50, 52.

20. *Achievement in American Poetry* (Chicago: Henry Regnery, 1951), 23.

21. I discovered the connection between Bogan and Robin Morgan at Harvard University's Widener Library, which contains a tribute put together by Morgan and others for Louise Bogan.

22. See *The Heath Anthology of American Literature*, Paul Lauter et al., eds., vol. 2 (Lexington, Mass.: D. C. Heath, 1990), and *The Norton Anthology of American Literature*, Nina Baym et al., eds. (New York: Norton, 1989).

23. My first insight into these poems came in 1976 when I encountered the theories of René Girard and was introduced to Girard's iconography, in which raging fire and epidemic image the contagion of mimetic violence. Triangulated desire, of course, does have considerable relevance to Bogan's concerns in this period. See particularly Girard's *Deceit, Desire and the Novel* (Baltimore: Johns Hopkins UP, 1965), *Violence and the Sacred* (1977), and *To Double Business Bound* (1978).

24. Edmund Wilson, *Letters on Literature and Politics 1912–1972*, selected and edited by Elena Wilson (New York: Farrar, Straus, 1977), 207.

25. Wilson, 404.

8. THE SOUND OF NIGHTINGALES

1. See William Butler Yeats, *Selected Poems and Two Plays* (New York: Collier Books, 1962), 55–56. Though rather cool to Yeats when she first read him, by the 1920s Sara Teasdale considered him the greatest living poet and "The Wild Swans at Coole" the finest poem of the twentieth century. Louise Bogan also elevated him above all others and measured everything she wrote against his aesthetic standards. Judith Farr insists that Yeats was Elinor Wylie's master, too. The influence of Yeats on the twentieth-century nightingale tradition is indisputable and deserves further study.

2. Kaplan, *Sea Changes*, 3.

3. Ibid., 211.

4. See Mossberg, *Emily Dickinson: When a Writer Is a Daughter*, and "A Rose in Context: The Daughter Construct," in Jerome J. McGann, ed., *Historical Studies and Literary Criticism* (Madison: U of Wisconsin P, 1985).

5. Carolyn Kizer, *Mermaids in the Basement: Poems for Women* (Port Townsend, Wash.: Copper Canyon, 1984), hereafter referenced in the text as MB.

6. Lisel Mueller, *The Need to Hold Still* (Baton Rouge: Louisiana State UP, 1980); hereafter referenced in the text as NHS.

7. Alicia Suskin Ostriker, *Green Age* (Pittsburgh: U of Pittsburgh P, 1989), 5.

8. Louise Gluck, *Descending Figure* (New York: Ecco Press, 1980), 39.

9. Jana Harris, *Manhattan as a Second Language* (San Francisco: Harper and Row, 1982), 55–56.

10. Cleopatra Mathis, *Aerial View of Louisiana* (New York: Sheep Meadow Press, 1979), 11.

11. *The Norton Anthology of American Literature*, 3d ed., 2773.

12. Rita Dove, *Thomas and Beulah* (Pittsburgh: Carnegie-Mellon UP, 1986), 72.

13. Dove, *Grace Notes* (New York: Norton, 1989), 41.

14. Ibid., 42.

15. Elizabeth Bishop, *The Complete Poems 1927–1979* (New York: Farrar, Straus, 1980), 159–61.

16. Sharon Olds, *The Dead and the Living* (New York: Knopf, 1985), 6.

17. Toni Morrison, *Beloved* (New York: Knopf, 1987), 275.

Index

CHERYL WALKER is Richard Armour Professor of English at Scripps College in Claremont, California. She is the author of *The Nightingale's Burden: Women Poets and American Culture before 1900*, winner of a Choice Award as one of the best academic books of 1983; she has also authored numerous articles on feminist theory and women poets from Anne Bradstreet to Margaret Atwood.